The Evolution
of Educational Theory
in the United States

The Evolution
of Educational Theory
in the United States

DICKSON A. MUNGAZI

Foreword by George M. Lubick

PRAEGER

Westport, Connecticut
London

Library of Congress Cataloging-in-Publication Data

Mungazi, Dickson A.
    The evolution of educational theory in the United States / Dickson
A. Mungazi ; foreword by George M. Lubick.
      p. cm.
    Includes bibliographical references (p.   ) and index.
    ISBN 0–275–96130–3 (alk. paper)
    1. Education—United States—Philosophy—History. I. Title.
LA205.M75   1999
370′.1—DC21   97–43946

British Library Cataloguing in Publication Data is available.

Library of Congress Catalog Card Number: 97–43946
ISBN: 0–275–96130–3

First published in 1999

Praeger Publishers, 88 Post Road West, Westport, CT 06881
An imprint of Greenwood Publishing Group, Inc.

Printed in the United States of America

The paper used in this book complies with the
Permanent Paper Standard issued by the National
Information Standards Organization (Z39.48-1984).

10 9 8 7 6 5 4 3 2

To the memory of Albert E. Shanker,
scholar, educator, and friend,
whose contribution to American education is invaluable

Every valuable end of government is best ensured by the
enlightened confidence of the people.
—George Washington, 1790

Our schools, by producing one general and uniform system
of education, will render the mass of the people
more homogeneous.
—Benjamin Rush, 1798

Contents

Foreword

As the United States enters the last few years of the twentieth century, it does so acknowledging that the educational system that sustained its social, economic, scientific, and democratic aspirations faces serious problems. In fact, for more than a decade, Americans have conceded that the country's public schools were in a state of decline. Government reports are not often widely read and discussed, but when the National Commission on Excellence in Education published *A Nation at Risk* in 1983, people quickly grasped its implications. The postwar advances in education, particularly those following Sputnik, seemingly had disappeared, leaving the country with an educational system best characterized as mediocre. Other problems were evident, too, comprising a litany that included school violence, drugs, lack of interest in formal education, rising illiteracy, and diminished involvement by parents. In response, some parents enrolled their children in parochial schools; others experimented with home schooling or opted for the curriculum of charter schools.

Dickson A. Mungazi, Regents Professor in Northern Arizona University's Center for Excellence in Education, does not dispute the condition of education in America. He suggests, though, that Americans ought to look back on the historical development of educational theory as the foundation on which to build the development of a new set of ideas to meet today's educational and social challenges and to guide the country into the next century. Although his *Evolution of Educational Theory in the United States* acknowledges European antecedents as important background to the evolution of educational theory in the United States, beginning with ancient Greek masters and continuing on through the Middle Ages, Renaissance, Reformation, and Enlightenment, its focus is on the American experience. New England's

Puritans, he notes, demanded conformity in local schools as a means to structure a society governed by religious principles that were clearly based on values different from those of England. Theory changed by the time of the Revolution, reflecting in particular the impact of Thomas Paine's pamphlet, *Common Sense*. This work not only denounced George III and made the case for independence, but it also argued that education was the foundation for a people struggling for freedom. Benjamin Franklin added to this emerging theory of education when he recommended that education in the new United States be designed to allow equality of opportunity for all students.

Later, in the antebellum era, educational reformers led by Horace Mann and Henry Barnard developed theories that reflected the democratic aspirations of Jacksonian America. Most important was the idea of a publicly funded system of common schools. Later generations consistently adopted theory to historical change, as schools responded to the new immigration of the late nineteenth and early twentieth centuries and also established public high schools and expanded state-supported colleges and universities. Professor Dickson A. Mungazi points out that the American court system forcefully shaped the evolution of new educational theory, beginning in 1938 with the *Gaines* decision and continuing on through *Brown v. The Board of Education of Topeka* in 1954. He credits the courts with finally enunciating "a theory that affirmed the right of African Americans to education."

Throughout this study, Professor Mungazi convincingly argues that educational theory has never been static but invariably has changed, although sometimes slowly, to accommodate historical circumstances. In recent history, the country has confronted serious economic, political, and social issues, and policy makers have responded with such measures as the 1958 National Defense Education Act and the 1964 Civil Rights Act. He writes that such laws, along with the *Brown* and *Tinker* decisions and *Roe v. Wade*, indicate how the country sought "to further create conditions that were conducive to the improvement of the lives of all people."

What does this relationship between history and educational theory suggest for late twentieth-century Americans who already were disenchanted with the existing system of education? Clearly, this is a time to search for new theoretical approaches. Professor Mungazi argues that Mortimer Adler, in *The Paideia Proposal: An Educational Manifesto*, provides some new direction when he observes that, "We are all suffering from our continued failure to fulfill the educational obligations of democracy. We are all victims of a school system that has only gone halfway along the road to realize the promise of democracy." Professor Mungazi then concludes that any new theory of education must ensure the development of all students as individuals and must also enable them to function in the larger society. He adds that educational theory depends on both *learning* and *teaching*. He is absolutely right when he says that the recent learning theory of cognitive psychology is based on the belief that students learn in a variety of ways and at different rates; capabilities vary from student to student. While cognitive psychology is a promising theory of learning, Mungazi cautions that the search for a new theory of education must also embrace the school and home environmental factors, social conditions, and the training of teachers. As for a theory of teaching, he explains that education is "far more meaningful when students are allowed to discover for themselves those critical aspects of knowledge associated with the educational process."

Professor Mungazi argues in a very logical fashion that broad educational objectives have not varied substantially since the colonial era. American schools typically have sought to ensure personal and individual growth, to prepare citizens to play an important role in society, and to train students for a vocation or occupation. To these important aspects of national life, Professor Mungazi adds that educational objectives would be defined to help students function within the environment of their culture. "Any education that negates the culture in which it is cast," he cautions, "loses the purpose for which it is designed," and has "no relevance to building a new national character." In a modern multicultural society, citizens must acknowledge that expanding the equality of educational opportunity is essential to building that new national character. Similarly, educational theory in the United States must embrace issues of social justice, the elimination of poverty, address the plight of homeless people, confront racism, and seek to end domestic violence. These are complex characteristics of contemporary society, and they demand that educational theory continue its historical precedent and journey of trying to reach out to address the problems that accompany the trust for meaningful social change.

The importance of Dickson A. Mungazi's synthesis of the evolution of educational theory rests on his solid argument that any society must search for a functional basis for its educational theory. This, in turn, shapes the agenda and thrust for national development. America's schools historically have responded to a changing world, and their proponents (teachers, politicians, and scholars) have evolved new theoretical contexts for public education. That was among the first tasks faced by seventeenth-century settlers, particularly New England Puritans. Mungazi argues that it was a challenge that confronted the revolutionary generation and that of Horace Mann. Similarly, that endeavor led to the development of high schools and expanded colleges, absorbed the progressive ideas of John Dewey, and embraced the idealism of the Civil Rights movement to integrate schools in the quest for equality of educational opportunity. At the end of the twentieth century, the United States faces other complex challenges as it seeks to accommodate educational theory to respond to global issues and to the most demanding domestic social issues that the nation confronts. This may not be the time to abandon a historical national commitment to equal educational opportunity in public schools in favor of vouchers and charter schools. Mungazi's challenge to the United States is to demonstrate unequivocal commitment to the development of contemporary educational theory as a guide to meet new challenges—not to retreat from them. This book provides critical insights that are important to the scholar, the educator, the graduate student, the politician, and the reader who seeks to understand the evolution of educational theory in the United States in order to shape new directions of development. One must read it with great care and interest.

—George M. Lubick, Professor
Department of History
Northern Arizona University

Preface

THE PURPOSE OF THE STUDY

The purpose of this study is to trace the evolution of the theory of education in the United States from the beginning of the colonial period to the present. In doing so it will discuss the implications that such an evolution has had on the national character of the United States and the kind of education that has developed as a result of this application. In order to adequately present components of this theory, this study begins with a discussion of the evolution of theory in ancient Greece as the origins of theory in Western education. Using this approach, the study focuses on seven specific areas of critical importance.

These areas are: (1) the conditions that affected education during the colonial period; (2) the influence of educational institutions in medieval Europe; (3) the theory espoused by certain individuals, both in Europe and in colonial America; (4) the inception of formal education; (5) the nature of the colonial society; (6) the kind of education that evolved during the colonial period; and (7) the impact of religion on both education and society. These combined to create an environment that required an evolution of theory. By its very nature, theory must seek to address various aspects of the educational process. It must address educational objectives and how their implementation determines the character of education and the society in which it is cast. Its effectiveness in serving national purpose must be determined by how well students are doing, both in school and in society. Theory must also address the curriculum, administrative system, and current problems.

THE APPROACH

This study begins by examining some theories of education in ancient Greece, especially those espoused by Plato, Socrates, and Aristotle. It then goes on to discuss the theory of early thinkers in colonial America, such as that of Jonathan Edwards, Cotton Mather, John Locke, and Adam Smith. It then discusses theory espoused by the masters of the Age of Reason, such as George Washington, Benjamin Rush, Thomas Jefferson, Jean-Jacques Rousseau, Samuel Johnson, and Benjamin Franklin. This examination suggests why, at the conclusion of the eighteenth century a concerted effort was made to give a new meaning to education. A collective enterprise was being made to diagnose the causes of conflict between the colonies and Britain.

The outbreak of the Revolution helped set an agenda to avoid such conflict in the future. This would not be, as another conflict broke out in 1812. What was wrong with the thinking of the British and the people in the United States to go through another conflict only thirty-seven years after the outbreak of the first one in 1775? This study then goes on to discuss the influence of theory on the reform movement led by Horace Mann and Henry Barnard to suggest the change that took place in both education and society. It then discusses the importance of theory as the basis for effective change in education in order to improve it. Education in the United States is facing problems that are discussed in the context of a response to theory. Some essential theoretical considerations that may make or break education are also presented.

The relationship that exists between society and the individual is the primary focus of education as a product of putting theory into practice. That the United States, as the principal proponent of the capitalist ideology of the Western world, is experiencing substantial difficulties in its educational system presents an interesting perspective from which to discuss the theory of education. This study then discusses educational objectives as an outcome of theory and examines how objectives determine the character of education, as well as discussing the curriculum as an instrument of fulfilling objectives and national purpose. How the curriculum is designed provides a fascinating account of how the United States sees itself in relation to its national agenda.

SUMMARY, CONCLUSION, AND IMPLICATIONS

The last chapter presents summaries of the preceding main features and arguments. It also draws some conclusions and discusses some implications. Following are some of these conclusions: (1) The evolution of the theory of education in the United States has made a difference between success and failure, between relevant education and irrelevant instruction, between mediocrity and a dynamic system. (2) The application of theory becomes a critical aspect of any national system. It is virtually impossible to initiate any undertaking in any area of human endeavor without initiating theory. The development of education in the United States fits into that model. (3) In its efforts to maintain technological superiority in a competitive world, the United States has strengthened its system of education in the educational interests of the students as a reflection of the interests of the country. (4) The thrust for educational reform was initiated in an absolute belief that only education that is available to all the people on the basis of equality can serve the interests of the nation. (5) The struggle of African Americans to secure an education must be seen in the context of a theoretical belief that education was good for the United States because it was good for all people. (6) The educational reform package announced by President George Bush in April 1991 received a mixed response because many thought it fell short of providing a clear direction for development. This situation contributed to his defeat by Governor Bill Clinton in the presidential elections held in November 1992. During the State of the Union address in January 1997 President Clinton indicated that he would make education the top priority of his second term of office as president of the United States.

However, in 1997 the United States, like other countries of the world, was facing serious problems with education. Drugs, violence in schools, truancy, lack of interest in formal education, social pressure, rising illiteracy, and lack of involvement by parents have all compounded the problems of education in the United States. Unless the United States makes concerted efforts to find solutions to these problems, the deterioration in education will have a negative effect on American society itself. This grim reality was recognized in 1983 by the National Commission on Excellence in Education. To find solutions to these problems, the United States needs to remember that no nation has sufficient resources to go it alone and will need to coordinate its efforts and to cooperate with other nations because these problems have global implications. Together nations can overcome their ideological differences and the impact of their different levels of development to find a common ground on which to cooperate in launching a new *safari* to educational development as a means to national development and international peace. This is an opportunity the United States should wish to utilize. To do so it needs to formulate new theory to guide its endeavor.

Acknowledgments

In the process of writing a book that covers the development of education for a period of three hundred years, one must rely on historical materials that one obtains from different sources, such as books, journals, and so forth. For this reason, the author wishes to thank the Interlibrary Loan System for making it possible to secure the materials needed to produce this study. He also wishes to thank the Library of Congress for allowing access to public materials needed to complete this study.

The author also wishes to thank several of his colleagues at Northern Arizona University for the support and encouragement they have given him. He is also grateful to members of the National Social Science Association, the Association of Third World Studies, and the Comparative and International Studies Society for the encouragement given while he was presenting papers at professional conferences during the past decade. The idea for this project came from those papers. The author wishes to express his special gratitude to L. Kay Walker, his colleague and professor in the Center for Excellence in Education, for allowing him access to rare books that formed an important part of the materials needed to complete this study.

The author also thanks Betty Russell in the Center for Excellence in Education at Northern Arizona University for programming the computer to produce the manuscript more efficiently. His special gratitude goes to Carolyn Hardison of Arlington, Arizona, for allowing him access to personal correspondence of her great grandmother, Janie Kerr, who was a teacher in Missouri in 1885. The author found this correspondence inspiring and insightful about conditions of employment for women as teachers during the nineteenth century. The author also wishes to thank Sandra Feldman, president of the American Federation of Teachers since May 6, 1997, for sending him a passage about her philosophy of education for inclusion in this study. He also wishes to thank George M. Lubick, professor in the History Department of Northern Arizona University for agreeing to write the Foreword.

The author wishes to thank his secretary, Charlene Wingo, and her assistant, Margo Gay, for assisting in the production of the manuscript, and the Office of Regents Professors as well as the Center for Excellence in Education, for support and financial assistance in the research and production of this study. Finally, the author wishes to thank the staff of Cline Library at Northern Arizona University for their readiness to help in securing materials, as well as the members of the Northern Arizona University community for their support and encouragement.

Introduction

THE PURPOSE OF THIS STUDY

The action that President George Bush of the United States and President Mikhail Gorbachev of the Soviet Union took in Moscow on July 31, 1991, in signing the nuclear arms reduction treaty ushered in a new era of relationships between the two superpowers and members of the international community. The signing ceremonies would not have taken place if the signatories were uninformed about the issues that had brought them to the negotiating table over the past decade or if they were not convinced of the intent of the treaty itself. This means that the two leaders and the two nations they represented had previously gone through the process of evolution to arrive at the conclusion that it was in the best interest of both countries to sign the treaty. Whatever reasons they used to arrive at that conclusion, the process demanded observation of theory. The purpose of this study is to discuss the evolution of the theory of education in the United States from the beginning of the colonial period to the present.

Because the signing of this treaty was so critical to the security of the world as a whole, it is important to discuss briefly some theoretical reasons and arguments that led to it. This will help put the evolution of theory in its proper broader context. In 1982 a national debate was initiated in the U.S. Congress about the real danger of a nuclear war between the United States and the Soviet Union. Senator Edward Kennedy (D., Mass.) and Senator Mark Hatfield (R., Ore.) introduced a resolution in the U.S. Senate calling for a freeze by both the Soviet Union and the United States in the experimentation, production, and deployment of nuclear weapons. Kennedy and Hatfield were joined by 22 other senators and 150 members of the House of

Representatives in supporting the freeze. Both President Ronald Reagan of the United States (born 1911) and President Leonid Brezhnev (1905–1982) of the Soviet Union supported the freeze.

What were the issues and the concerns that had ignited this debate? Here are a few answers. The suspension of SALT II in 1980 had actually resulted in the increase in the nuclear arsenals of both countries by more than 10 percent. NATO planned to deploy 572 new Pershing II and cruise missiles in Europe by the end of 1983, while the Warsaw Pact planned to deploy 300 SS–20 missiles in the same year. In 1972 the United States had 6,700 warheads, and the Soviet Union had 2,500. By 1982 it was reported that both the Soviet Union and the United States each had a nuclear arsenal that would destroy the world fifteen times over (as if to suggest that once is not enough). Experts tell us that no side can a win a nuclear war. Speaking on the danger of a nuclear arsenal, Brezhnev said, "Only he who has decided to commit suicide can start a nuclear war. However, if NATO stations any new missiles in Europe, there would arise a real additional threat to our country. This would compel us to take retaliatory measures that would put the other side in its own territory" (*Time*, March 29, 1982). There is no question that Brezhnev was enunciating theory on nuclear weapons.

This situation seemed to represent the worst crisis between the two superpowers since the Cuban missile crisis of 1962. The question is: Can one realistically believe that this crisis developed overnight or did it evolve over an extended period of time? One can conclude that this crisis was a product of history. Since the end of the war in 1945 the United States and the Soviet Union transformed their relationships from being allies to being adversaries due to ideological differences. But the emergence of ideological differences was an outcome of the application of theory about political, social, and economic activity. Once this theory came into place, the two nations could not reconcile themselves to the need for cooperation rather than competition. The evolution of the theory that the two nations utilized to structure relationships between them can be traced to the Russo-Japanese War of 1901. In the Soviet Union this evolution adopted a faster pace in 1905 and 1917. Theory becomes the guiding principle to human endeavor. It is an operational mover, the basis of meaningful action, the rationale behind human behavior, whether it is in politics, international relationships, the economy, or a study of sociology or education.

The approach made in this study is quite different from the conventional approach to the study of history of education in the United States in some important respects. Instead of discussing the development of education in itself, this study attempts to present the evolution of theory in proper chronological order and in an integrated approach where the components of theory relative to a specific period of time are presented in the context of the developments that were taking place. In the discussion of this evolution one sees the discussion of a society struggling for development. Specific educational features are discussed in this study as a response to the application of theory. As time went on, the evolution of theory became complex because American society was becoming increasingly complex.

This approach enables the author to develop a coherent argument and enables the reader to see and follow the critical nature of the influence of education in national development as a result of theory. Why, for example, did the Soviet Union, as it had been known since the Bolshevik Revolution of 1917, go out of existence in 1992 and become the federation of independent republics? Does this negate the reality that for seven decades the Soviet Union operated under a socialist system that, by 1992, was no longer relevant to conditions of today? The answer lies in theoretical reasons that were advanced for the demise of the Soviet Union. Having recognized that major adjustments would have to be made in socialism and had to be maintained, Mikhail Gorbachev took six years to formulate a new theory based on *glasnost* and *perestroika* to bring about change.

RATIONALE OF THIS STUDY: EXAMPLES OF EVOLUTION OF THEORY

A study of all areas of human endeavor and achievement shows that it is based on theory that has evolved over an extended period of time. The evolution of theory, like the evolution of a living species, is a slow process. It is a well-known fact that human action is based on prior thought. Prior thought is the process of developing theory. Let us cite some examples. Perhaps the best example relates to the master of the theory of evolution himself, Charles Robert Darwin (1809–1882). When Darwin published his *Origin of Species* in 1859, he had spent many years studying and developing the framework of a theory that his grandfather, Erasmus Darwin, had put in place during the Age of Reason. The publication of *Origin of Species* coincided with the rapidly developing new ideas that became part of the Industrial Revolution. Darwin's work was based on his theoretical principles that variations exist on such a scale that no two living things are exactly alike. Members of each species compete with each other and with other species for a chance to live. The strongest species will survive, and the weakest will die. Darwin called this process natural selection. As the Industrial Revolution reached its peak in 1885, politicians and entrepreneurs applied it to the human condition—social, political, and economic. Colonial adventure in Africa was based on this application.

History says that the ancient Greek philosopher and mathematician, Pythagoras, became famous for spending years studying and formulating his theory that is famous to this day. The theory states that in any right-angled triangle the square of the hypotenuse is equal to the sum of the squares of the other two sides. Pythagoras also formulated a supplementary theory that numbers are the essence of all things. He also associated numbers with virtue and many other ideas, such as his conclusion that Earth was spherical and that the Sun, the Moon, and planets have movements of their own. This theory is the basis that Nicolaus Copernicus utilized in 1543 to formulate his own theory that the motions of the Earth influenced the motions of other heavenly bodies. One wonders how the world would function without the knowledge of the theory that Pythagoras and Copernicus developed.

When the American Revolution finally broke out with the Boston massacre on March 5, 1770, it was a sequel to the application of theories that had evolved over a long period of time in response to the action that the British government had taken in applying its own theories. British policy toward the American colonies took a dramatic turn in 1763 when the British government decided to keep a standing army in the colonies and proposed to support it by taxing the colonies. The British government began to pass legislation to control colonial trade and navigation in a way that promoted its own economic interests at the expense of those of the colonists. The British Parliament passed the Sugar Act in 1764, the Stamp Act in 1765, the Tea Act of 1773, and the Intolerable Act of 1774 to ensure maximum benefit from the colonies. The colonists responded to these laws by enunciating their own theories. "Taxation without representation is tyranny," "Give me liberty or give me death," and "All men are created equal" were theories which, when put into action, led to the American Revolution.

Here are a few examples of the evolution of theory in various areas of human endeavor. History tells us that before Orville and Wilbur Wright invented a machine that could fly, they had spent a lot of time watching birds fly. In 1896 they began an intense study of the ideas of a German pioneer glider, Otto Lilenthal, and by 1899 had acquired considerable observations and knowledge of flying. From these observations the Wright brothers formulated some theoretical perceptions about their belief that man could also fly. These ideas turned into theory. Although their father, a traditional Methodist preacher, discouraged them by advancing his own theory that if God intended for man to fly, He would have given him wings, the two brothers refused to give up their theory. Today we jet across the world in hours using the machines that have been created using the application of that theory.

In 1895 an Italian entrepreneur, Gugliemo Marconi, tested the theory he had been working on for some years about sending messages by wireless communication. The influence of the Industrial Revolution of the nineteenth century persuaded him to refuse to give up the efforts he was making in formulating his ideas of sending messages without wires. His contemporaries thought that he was insane trying to conceive an idea that they thought was impossible to implement. In 1909 Marconi received the Nobel prize for his work because it was now beginning to show results. Today we routinely enjoy radio FM/AM transmissions in our cars. By the time of his death in 1937 Marconi had become a household name in radio transmission.

In 1894 George Washington Carver, a former slave born in Diamond Grove, Missouri, graduated from Iowa State College with a degree in botany. While he was still a baby he and his mother were abducted by thieves. Later his mother's master brought him back in exchange for a horse. He never knew his father, and his mother had vanished. Born in 1864, a year before the ratification of the Thirteenth Amendment ending slavery, Carver endured the pain and suffering of not knowing his parents. A brilliant and dedicated student, Carver applied himself to learning in a manner that surprised those who knew him. He showed an intense interest in plants. Upon his graduation from Iowa State College he was persuaded to remain there as director of the greenhouse. He began immediately to collect varieties of plants that numbered 200,000 by the time he moved to Tuskegee in 1896. In 1916 Carver was named Fellow of the Royal Arts in London in recognition of his work in botany. He began soon to formulate his theory about converting peanuts into many products that we take for granted today. In 1923 he received a distinguished medal for his contribution to the evolution of theory of botany. In 1939 he received the Roosevelt medal for many of his inventions and contributions to the study of botany. His study of botany presents Carver's theoretical exploits and the impact that they had on the evolution of theory of education. Just as Carver defined theory as the mother of invention, one can define it as the origin of human endeavor.

In 1913 Daniel Hale Williams (1856–1931) was named the first African American member of the American College of Surgeons for his contribution to theory of medical science. Beginning in 1896 Williams was the first to formulate a theory of plasma, the straw-colored liquid part of blood that remains when the red and the white blood cells are removed. Williams discovered that plasma contains water, salts, proteins, and other food materials. He discovered that plasma carries dissolved food materials to all parts of the body and picks up waste materials produced by the body cells and carries them to the organs that remove waste materials from the body. Williams concluded that plasma can be used for blood transfusions when whole blood is not needed or cannot be obtained. Williams advanced his theory that plasma can be used during surgery to combat shock and that it can successfully be used to restore blood volume lost during severe bleeding. Williams also concluded that plasma generates antibodies that help destroy germs and help prevent infection. Today a variety of uses of plasma is part of the medical practice utilized to save lives that would otherwise be lost.

In 1967 Christiaan Barnard, a heart surgeon at Groote Schuur Hospital in Cape Town, performed the first heart transplant on Louis Washkansky. Barnard repeated this feat in 1968 on Philip Blaiberg. Although both patients lived only a short period of time, the experiment proved that the transplant could work. When the author was in Cape Town in December 1994, he visited the Groote Schuur Hospital because it had become a major tourist center due to the work that Barnard had done there, and he was told that

Barnard had studied and developed his theory of transplant over many years. He had watched patients die who could otherwise survive if a compatible heart was found. Although many of his colleagues dismissed the idea of heart transplant, Barnard refused to give it up because be believed that it would work. Today heart, lung, and kidney transplants are routine.

On February 24, 1997, the world woke up to sensational news. It learned that scientists had successfully cloned a sheep, named Dolly, in Scotland. Dolly, unlike offspring produced in the usual manner, did not merely take on characteristics of her mother; she was, in effect a duplicate, a scientific counterfeit so real that she was considered her mother's identical twin (*Time*, March 10, 1997). The process of making an identical duplicate of one sheep is the latest major scientific breakthrough. For many years the idea of cloning had belonged to the movies and fiction only. All of a sudden a new and frightful world of reality had been created with enormous implications for human life. This latest human accomplishment would make such successes as in vitro fertilization of twenty years earlier seem minor. Although many people considered cloning repugnant to human moral values, those who supported it hailed it as a remarkable success in a critical era of human enterprise. They saw it as important in the struggle to enhance agricultural production to feed a rapidly increasing population. But it would also expose human beings to chemicals that could cause illness. Like other successful experiments of this age, this latest scientific achievement had taken years to develop the theory on which it was based.

If successfully used, this scientific accomplishment would join the exploits of people such as Louis Pasteur (1822–1895), one of the greatest scientists who made invaluable contributions to the development of theory of chemistry, and Thomas A. Edison (1847–1930), an American whose inventions are part of our daily lives. The evolution of Pasteur's theory, that bacteria spread disease, led to the evolution of methods of successfully combating disease. Today we use pasteurized milk with no fear that it may be contaminated with germs. Pasteur developed his theories over many years. One reaches two conclusions from these examples. The first conclusion is that it takes time for theory to evolve. Like good wine, theory cannot be functional before its time. The second conclusion is that the evolution of theory is highly essential to address all areas of human endeavor. Such is the case with the evolution of theory of education in the United States.

THE ILLUSION OF MILITARY POWER
IN HISTORICAL PERSPECTIVE

As the United States began to build itself as an independent nation, it became aware of its military vulnerability. The Revolutionary War had drained its resources and left its defense forces spread thin. To rebuild its armed forces it was necessary to seek the assistance of nations that were friendly, such as France. The war with the British in 1812 came as a reminder of the need to strengthen its military forces. The war with Mexico from 1835 to 1836, from which Texas was created, the war with Spain in 1894, and U.S. mediation in the war between Russia and Japan in 1904 all suggested the need to coordinate national efforts with other countries to ensure its security. By the beginning of World War I in 1914, opinion was increasing that the United States was either involving itself too much in international affairs or that it was too dependent on other nations to ensure its security.

Many politicians argued that the United States should chart an independent course of action to insure its own long-term security. Thus Senator Henry Cabot Lodge led a campaign to stop the United States from becoming a member of the League of Nations. Indeed, the United States tried hard to stay out of involvement in world events until the Japanese surprise attack on Pearl Harbor in December 1941. In 1947 the United States became part of NATO. Since that time the United States has been active in international events. Over these years the United States has spent huge sums of money to ensure its security to the extent that financial resources needed for educational development has been limited. Since the end of World War II successive U.S. governments have operated on the theoretical assumption that military power ensures national security. The Reagan administration formulated a theory that it defined as an intent to ensure the security of the United States and maintain international peace through strength.

There are two disturbing aspects of the theory of military power as the ultimate cause of the illusion of national security. The first is that it gives politicians a false sense of security and an intransigence that makes them arrogant and refuse to see issues of international relationships from their proper perspective. The world witnessed this tragedy in the crisis in the Persian Gulf caused by Iraq's invasion of Kuwait on August 2, 1990. The level of destruction that is always evident in war does not seem to influence the thinking or the action of national leaders; all they think of is the political gain they make in the pursuit of their own political agenda and purpose.

Quite often, as the world saw in 1991 when hostilities mounted between Iraq and the Western coalition forces, national leaders whose own political positions were weak took advantage of the conflict to improve their standing with the people. In this way an opportunity was lost to put in place elements that are needed to find genuine solutions to the problems of international conflict.

The second aspect is that to achieve their own political objectives, many national leaders deny their people the opportunity to utilize national resources to ensure development. Instead, they use resources to bolster their own political positions. For example, in the United States it was widely reported in 1991 that the White House chief of staff, John Sununu, had used taxpayers' money to make frequent trips of a personal nature. This is not to suggest that there was wrongdoing in this practice, but to indicate that public officials are constantly faced with the problem of trust when it comes to using national resources. They claim that the pursuit of military objectives is in the national interest and international interests. They portray the party with whom they are in conflict as the aggressor. They convince the military establishment that theirs is a mission to save the world, or, as President Woodrow Wilson put it in 1917, their objective is to "make the world safe for democracy." In the conduct of U.S. policy in recent years the theoretical assumptions that have been the basis of this policy need to be reexamined. The process of formulating theory on which to base policy requires a deliberate and logical thought process. Neither theory nor policy can hastily be designed.

THEORY AS THE ESSENCE OF POLITICAL BEHAVIOR

It is a troubling fact that whether or not national leaders are democratically elected, they utilize legislatures as an instrument for carrying out their own political agendas. The sad part of all this is that the people often regard national leaders who take them into war as heroes. This is why President Bush's popularity rose sharply at the beginning of the hostilities in the Persian Gulf in 1991. The people tend to believe anything their national leader says and give him the support he says he needs to carry out a national policy he claims to be in the interest of the nation. Any segment of the community that questions the policies and actions of such a leader are considered unpatriotic. These are characteristic features found in all national leaders, but they do not contribute positively to national purpose. In January 1992, for instance, the economy of the United States was weakened by a combination of powerful factors that included the aftermath of the war in the Gulf of Persia.

The second disturbing aspect of the illusion of military power is that because national leaders are not able to see their own errors, they operate on the assumption that the party with which they are in conflict is always wrong and that they are always right. This is the environment in which President Saddam Hussein convinced his followers to see President George Bush as the ultimate threat to the world of Islam. This is also the same environment that President Bush utilized to convince his fellow Americans to believe that Hussein was the embodiment of Moslem extremism that must be stopped to deny Hussein an opportunity to become another Adolf Hitler. The frequent use of such terms as "the Great Satan" and "the Infidel" to characterize Western leadership, "the brutal dictator" to characterize Saddam Hussein, and "the evil empire" to characterize the Soviet Union contributed nothing to the creation of a climate of real knowledge of the issues that cause conflict between nations and the need to initiate dialogue to resolve problems. Refraining from using extreme language would have enabled the parties to understand and appreciate the concerns of the other. The process of understanding and appreciation requires education. Indeed, the conflict in the Persian Gulf underscores the importance of the belief that national leaders need education to understand the essence and the art of diplomacy.

Another critical factor that stood in the way of seeking a peaceful resolution to the crisis in the Persian Gulf was the enormous ego that manifested the attitudes and actions of both President Hussein and President Bush. This problem was caused primarily by previous international events whose impact they sought to turn into an advantage. On the one hand, having come out of a six-year war with Iran, Hussein, seeking to fill the regional leadership void left by the death of Anwar Sadat, wanted to assert himself as the undisputed leader of the Arab world. On the other hand, having endured the humiliation of the war in Vietnam and the tragic drama of the hostages held in Iran and Lebanon in 1979, Bush sought to assert his own leadership role in the Western world.

Indeed, the personality of both men left no room for dialogue or accommodation. Instead, they acted in ways that accentuated rhetoric that was partly carried out by the media. This is why, at the conclusion of the war with Iraq in 1991, Bush proudly proclaimed that the Vietnam syndrome was finally over, suggesting that he used the war with Iraq to eliminate the lingering effect of the defeat the United States had endured in the conflict in Vietnam. President Bush's proudest moment was his claim that the Patriot missiles had elevated the American national spirit to a new level of national pride and self-confidence. But was there a price to pay?

But, like Hussein, President Bush appeared to neglect the importance of developing the ability to reason things out rather than to utilize military power to seek solutions to international problems. Indeed, it is quite clear that both men needed a new form of theory of education to help them understand that humility and self-restraint are distinct qualities of national leaders and that they do not diminish the power of leadership and the office they hold simply because they seek to understand the concerns of their potential adversary as a condition of dialogue. This suggests that the theory of education is the essence of political behavior and action. To neglect its evolution and application in favor of strengthening the military is to undercut the very essence of national endeavors.

THEORY IN CONTEMPORARY WORLD SETTINGS

The situation discussed above is a reality that delegates in San Francisco took into account in their deliberations. But by 1992 too many leaders had already forgotten this basic principle of human behavior. The world of 1991 showed much that could be related to events of earlier times. The change of leadership in Britain from Margaret Thatcher to John Major, the continuing saga of apartheid in South Africa and its final collapse in 1994, the conflict between Mikhail Gorbachev and the Baltic states, the political crisis in eastern European countries, and the end of the Soviet Union—all were manifestations of conditions that could easily have led to a major global conflict unless nations were prepared to learn what they must to bring about a lasting peace.

The sad part of the tragedy in the Persian Gulf is that in this kind of environment the real causes of the conflict were not addressed. On the one hand, Hussein, claiming to be the guardian of the Palestinian cause, wanted linkage to the crisis caused by his invasion of Kuwait. On the other hand, Bush, believing that he was the guardian of Western democratic values, rejected the idea of linkage and argued that the invasion was nothing less than naked aggression that must not be allowed to stand. Failure to resolve this difference through dialogue is what caused the war in the Persian Gulf in 1991. Must one assume that differences of opinion on issues of international relationships and human existence could be resolved only by military means and not by applying reason? It would be a sad day for the international community to be forced to accept such thinking. Yet, in 1991, this kind of thinking became the norm of international relationships when the UN itself voted to authorize military means to force Iraq out of Kuwait. Then, on January 12, the U.S. Senate voted 52 to 49 and the House of Representatives 250 to 183 to authorize President Bush to use military means to force Iraq out of Kuwait. While this action yielded considerable political fallout, it had its dark side—a lingering and devastating effect that would last for years. Victorious in military action, the United States entered a new phase of economic decline that forced Bush to undertake a mission to Japan in January 1992 in an effort to revive the declining U. S. economy.

In examining the role that education must play in helping nations seek an improvement in the human condition and relations between nations, one must be reminded of the diagnostic approach that the world community made at the conclusion of the war in 1945. This is the place and time that this study begins. Painful as this exercise was, the delegates to the San Francisco conference concluded that rather than blame the Axis powers for causing the war, all nations must share the responsibility for its outbreak. If nations had realized this in 1939, the war would have been avoided in the first place, and in 1991 the devastation caused by the war in the Persian Gulf would have been avoided and the billions of dollars used to wage the war could have been directed at the much needed social services that all countries have not been able to extend to their people.

Neither the U.S. Senate nor the House of Representatives predicted the setting on fire of oil fields in Kuwait and the displacement of the Kurds as outcomes of the war. If the restoration of Kuwait was accomplished at the price of the displacement of the Kurds and the destruction of natural resources in Kuwait, then one must conclude that the victory the allied coalition forces thought they scored against Saddam Hussein must be considered a disaster. This means that using military means to force Iraq out of Kuwait had a much darker side in the form of human cost that could not be measured.

There is another cost to this tragedy: prospects for peace in the Middle East, which Western nations thought would become possible with the defeat of Iraq, have remained as distant as ever. The shuttle diplomacy that Secretary of State James Baker initiated at the conclusion of hostilities did not yield any tangible results. Indeed, Baker's efforts amounted to the days of Henry Kissinger reincarnate, shuttle diplomacy with its weak side. As the presidential campaign got underway in August 1992, President Bush removed Baker from the State Department and appointed him manager of his reelection efforts. The fears that Israel and its Arab neighbors had about the intention of the other even intensified as both sides hardened their respective positions, refusing to see the critical issues they faced from the other's perspective. With Baker out of the negotiations, the crisis in the Middle East took a dramatic turn for the worse.

MILITARY ACTION AS A CONSEQUENCE
OF THE LACK OF THEORY

There is yet another disturbing aspect of the war in the Persian Gulf that the Western forces had not anticipated. As war progressed and allied forces were reported to be within striking distance of victory, social and economic conditions in the United States began to deteriorate rapidly. In his PBS television program on June 2, 1991, Bill Moyers gave the following facts as an outcome of the war. Nearly a million Americans were lining up for welfare benefits that were not there. The recession was having a devastating impact on education as nearly 54 percent of programs were being cut. Hospital care and other services were being reduced. The scourge of homelessness was rapidly increasing, and the plight of the less fortunate was deteriorating. In New Jersey the Office of Social Services was advising those fifty-five years and older to seek economic and financial help from their children in order to survive.

Many American servicemen returned home from the Gulf to find their families in a state of economic ruin. Some experienced family trauma that they had not anticipated, such as divorce. Even conservative journalist George Will argued in June 1991 that the war with Iraq had left behind "broken homes, broken hopes, and broken hearts" in both Iraq and the United States. Tom Foley, the speaker of the U.S. House of Representatives, added on June 16 that the preoccupation with the war in the Persian Gulf had created an array of problems at home that the nation was now finding hard to resolve. On August 2, ABC published the results of a poll that indicated that those Americans who had generally supported going to war with Iraq now questioned the decision to do so by a margin of 54 to 46 percent.

While this was happening, controversy between the president and the Democrats in Congress over the civil rights bill of 1991 was having a paralyzing effect on the political process. Can one conclude that all these adverse

tion of theory to seek solutions to the problems of national development from the time of Warren G. Harding to that of Bill Clinton.

Chapter 8 offers a summary of the essential features of education, and notes the problems that the United States is facing, as well as some implications they pose. This last chapter offers some interpretive analysis of the implications of the application of theory from the beginning of the colonial period to the present. The developments that are presented are critical to a national approach to education. The fundamental consideration is: What must the United States do to provide an education that reflects the conditions of today? The answer demands a formulation of theory, not just for the present but also for the future. This is where the study of history becomes important—especially the evolution of theory. It is virtually impossible to undertake this task without acquiring a functional knowledge of the evolution of theory. That theory must be designed so that it adequately responds to the needs of the people as a condition of meeting those of the nation. In approaching this task of seeking to address the needs of people, the United States can hope to accomplish its national agenda. The author hopes that this study provides some important insights into that task.

1

The Origins of the Theory
of Western Education

> Plato placed strong emphasis on method of study as the road to proper
> knowledge. The acquisition of knowledge required intellectual exercise
> and the use of reason.
>
> —William van Til, 1974

MIGRATION TO THE NEW WORLD

Theory is defined as a statement of principles which, when applied, would
lead to action that is consistent with given objectives. Evolution is defined as
the process of change from one form to another but providing a continuum.
Applied to its original definition, evolution implies that living species slowly
change from one form to another over a long period of time. For example,
one can say that buds evolve into flowers, or that modern automobiles have
evolved from ancient carriages, or, as is often stated, man has evolved from
the ape. When one speaks of the evolution of climate, continents, planets, or
heavenly bodies, one speaks of them as taking a slow and orderly change.
Therefore, the evolution of the theory of education in the United States must
begin with a discussion of thought processes in ancient Greece. It is not possible to discuss any aspect of the history of the United States without taking
into account developments in Europe. The discussion of the evolution of the
theory of education is no exception.

As Charles Robert Darwin defined it, the theory of evolution states that
plants and animals have changed from one generation to the next and are
still changing today. This study takes this line of thinking in discussing the
evolution of the theory of education in the United States as having its origins
in ancient Greece. Theory, as it was applied to the educational process in the
colonial period, went through a process of change and is still changing
today. It has evolved from placing emphasis on the teaching of religious and
moral values to the teaching of secular values and racial tolerance. It has
evolved from utilizing the Bible as the main textbook to utilizing videos or

the overhead projector as instructional materials. Indeed, from the colonial period to the present, the theory of education has taken various forms. We know that Darwin's theory of evolution carries three important elements. The first element is that living things change from one generation to the next producing descendants with new characteristics. The second element is that this process has been going on for so long that it has produced all the groups and kinds of things now living, as well as others that lived a long time ago. The third element is that these different living organisms are related to each other. This is how a particular species manages not only to survive but also to improve.

The settlement at Jamestown, Virginia, in 1607 marked the beginning of English migration to the New World. With this migration came a new way of life and evolution of a new culture demanding a new approach to government, social and economic systems, and a new education. One gets the impression that to those who settled in this area the land was a vast wilderness sparsely occupied by various groups of Native people whom they found there. The perception that the New World was a vast wilderness persisted from 1492 when Christopher Columbus (1451–1506) arrived in the Bahamas[1] to the present. But since 1607 the territory that later became known as the Thirteen Colonies was actually occupied by people who moved there long before the settlement at Jamestown. By some accounts there were 200,000 people known as Indians east of the Mississippi.[2] This means that this area was still a vast wilderness.

However, the settlement at Jamestown attracted more settlers from Europe. Thousands of those who came to the New World were seeking the right to worship in their own way. During the reign of James I of Britain from 1603 to 1625 and of Charles I from 1625 to 1689, religious tolerance reached a low point because kings of that era sought to strengthen their political power through the practice of religion.[3] In various ways, this practice has continued to this day, even in the United States. From the days of Henry VIII (1491–1547) from 1509 to 1547, British monarchs tolerated religious freedom only if the practice of religion did not interfere with their political power. When Henry pressured Parliament to pass legislation in 1534 that made the break with the Catholic Church complete and made him the head of the new Church of England, he set a precedent that future monarchs used to limit religious freedom.

By the time that Oliver Cromwell (1599–1658) assumed the office of head of the government[4] in 1652 following the conclusion of the civil war that broke out in 1642, life in Britain was increasingly becoming difficult for many people who were caught between their political activity and their desire to exercise religious freedom. The period of Cromwell's dictatorial rule did not suddenly bring to an end the social, political, economic, and religious conflict that was making life difficult for the people. When Cromwell was succeeded in 1658 by his son, Richard Cromwell (1626–1712), conditions of life continued to deteriorate. Fortunately, Richard was in office for only about a year, resigning in 1769 due to his inability to enjoy the confidence of the people.

The conflict that Britain experienced during this time was also experienced by people of other countries of Europe. The Thirty Years' War from 1618 to 1648 was devastating in many ways. Recognized as the last of the great religious wars, this conflict began as a civil war between Protestants and Catholics in Germany.[5] Before it came to an end most nations of Europe were involved causing a general decline both in the standard of living and human relationships. The cause of the war was the old hostilities that emerged between Protestants and Catholics due to the disagreement over interpretation of the Treaty of Augsburg of 1555. This treaty had been intended as a settlement of the religious question in Germany.

In 1618 conflict broke out throughout Europe caused mainly by the religious intolerance that had spread to all parts of Europe. Although a comprehensive peace was concluded by the Treaty of Westphalia in 1648, confidence among Europeans in a long-term peace and development was not restored. This is why people sought their future in the New World. The ordinary human impulse to be free provided an impetus to romanticize about the limitless opportunity in the New World. In spite of the dangers on the high seas and the hostility of the people who had settled the land many years before, the immigrants decided to take chances with beginning a new life rather than staying in Europe where there was no hope of an improved standard of living.

Perhaps the most important group of immigrants to the New World was the 102 passengers that came on the *Mayflower* that set sail from Southampton, England, on September 16, 1620, and arrived at Plymouth, Massachusetts, on December 26, 1620.[6] The new immigrants sent back to Europe reports of the extent of freedom they enjoyed in the New World. Eight years later another group arrived and settled in Salem, a community that became known for the trials of witchcraft. In 1630 a group of immigrants founded Boston. During the next ten years nearly 20,000 immigrants arrived in the area. Most were Puritans who came to the New World in search of religious freedom and would later play a major part in shaping the role of religion in society.

As the number of immigrants increased, several groups settled in different parts of the New World. For example, in 1636, the year that Harvard College was chartered, Thomas Hooker led a group to settle in the valley of the Connecticut River where they raised crops and livestock and practiced religious freedom. Another group moved and settled in New Hampshire because its members would not accept the religious intolerance of the Puritans. In the same year, 1636, George Calvert, who later became Lord Baltimore, obtained land in Maryland where his son, Cecilius Calvert, established the principle of religious tolerance. Thus, both Protestants and Catholics enjoyed religious freedom in Maryland. In the same way William Penn led a group of Quakers in 1681 to the territory that later became known as Pennsylvania.

Until 1680 those who came to the New World came from Britain in search of religious freedom. After that date most of the immigrants came from France and Prussia. Those who came from France were Huguenots who were persecuted by Catholics. In the New World they mainly settled in seaport centers where they became successful merchants and traders. Those who migrated from Prussia were members of various religious faiths who believed that church and state should remain separate. In the New World as a whole, immigrants enjoyed abundant land, fertile soil, plentiful game and fish, which they needed to survive and get started in their new life.

In spite of these hopeful indications for a bright future the settlers faced some serious problems. Jamestown was founded in an area that was infested with mosquitoes, which carried malaria. Inadequate methods of controlling malaria made it difficult to maintain good health. As a result more than half the immigrants who arrived in 1620 died. Between 1620 and 1624 other epidemics took a heavy toll on these immigrants. During the following spring many considered returning to Europe. But the prospects of facing old problems they thought they had left kept them hoping for a better life in the future. Indeed, new hope for a better future grew in the summer of 1621. The abundant harvest rejuvenated the confidence of the immigrants and their courage and determination to withstand adversity. Governor William Bradford decided that a three-day feast, thanks, and celebration be scheduled to begin on July 30, 1623.[7]

In addition to health problems, immigrants faced the hostility of the original settlers, known as Indians. At first these proud people were friendly and kind. They showed the new settlers how to raise crops and trap wild animals. They also taught their guests how to blaze trails through the forests, construct canoes, and make clothing items from raw materials that the wilderness provided. In 1614 Pocahontas (1595–1617), the daughter of Chief Powhatan, married John Rolfe (1585–1622), one of the settlers helping to improve relationships between the Powhatan and the settlers. But after the death of the chief in 1618 the Powhatan began to doubt the intentions of the settlers and conflict between the two groups began to grow. Thus began the conflict between the settlers and the Indians that lasted well into the nineteenth century.[8]

PATTERNS OF SETTLEMENT IN THE NEW WORLD

With increasing confidence in their ability and determination to overcome adversity, the settlers began in earnest the process of developing the territory so that it would become more habitable to support life. The study of the settlement patterns in the New World shows that there would be three major areas of settlement (New England, the mid-Atlantic, and the South). These developed according to climatic conditions, geography, and the needs of the settlers themselves, such as religion, commerce, trade, and agricultural activity. Amerigo Vespucci (1451–1512), known also by his Latin name, Americus Vesputius, an Italian friend of Christopher Columbus who went on subsequent voyages to the New World, kept an account of the land he had seen. In 1492 Columbus had no idea that he had discovered the Western Hemisphere. He believed that the islands he had discovered were part of the Indies. Even in 1498, his third voyage, when he first set foot on the North American continent he still believed that he had discovered India. That is why he called the people he found here Indians. Vesputius knew better, but he could not convince Columbus, the more famous explorer, that they had discovered a new land.

Some years later a Prussian explorer and adventurer, Waldsee Muller, released the results of his study of the land forms in the New World and described it in greater detail than had been done in the past. Vesputius compared Muller's description with his own and found that the two descriptions were quite similar. Muller suggested that the New World be named America in honor of Americus Vesputius.[9] Muller's account of the three regions that immigrants settled in proved valuable to future immigrants. In doing so Muller provided valuable information about the three regions using the methods that Vesputius had developed. The settlers in these three regions (later known as New England, the Middle Atlantic region, and the South) learned valuable things about the conditions that prevailed there. Each area had geographical and climatic features that were different and would influence the development of the regions in their unique ways.

NEW ENGLAND

The characteristics that were part of each of these regions formed the thrust for the evolvement of the theory of education that was applied to develop them.[10] New England was settled by Puritans who demanded nothing less than complete conformity in order to structure a society that was governed by religious beliefs and principles different from those applied in Britain. The Puritans based these principles on the theology of John Calvin (1509–1564), a Swiss religious leader whose ideas were influential in shaping the course of the Protestant Reformation movement in Europe. Born in Noyon in Northern France, Calvin received his early education in Paris. Later he studied theology and law at the universities of Orleans, Bourges, and Paris. Because he acquired a high level of education, Calvin became highly influential in the reform movement. In 1532 he expressed dissatisfaction with some of the teachings of the Catholic Church. In 1536 he explained some of his own theology contained in his book, *Institutes of the Christian Religion*, which many regarded as an important contribution to the reform movement.

As a result Calvin attracted a considerable following in most countries of Europe. Calvin's theology included five components that had special appeal to those who settled in New England: (1) God is sovereign and knows all things including human destiny; (2) God is the creator of the universe and He is absolute in all creation; (3) man is pure at creation because God creates him in His own image, but man has fallen from the status of perfection through his own action; (4) man can be saved only through the unmerited grace of God through the sacrifice that Christ made on the cross; man can do nothing to ensure his own salvation and no amount of good work can save man; (5) only those predestined for salvation will be saved.[11]

The significance of Calvin's theology to life in New England is the application the Puritans used to define the role of education to prepare children for an effective place in society. The Puritans also utilized Calvin's theology to express some theoretical precepts that included their conclusion that children were born from an act of sin and corruption.[12] The Puritans saw their task as one of educating children so that they conformed to the rules and requirements of society. On their own, children are unable to learn these requirements. In accepting this theology as their modus vivendi the Puritans operated by the belief that all human beings, especially young people, are savage creatures who need constant discipline and supervision to control their inclinations and desires to operate outside the norms established by society. The function of education is to help them redirect the behaviors beneficial to society as a whole. As a result of applying this theoretical precept, discipline of all people in society was considered essential in an effort to give it a cohesive and orderly structure. Obedience to both the laws of society and to parents was also considered important to the formation of good character needed to develop society.

From 1620 to 1700 the Puritans embraced fully Calvin's theology to become part of life in New England. By the mid–eighteenth century Calvinism had become fully established as a theory of education. In 1754 Jonathan Edwards (1702–1758) published his *Freedom of the Will* in which he reminded the Puritans of the importance of upholding Calvin's theology. Edwards based his own theology on that of another Puritan thinker, Cotton Mather (1663–1728). In 1710 Mather published *Essays to Do Good*, in which he fully supported Calvin's theology. Edwards stressed the importance of teaching children, early on, the acceptance of Puritan values, saying, "Let children obey their parents and yield to their instructions and submit to their orders as they would inherit a blessing and not a curse. We have reason to think from many things in the world of God that nothing has a greater tendency to bring a curse on persons in the world and on all temporal concerns than undutiful, unsubmissive, disorderly behavior in children towards their parents."[13]

Gerald L. Gutek concludes that various religious leaders that included Jonathan Edwards and Cotton Mather embraced all the essential components of Calvin's theology in order to elevate Puritan ideals to a new level of meaningful living.[14] The question that one must ask is: Why did religious leaders of that time exert so much influence on society? The answer is that religious leaders were more educated than other members of the community. For example, Jonathan Edwards received both a B.A. and M.A. degree from Yale University. Yale University was chartered in 1701, the third oldest college after Harvard (1636) and William and Mary (1692).[15] Edwards was therefore well read. In 1727 he was ordained and appointed as assistant in the church of his grandfather, Solomon Stoddard, who was stationed at Northampton, Massachusetts. When Stoddard died in 1729 Edwards was appointed to succeed him. He delivered his famous sermon, "Sinners in the Hands of an Angry God," in 1741 during a period of the Great Religious Awakening. The fact that Edwards was well educated is the reason why colleges were founded to prepare the clergy for an effective role in society.

In the same way Cotton Mather was exerting considerable influence on Puritan society—he had a good education and a strong family background. His grandfather, Richard Mather (1596–1669), was born in Britain where he studied at Oxford University. His Puritan beliefs led to serious conflict between him and the authorities in the Church of England. He left Britain to begin a new life in Massachusetts. From 1636 to his death, Mather was appointed pastor of the Congregational Church in Dorchester. Because of the power of his message, Mather's influence quickly spread to other areas of New England. Richard's son, Increase Mather (1639–1723), was born in Dorchester and went much further than his father in his pursuit of education and knowledge based on Puritan theology. Increase attended Harvard College where he distinguished himself as a student of biblical studies and other areas of intellectual pursuit.

Increase's best contribution to the development of the Puritan theology and society in New England came with his publications. In 1693 he published *Cases of Conscience Concerning Evil Spirits*. Later he also published *A Brief History of the War with Indians*. Although the book was well written, it appears to be based on considerable bias against the Indians. Increase knew this, but he felt that he needed to write the book the way he did to leave something for posterity. Increase also wrote a number short publications that addressed social, political, and religious issues of the day. This is the environment that produced Cotton Mather. History says that Cotton wrote more than 400 short books, among them *Magnalia Christi America*, which was published in 1702. The book is a classic presentation of the history of religious thought and its development in New England. Mather was clearly worried about the increasing number of individuals who were coming to the New World for reasons other than fear of persecution. He believed that this enclave of religious purity, which the Puritans represented, be preserved by not allowing those who did not subscribe to its theology to settle among them. Thus Cotton Mather contributed to the intolerance that those who came to the New World were trying to escape in Europe.

As this critical region of the world steadily attracted more people, it mobilized them to structure a new society that was increasingly becoming intolerant of any religious and social ideas that were incompatible with Puritan theology. In adopting this strategy of preserving itself, New England excluded a wide range of individuals with remarkable resources to contribute to its development. They—like the members of the Mather family who thought that only Puritan theology was the best that could have happened to New England—lost an opportunity to view their society from a broader and more inclusive perspective that was needed to make society more representative and diverse as a basis of its richness.

MIDDLE ATLANTIC COLONIES

Next to New England was a number of settlements that became known as Middle Atlantic colonies. These included Delaware, New Jersey, Pennsylvania, and New York. There were important differences between New England and the Middle Atlantic colonies. The first difference was that the land of the Middle Atlantic colonies was less hilly and rocky than the land in New England. This meant that the land was more fertile than in New England, making it possible to support considerable agricultural activity.[16] The second difference was that while New England attracted conservative Puritans from Britain, the Middle Atlantic settlement attracted people from major countries of Europe such as Prussia, Holland, France, and Scandinavia. This meant that the Middle Atlantic colonies were settled by people from diverse backgrounds bringing with them diverse perspectives of the world in which they lived.

These groups spoke different European languages that created an environment of diversity and richness in social practice. This was necessary to bring about tolerance, understanding, and cooperation. The third difference between New England and the Middle Atlantic colonies was the practice of religion. In New England the Puritans' practice of religion was based on the theology of John Calvin. Gerald L. Gutek concludes that in the Middle Atlantic colonies religious pluralism was regarded by different religious groups that included the Dutch Reformed, Quaker, Lutheran, Anglican, Presbyterian, Jewish, and Roman Catholic[17] as faiths all living and operating in harmony without any show of conflict. The presence of these diverse religious groups in this region suggests the extent to which they decided to allow religious tolerance for the good of all the people and of society itself.

Of the Middle Atlantic settlements, New York was more inclusive than the others. Known as New Amsterdam until 1664 when the British seized it, New York had been a Dutch colony since 1626, twenty-six years before they founded a colonial settlement at the Cape of Good Hope at the southern tip of Africa.[18] The Dutch exerted considerable influence on the development of New Amsterdam as they did in South Africa. After the region was taken by the British the Dutch tried hard to maintain their cultural and religious practices. In the Middle Atlantic area there was no effort made by any religious group to demand conformity by other groups. As no religious group exerted greater influence than others, religious development of all groups had equal opportunity for growth. What is even more important is that religious tolerance extended to other areas of life such as economic and social development. Robert E. Potter concludes that religious freedom was granted to New Jersey when the Duke of York granted the land to two friends who established an administration in 1665.[19] The people of the Middle Atlantic colonies operated on the theological belief that because people were different they became the means through which God communicated to them in different ways. They also believed that this difference was an enrichment of both their religious experience and society itself.

Although the different groups that settled in the Middle Atlantic region were sensitive to the need to exercise religious tolerance, each group aspired to promote its own cultural, social, and religious traditions. In the absence of a single religious system, such as the Puritan system of New England, there was no single system of education that began to take on an established pattern and direction. However, those who settled in the Middle Atlantic region held one common belief that every person must be able to read the Bible in order to lead a meaningful and fulfilling life.[20] This theoretical belief became the basis of a common approach to education. This heterogeneous approach to education led to the establishment of parochial schools that required orthodox religious knowledge as the principal qualification for those who aspired to become teachers.

In this common approach the Middle Atlantic colonies put together elements of a theory of education that began to form as the new destiny of the region (and the New World as a whole) was being slowly shaped. When the Dutch West India Company received the charter in 1626 it was granted the right to govern itself. In order to make the people under its administration happy, the system of government formulated policies and a program of action that recognized religious freedom of the people. Although the Dutch Reformed Church became part of the administrative system, the colonists enjoyed the freedom of religion more than the Puritans in New England. It is the practice of this freedom that soon became the basis of the evolution of a theory of education. The belief that religious freedom was important to individual liberties was also important to the educational process.

SOUTHERN PLANTATIONS

The third region of settlement in the New World was the South. There, climatic conditions were suitable for growing a variety of crops that included sugar, tobacco, and cotton. This made it possible for the system of plantations to exert as much influence on society as the Puritans did on New

England and as the various religious sects did in the Middle Atlantic colonies. Therefore, the plantations were the religion of the South. Gerald L. Gutek suggests that the society that developed in the South was essentially agricultural in character and, since 1619, was supported by the growing number of slaves imported from Africa.[21] In time, slavery became so institutionalized that it became the cornerstone of the society in the South.

Until the Emancipation Proclamation issued by President Abraham Lincoln (1809–1865) on September 22, 1862, which took effect on January 1, 1863, slavery sustained the economic, social, and political system of the South. Because slavery was engrained in all aspects of society in the South, it could not be ended without causing major disruptions to institutional operations. By the time the Thirteenth Amendment was proposed on January 31, 1865, and proclaimed December 18, the United States had gone through a devastating civil war[22] resulting in the assassination of the president on April 14, 1865.[23] Bitterness between the South and the North would form the nature of relationships between the South and the North and between whites and Negroes for the next century.

The presence of slaves from Africa early in the society of the South created problems that would not be solved for well over 300 years. Slavery created a climate that compelled the colonists to exercise limited resourcefulness needed for the development of a new society. It compelled the colonists to believe that some people were more important than others and so must be treated differently. Slavery also produced a new theory that a person's place in society must be determined by what he did, and what he did must be dictated by who he was. In this and other theoretical principles, fairness and justice, so crucial to peace and harmony in any society, were rendered meaningless. The society of the South ignored the fact that slaves were yearning for freedom as much as the colonists. The search for freedom by slaves became a preoccupation from the inception of slavery since 1619 when twenty slaves were brought to Jamestown. John Hope Franklin and Alfred A. Moss Jr. state, "In 1774 a group of blacks expressed their astonishment that the colonists could seek independence from Britain yet give no consideration to the slaves' pleas for freedom. Slaves made literally scores of such representations and, in so doing, contributed significantly to broadening the ideology of the struggle to include at least some human freedom as well as political independence."[24]

In 1845 Frederick Douglass (1818–1895) described the negative impact that slavery had on the society of the South and the efforts slaves made to overcome adversity saying:

I lived in Master Hugh's family about seven years. During that time I succeeded in learning to read and write. I had no regular teacher. My mistress, who had kindly commenced to instruct me, had, in compliance with the advice and direction of her husband, not only ceased to instruct, but had also set her face against my being instructed by any one else. It is due, however, to my mistress to say of her, that she did not adopt this course of treatment immediately. She at first lacked the depravity indispensable to shutting me up in mental darkness. It was at least necessary for her to have some training in the exercise of irresponsible power, to make her equal to the task of treating me as though I were a brute. However, my mistress, in teaching me the alphabet, had given me the inch, and no precaution could prevent me from taking the ell.[25]

There is no question that this form of dysfunctional characteristic of the society of the South had its origins at the time slavery was institutionalized as part of the plantation society. But it is troubling to think that social practices in the South were based on slavery until emancipation. This is because once the plantation society saw the benefit that the institution of slavery accrued politically, socially, and in the form of labor, it was not likely to initiate the search for improvement based on emerging social and economic practices that would give new meaning to the future.

The increasing demand for agricultural production to feed the growing population demanded a more stratified society to delineate activity related to agricultural industry. The production of tobacco by England made the settlements in the South require that the plantation system be improved to make it more effective. Trade owners forced small tenet farmers to surrender their operations and move away to make room for the farmers who were able to consolidate their own operations. As the demand for tobacco grew, the price rose as did the acreage. This caused a corresponding increase in the need for labor. This meant an increase in the number of slaves. By 1680 there were as many slaves as white indentured servants. Soon after, the number of slaves steadily increased as they proved more efficient in agricultural operations because that was what they had learned to do in Africa. Back in Africa the economy was based on agricultural production, and most Africans had learned early to be efficient agriculturists. This is why most slaves were sent to the South.

By 1700 the production of rice as a commodity had equaled that of tobacco in importance. It was grown mainly in South Carolina where the marshy coastal lands and a moist climate were well suited for its growth. The colonists and white indentured servants refused to work in the fields infested with malaria because they saw the threat to their health as an indication that conditions of work in general were so bad that they would not sacrifice their health for a small income. This meant that the agricultural operations relative to the growing of rice had to be done by slaves who did not have the same choice as did the indentured white servants. The colonists also began to raise livestock. Herds of cattle, pigs, and chickens became common in the southern colonies. Because the weather in the South was humid, it was quite possible to raise livestock easily. The combination of the increase in the importance of rice and the raising of livestock raised the importance of slaves so as to institutionalize slavery itself. By 1750 it was no longer possible to separate slavery from any aspect of life and society in the South. Slavery had become both the engine and the fuel that were needed to move the social, economic, and political vehicle that the colonists were traveling in to their destination.

As the population steadily increased, urban centers began to grow rapidly. Centers like Boston, New York, Baltimore, Philadelphia, and Charleston were growing rapidly due the number of people who were moving there. Boston, having been founded in 1630, had the largest population. But in 1750 Philadelphia had become a more important center of trade than Boston. In 1751 street lamps were installed in Philadelphia. In 1736 Benjamin Franklin (1706–1790) founded a company of volunteer fire fighters. Industrial development was also becoming important in shaping the nature of society. The important thing to remember here is that the development that was taking place in the North had a profound impact on the South, which needed facilities in the North to accommodate trade and commerce. During the early days of the settlements the three regions do not appear to have coordinated their activity due to differences in religious practices. But by 1750 it was clear that each region needed the other two to improve their economic development.

This realization became a powerful influence on the formation of a theory of education in the South. The theory of labor as a definite form of education became a fundamental tenet of thinking among members of the South. At Tuskegee, Booker T. Washington (1856–1915) fully embraced it, urging his students to remember that there was as much honor in tilling the soil as there was in writing a poem. Washington added, "I not only learned too, that it was not a disgrace to labor, but I also learned to love labor, not only for its financial value, but for labor's own sake."[26] Indeed, the evolution of a theory of education relative to labor as a form of education in the South came from different directions.

During this formative period of the plantations the colonists spent a great deal of their time and energy in the production of food, making clothes, and providing shelter. There were few markets for their small amount of excess products, and manufactured goods were produced on a small scale. Through various legislation Britain controlled the markets for its own benefit. From 1361 to 1835 Britain maintained the infamous corn laws, which it used to control the production, distribution, and prices of the goods from the colonies. The British landlords, many of them powerful members of Parliament, supported these laws to enhance the margins of their profit. They did this by forcing the colonists to pay heavy taxes and various fees that forced farmers to endure considerable economic difficulties. The brand of these difficulties was borne by farmers in the South. This is why George Washington, Thomas Jefferson, and James Madison[27] all took the initiative to register protests against the application of British laws.

The application of the corn laws generated a set of circumstances that increased tension between the colonists and Britain. Differences of opinion began to emerge between the two sides about the economic impact of the British laws and the political implications the colonists saw. The two sides were heading for a showdown. By the time Adam Smith (1723–1790) published his famous book, *Wealth of Nations,* in 1776—a fateful year for the colonists—relationships between the two sides had been damaged beyond repair. In his book Smith outlined economic theories that had direct application to economic conditions in the colonies. He argued that labor, not land or money, was the real source of a nation's wealth. Nearly seventy-two years later, in 1848, Karl Marx (1818–1883) and Friedrich Engels (1820–1895), German social reformists, took this same line of thinking in publishing *The Communist Manifesto.* In it they argued that the emphasis that the entrepreneurs were placing on making profit as a result of the conditions created by the Industrial Revolution would soon cause conflict between laborers and management because the former would not sell their labor cheaply to the latter allowing them to make an enormous profit.

ORIGINS OF A THEORY OF EDUCATION
IN BRITISH NORTH AMERICA

Now that we have given a brief account of the patterns of settlement in the New World, two questions must be asked. The first question is: What kind of theory of education did the society of the New World initiate in order to provide the settlers with the kind of education they needed to lead a successful life style and to ensure the development of their society? The second question is: What were the origins of such a theory? It has been established earlier in this chapter that the evolution of a theory of education took different directions in the three regions of settlement according to their religious orientation. Although the New World progressively led to the evolution of a new culture, the emergence of a new language pattern, economic, political, and social life, its origins were closely related to practices and traditions that had existed in Europe for many years, both ancient and modern. To have a clear picture of the evolution of a theory in the New World it is necessary to discuss some theoretical perspectives of two masters in ancient Greece because that is the origin of Western thought and its influence on society—Plato and Aristotle. This is not to suggest that they were the only two who influenced the evolution of a theory of education in the Western world, but just to cite them as examples of that influence.

THE INFLUENCE OF PLATO

Among the individuals whose ideas formed part of the origins of a Western theory of society in general and education in particular is the ancient Greek philosopher, Plato (427–347 B.C.).[28] Plato's theories still constitute the frame of reference in any discussion of philosophy of education. He formulated a logical application of human thought process to human activity, including the learning process and involvement in confronting problems of society. Gerald L. Gutek suggests that one good approach to the study of Plato's philosophy is to examine events in his society and the experiences in his life that influenced him in formulating his theory the way he did.[29] Plato realized that while society was by no means perfect, it was quite possible to educate its members to the extent that they would be trained adequately to play a meaningful role in society and so improve it.

The emphasis he placed on education as an instrument of sharpening human qualities, such as truth, honesty, and beauty of the mind as his definition of human goodness, formed the basis of his theory that man, by his very nature, is good because he has a spirit that enables him to discern good from evil. He concluded that with proper education man can become even better, poising him for service to his society. This is why, in its formative phase, the evolution of a theory of education in the New World stressed the importance of religious and moral instruction in order to elevate the human spirit to a higher level that made human life more meaningful. Although Plato's concept of the human spirit was not directly related to the practice of religion, those who were part of the evolution of a theory of education in the New World saw a direct relationship between the human spirit and religion.[30] For them the human spirit could not be separated from the practice of religion. This belief became an essential consideration in the process of elevating the human being to the level where his action and behavior would assist in creating a great society. This is why, in 1967, President Lyndon B. Johnson (1908–1971) based his war on poverty and his efforts to create what he called the Great Society on expected contribution of individuals as a result of receiving the kind of education he hoped they would receive from applying the theory his administration had formulated.

To understand Plato's theory—that society is best served by the role that individuals play—one needs to appreciate the existence of social systems that were ruled by despots in the areas around Greece. In the famous Fertile Crescent of the Tigris and the Euphrates, the Assyrian and Persian empires were ruled by despots. In the same way along the Nile River there existed powerful rulers in Egypt that were not as despotic as those of Assyrian and Persian societies. The empires in these two societies were kept together by the force of military power. The people had no role in shaping the character of their society. Absolute obedience to the emperor was required of all subjects to keep society cohesive as he defined it. But in Egypt society was kept together by common love of tradition and culture. Plato closely studied these empires and came to the conclusion that the reason the pharaohs of Egypt were less despotic than those of Assyria and Persia was the emphasis that was placed on education.

Early in the process of developing his theory Plato thought that his own society should follow a different line of development from that in Assyria and Persia. He therefore developed the theory of education that he believed, by its application, would create a society that was capable of understanding and embracing values that would serve the needs of all the people from one generation to the next without any individual emerging to resort to despotic rule. In developing his philosophy of society and theory of education Plato wanted the members of his society, especially those who lived in Athens, to have the kind of life that was totally different from that which people in despotic systems led. The principles of democratic behavior that became the basis of education in the New World would have their origins in Plato's philosophy and theory.

As Plato continued to study the meaning of human life and the role of the individual in society, he discovered new dimensions that he believed education could make possible. Among the conclusions he reached as a result of his study was that every person possessed a potential for making a viable contribution to the development of society. He further believed that that contribution came from one's talent, which could be improved and sharpened by education. He also concluded that the organizational structure of society was a result of political activity that every individual was entitled to. In that context social interactions give a deeper meaning to the structure of society when each member is free to explore his own capability to benefit first himself as a prerequisite of benefiting his society. To realize this benefit society must allow freedom to the individual so that he can develop and express his ideas in an unrestricted manner. However, Plato argued that his function is seriously limited unless education becomes the principal means of fulfillment. Therefore, the fulfillment of any objectives defined or expected by society is a result of the combination of the interests of the individual and those of society.

In his study, *Protagoras*, Plato presents his definition of the purpose of education that is inclusive and comprehensive. Plato defines purpose as producing an individual who not only understands himself in terms of his needs, but who also has a comprehensive understanding of his world so that he relates his activity to playing a role that makes his community a better place for all to live in.[31] Plato's definition of the purpose of education includes that kind of pursuit of knowledge that enables the individual to acquire ethics and morality and enables him to distinguish himself from other living species in terms of an ability to make a difference between what is right and what is wrong. He suggested that to enable the individual to accomplish what he is capable of, society must recognize his basic freedoms. These freedoms include the freedom to think, to form new ideas, and to apply them within the environment of learning. The best environment is one in which learners interact with one another in a meaningful way. These elements played a major role in an effort to structure social systems and education in the New World.

Plato was also at his best in defining his theory of education in *The Republic*.[32] In 368 B.C. Plato went to Sicily to educate the young prince, Dionysius II, in the virtues necessary for a just and good ruler. The experiences and observations he made there became the basis of *The Republic*. In this book Plato advances his theory that for society to serve its purpose it must be cohesive. This cohesion comes from the relationships that members have with each other. He argues that harmonious relationships cannot be assumed. They have to be developed from the positive attributes that each member possesses and which appropriate education can improve. He goes on to argue that man must envision himself as living a life of fulfillment beyond the material world in order to understand the world of ideas. He admitted that the ideal society can emerge not only from wisdom, justice, and fairness, but also from living a life that is controlled by spiritual values. When the individual has lost his sense of justice and fairness because they have been denied him, he loses his sense of his role in society. In turn society itself pays the price. In this setting society degenerates and decays.

Although Plato recognized the importance of the political, economic, and social changes that were taking place in Athens at the time, he felt that education could be utilized to facilitate the creation of a more democratic and egalitarian society. His efforts in this direction contributed to the thinking that while Sparta was developing as a military state, Athens was developing as a democratic state. As Plato saw things, the thinking that the challenge for those who taught students—to inspire the process of meaningful social change to improve society—was a central purpose of education. *The Republic* was therefore a blueprint for both social change and educational endeavor. Plato was one of those thinkers who argued that the educational process must begin early in the life of the learner because his values and attitudes can be influenced more readily with good education.

This line of thinking is the reason why he argued in *The Republic* that the state school establish nursery schools. Their major function would be to introduce children to a sound environment that was conducive to social adjustment making it possible for them to learn social responsibility. The nursery schools would also help children learn to form proper habits of good life so that when they were adults they would appreciate and play their role in society. In the nursery schools children would learn music, drama, games, and other recreative activities that would help them in their coordination. These activities are important to social harmony. In any society social harmony cannot be assumed; it comes as a result of making a concerted effort to create conditions that bring it about. Among these conditions are the willingness of individuals to recognize that their civil liberties are directly related to those of others. If all people in society recognized this reality, then they would come close to eliminating the possible cause of social conflict.

Plato advocated the kind of education that would combine with law and order to serve the ultimate good and the promotion of human virtue as a prerequisite of an ideal society.[33] He regarded the ability of society to provide good government and to structure and preserve elements of freedom as inherent qualities of the human being. This is the reason why he concluded that education must be provided to all people on the basis of equality. However, Plato argued that there were those areas that manifested human potential for service. These are the ability to govern well, the ability to defend society, and the ability to perform social services.[34] Regardless of these three forms of potential, education cannot be separated from human potential because they have a reciprocal and symbiotic relationship. Society must design education to train people to serve the needs of the individual and those of society, and in turn education must serve the purposes of society. Only education that is provided on the basis of equality can meet the needs of society.

Among the strongest elements of Plato's theory is his view that education and society cannot be separated because they depend on each other. An individual's civic responsibility is to promote the broad interests of society such as its security, its goals and purpose, and its general welfare. His pursuit of goals which, when fulfilled, serves the needs of society and provides a satisfaction that becomes a motivation to do more good. But for individuals to operate under this basic human virtue requires education. Virtue requires total commitment and dedication. Only those who have dedicated themselves to gaining virtue must be called upon to serve society. Plato advanced his view that only those who have demonstrated high intellect and morality should come forward to offer their special talent for the benefit of society. William van Til sums up Plato's contribution to the evolution of theory and its application to society of today saying, "In *The Republic* Plato placed strong emphasis on method of study as the road to proper knowledge. The acquisition of knowledge required intellectual exercise and the use of reason properly censored to ensure a suitable moral tone."[35]

Van Til goes on to conclude that Plato's contribution to the theory of Western society and education is that he endeavored to develop several ideas that are still in use in American schools today. These ideas include state financial support of education, passing legislation that safeguards the educational interests of students, directing the development of education, ensuring the safety of students, encouraging discipline among students, setting regulations to ensure the security of teachers and determining their qualifications, outlining conditions of student promotion, and enforcing compulsory education. However, the society of today still faces the problems that the society of Plato faced. These include poverty, inequality in spending for education, lack of financial resources, confusion in educational priorities, limited success in teaching students to seek solutions to problems of society as an adult, too much emphasis being placed on material well-being, and failure to help students understand and appreciate moral values. This means that while Plato has left a legacy of good ideas about education in Western society, he has also left a legacy of problems that have yet to be resolved.

THE INFLUENCE OF ARISTOTLE

History says that Aristotle (384–322 B.C.) was a student of Plato. Aristotle proved to be a focused student who was able to learn as much as he could from his teacher. In time Aristotle acquired the reputation of a savvy statesman who became a tutor of Alexander the Great (356–323 B.C.) who was then fourteen years old. Aristotle inspired Alexander with a love of learning. When he was twenty years old Alexander became the king of Macedonia and tried to apply the ideas he had learned from Aristotle. Encouraged by the success of the relationship that he had with Alexander, Aristotle opened a school in Athens so that he could influence other youths with the quality of his instruction. Aristotle operated under his theory that all learners have a potential for excellence in the pursuit of learning if the right environment exists, and the society has the responsibility to structure that environment so that learning can take place.[36] It is ironic that Alexander, who learned the intellectual pursuit from a great master should turn out to be a military leader, rather than a statesman.

There were three features that were part of Greek society of Aristotle's time that he tried to address by his theory. The first feature was the rise of Hellenistic civilization that reached its height of influence during the time that Alexander was most powerful. The second feature was the increasing role of intellect in shaping the character of society. The third feature was the increasing importance of Greek culture in the existing world. Aristotle was trying to promote all three features as being closely related to the development of society. He felt that his society needed to intensify its intellectual pursuits and efforts to sustain traditions that had served it well in the past so that future generations would build great institutions. In this endeavor Aristotle was highly sensitive to his role in formulating his theory to shape the destiny of Greece. Making a claim to being the heir to the Greek educational tradition,[37] Aristotle tried to make Athens the ideal state in which to achieve excellence in academic achievement. He tried to promote an educational system that he believed would leave a legacy of what is known today as liberal studies.

Aristotle also operated under his theoretical belief that an educated person was a civilized human being whose worth was measured by his participation in all forms of human endeavors. These forms included art, politics, law, civic activity, and creative activity such as music, literature, drama, and service to the community. He shared Plato's view that all people had a unique contribution to offer society and that all must receive education on the basis of equality. It is important to remember that Aristotle lived during the time when Greece was subjected to major political change from the period of free city-states to the era of great change.

During that time Philip, the king of Macedonia from 359 to 336 B.C., defeated those who were trying to end the system of city-states at the battle of

Chaeronea in 338 B.C. Thinking that the system of city-states was secure, Philip began to relax some security measures including his own security. Two years later he was assassinated, and Alexander, his son, succeeded him. Immediately Alexander adopted a hard-line policy and increased his army to a point where it was the strongest in the region. Aristotle was disappointed to see that his student was abandoning the essential principles of behavior he had taught him. But given the threat to the security he was helping to build, he understood what Alexander was doing.

Perhaps the most important contribution that Aristotle made to the evolution of a theory of education was his involvement in the development of the Lyceum, an important school that played a critical role in the education of Athenians. The Lyceum was more of a moving institution rather than a fixed place. Aristotle moved from one place to another as he became an itinerant master reaching out to students where they were. Streets, public places, and parks became his classroom. Aristotle quickly acquired a reputation of a highly intellectual person who imparted to his students complete knowledge of the subjects he taught them. These included ethics, natural sciences, politics, metaphysics, and moral values.[38] He used the Lyceum to develop his theory of education and of society. One of the components of his theory related to natural progression in which he placed natural phenomena into structured hierarchical order. He placed lifeless objects at the bottom and living organisms on a higher scale beginning with man. He placed other animals below. The reason Aristotle placed the human being at the top of the ladder is that man possessed the power of rationality, which could even be improved upon by education. He argued that other animals could exhibit limited rationality, but it was the human being who exercised it more than other living species.

Aristotle was an impressive writer. Most of his writings were developed as lectures to his students.

Metaphysics outlines his theory of realism, that things are what they are because there is a real order.

Nicomachean Ethics presents his ideas about virtue as an essential human quality.

Politics presents his theory of the relationship that exists between education and social service.

On Justice discusses the logic of justice.

These examples show that Aristotle presented a theory of various subjects he considered important to human endeavor and society such as biology, law, botany, science, mathematics, psychology, and physiology. The breadth of his knowledge on different subjects of study placed him in a position that enabled him to have a profound influence on not only his students, but also on other societies 2,000 years later.

SUMMARY AND CONCLUSION

The purpose of this chapter was to trace the origins of the evolution of a theory of education in the New World beginning with migration from Europe as a result of the conflict that existed there. This conflict was caused by religious practices and political systems of varying forms, and it was not quite possible to have agreement on what was good for both people as individuals and society as a whole. Religious practices and political systems undercut the freedom of worship and expression. As Europe went through the period of the Renaissance and Reformation, those who contributed to the evolution of a new theology and political thought did so from the desire to improve the systems so that they would respond to the needs of the people. But in initiating a change of thought process in both religion and politics, they created an environment that led to conflict forcing individuals to consider going elsewhere. The New World presented an opportunity to start a new life free from the interference of the conflict in Europe.

This chapter also discussed three types of settlements in the New World and the kind of life each led. This leads to a discussion of the need to initiate a new type of education designed to meet the needs of society. But cast in a new environment where there were no traditions on which to build new institutions, the colonists adopted systems of education that had existed in Europe since the Medieval period. These systems were based on ancient Greek philosophy. This is why a discussion of Plato's and Aristotle's theory of education was initiated. These ideas form the basis of the theory of education in the Western world, and Plato and Aristotle form the major thrust of the type of education that began to form in the New World as soon as it came into being.

NOTES

1. The record shows that Columbus sighted the island of San Salvador, now Watlings Islands, in the Bahamas on October 12, 1492.

2. Barnes's Historical Series, *A Brief History of the United States* (New York: American Book Company, 1885), p. 10.

3. Ibid., p. 11.

4. A study of the political history of Britain shows that Sir Robert Walpole (1676–1745) was the first leader of the government to carry the title of prime minister in 1718.

5. For details see Lynn Miller, *The Global Order: Values and Power in International Politics* (Boulder, CO: Westview Press, 1994).

6. History shows that the *Mayflower*, a double-deck ship, was built in 1609 and measured 90 feet long and weighed 180 tons. It dropped anchor off what is now Provincetown Harbor on November 21, 1620, and then set sail to Plymouth, Massachusetts, where it arrived on December 26, 1620.

7. This event was the beginning of the now-famous Thanksgiving celebration in the United States. On November 26, 1789, President George Washington issued a

general proclamation for a day of thanks after the Revolutionary War. Since 1941 the fourth Thursday in November is observed as Thanksgiving Day.

8. The battle at Wounded Knee in South Dakota in December 1890 finally put an end to the military conflict between the two sides but tension has continued to this day.

9. Barnes's Historical Series, *A Brief History of the United States*, p. 24.

10. Gerald L. Gutek, *An Historical Introduction to American Education* (Prospect Heights, IL: Waveland Press, 1991), p. 3.

11. Ibid., p. 4.

12. Stanford Flemming, *Children and Puritanism: The Place of Children in the Life and Thought of New England, 1620–1647* (New Haven, CT: Yale University Press, 1933), p. 14.

13. H. Norman Gardiner, ed., *Selected Sermons of Jonathan Edwards* (New York: Macmillan Company, 1904), p. 147.

14. Gutek, *An Historical Introduction to American Education*, p. 15.

15. Barnes's Historical Series, *A Brief History of the United States*, p. 92.

16. Ibid., p. 91.

17. Gutek, *An Historical Introduction to American Education*, p. 11.

18. Dickson A. Mungazi, *The Struggle for Social Change in Southern Africa: Visions of Liberty* (New York: Taylor and Francis, 1989), p. 18.

19. Robert E. Potter, *The Stream of American Education* (New York: American Book Company, 1974) , p. 47.

20. Ibid., p. 48.

21. Gutek, *An Historical Introduction to American Education*, p. 8.

22. History shows that the Civil War broke out on April 12, 1862, and lasted until April 9, 1865.

23. The record shows that President Lincoln died on April 15, 1865, from an assassin's bullet fired by John Wilkes Booth (1837–1865) on April 14. The president was watching a play, *Our American Cousin*, at Ford's Theater in Washington, D.C.

24. John Hope Franklin and Alfred A. Moss Jr., *From Slavery to Freedom: History of African Americans*, 7th ed. (New York: McGraw-Hill, 1994), p. 79.

25. Frederick Douglass, *Narrative of the Life of Frederick Douglass, An American Slave, Written by Himself* (New York: New American Library, 1845), p. 52.

26. Booker T. Washington, *Up From Slavery* (New York: Doubleday, 1916), p. 73.

27. In addition to these three Virginians, there are five others who served as presidents of the United States from Virginia. They are James Monroe (1758–1831), from 1817 to 1825; William Henry Harrison (1773–1841), who died suddenly on April 4, 1841, shortly after he was inaugurated at sixty-eight years of age; John Tyler (1790–1862), from 1841 to 1845; Zachary Taylor (1784–1850), from 1849 to 1850; and Woodrow Wilson (1856–1924), from 1913 to 1921. These presidents give Virginia the title of "The Mother of Presidents."

28. Plato, a nickname meaning broad-shouldered to signify the broadness of his mind and ideas, was used in Greek mythology as a god who ruled the underworld. The belief that good physique was essential to mental prowess, which Plato represents, was widely held until the nineteenth century. It was applied to the colonization of Africa, where the ideas of S. T. von Soemmering of Prussia and Charles Whites of Britain were applied with impunity. For a detailed discussion see Dickson A. Mungazi, *The Mind of Black Africa* (Westport, CT: Praeger Publishers, 1996).

29. Gerald L. Gutek, *Historical and Philosophical Foundations of Education: A Biographical Introduction*, 2nd ed. (New York: Merrill, 1991), p. 10.

30. This reality suggests the conclusion, as discussed in the examples cited in the introduction to this study, that the evolution of theory, like the evolution of species, goes through a transformation over a long period of time taking into account developments that are pertinent to the environment in which it is applied.

31. Gutek, *An Historical Introduction to American Education*, p. 19.

32. Benjamin Jowett (1817–1893) is one the best-known authorities on Plato. His translations of Plato's works are among the best.

33. William van Til, *Education: A Beginning* (Boston: Houghton Mifflin Company, 1974), p. 409.

34. Ibid., p. 410.

35. Ibid., p. 411.

36. Ibid., p. 142.

37. Gutek, *An Historical Introduction to American Education*, p. 30.

38. Ibid., p. 33.

2

Theory During the Colonial Period

The Renaissance had influence on American development . . . English Calvinists who wanted to change or purify the Anglican Church became known as Puritans and were very important in the settlement of New England.

—John D. Pulliam and James van Patten, 1995

JOHN LOCKE: BRIDGE FROM THE ANCIENT WORLD TO THE NEW WORLD

The various theories formulated by ancient Greek masters discussed in chapter 1 did not end with their application to Greek society, but they found their way into the New World as it began to form. If there is one individual who deserves credit for transmitting the thoughts of the Greek masters to the New World, that individual is John Locke (1632–1704). Adam Smith, who gained so much from Locke's work, was born nearly twenty years after Locke had died. By the time Smith published his *Wealth of Nations* in 1776 Locke's reputation as a thinker had reached major proportions. Therefore Smith's success and fame came partly from the ideas he learned from Locke.

Writing in 1996 about Locke's contribution to the evolution of theory of the character of society in the New World, Lloyd Duck of George Mason University concludes that Locke's ideas came into application at the right time.[1] Duck goes on to add that Locke's ideas were influential to the development of society in the New World because he expressed them in a clear and forceful manner that left no room for doubt as to what he said. During and after his life Locke has appropriately been known as the predominant influence on the development of the New World. His theory of government, society, and education had a tremendous impact on the evolution of ideas. Among those who utilized Locke's ideas was Thomas Jefferson (1743–1826), who was born thirty years after Locke's death. Jefferson utilized Locke's ideas in writing the Declaration of Independence.[2]

Locke was at his best in presenting his theory of politics and education. His ideas contrasted with those of Rene Descartes (1596–1650), a French philosopher, scientist, and mathematician. Even though Descartes was thirty-six years older than Locke, he was so impressed with Locke's work that it had an impact on the formulation of his own ideas. Locke formulated his political theory in *Two Treatises of Government* (1690) and in four letters on *Toleration* (1689). Locke defended freedom of thought and religion both on moral and practical grounds. He argued that the sole responsibility of government was to protect the lives, liberties, and property of the people so that they led a happy life and that the government would be secure only when the people were happy. The government must never restrict the people in their search for freedom and happiness. If the government fails to ensure the happiness of the people, then the people must be at liberty to choose another government.

Locke was equally forceful in formulating and stating his theory of education. His *On Education* (1693) was a natural follow-up to his *Concerning Human Understanding* (1691). In these two books Locke argued that almost all of the knowledge that man acquires comes from the perception and utilization of past experiences. John Dewey (1859–1952), the great American philosopher, takes this line of thinking to present his theory of perception as the process of utilization of experience, saying, "Wholly independent of desire or intent, every experience lives on in further experiences. Hence the central problem of an education based upon experience is to select the kind of present experiences that live fruitfully and creatively in subsequent experiences."[3] Dewey advanced this theory as part of his articulation of his theory of progressive education, which he promoted in opposition to traditional education. It is a remarkable fact that Locke presented his theory of perception and experience in a manner that translated into practical realities of education in the twentieth century.

Locke also advanced his theory that at birth the human mind is a blank tablet on which experience later makes inscriptions. One of the principal mental processes is the nature of association of ideas that the human mind gains as it develops. Locke and Descartes seem to agree on one theoretical perception—that a human being can reach important conclusions in the process of learning by deductive reasoning. Both men also argued than human beings can doubt all things, but one must never doubt one's existence because existence is the basis of one's knowledge of the universe. Both men concluded that because the human being is the most important form of creation, he must learn all he is capable of learning in order to know all he needs to know so that he can influence his society in its struggle for development.

In formulating his theory Locke utilized the basic theoretical tenet outlined by Plato—that all ideas are innate and that they are developed by the process of gaining experience. Both Plato and Locke defined this process as education.[4] To substantiate the applicability of his theory Locke outlined a basic principle of logic as it relates to the process of learning in children. He observed children at play and deduced that in games they concluded that if an object was out of sight it was out of existence. To Locke this discovery suggested doubt on the part of children about the existence of the object. This is where experience becomes an important tool of learning the fact that although the child does not see the object, it is still in existence. All the child needs to do is learn to locate it.

Locke contributed to the tabula rasa concept, that at birth the child's mind is blank. As one remembers that in Britain, a nation that takes tremendous pride in its traditions and places value on nobility and privileges that come with birth and the system of monarchy and rules that come from the origins of birth, it came as a surprise for people to hear Locke state that at birth the kings and queens were born with a mind as blank as that of all other people.[5] Locke made this theoretical argument to stress the importance of environmental factors that he said were critical to the success of education. He also argued that without proper environment the student cannot learn, and that if the student fails to learn he and his society pay the price. He concluded that society has a major function to create and provide an adequate environment so that learning can take place.

Locke was also at his best in presenting his theory that the human mind was quite capable of exercising functions or operations that were derived from similar functions or operations that have been carried out in the past. This is where experience becomes part of the learning process. This author reaches the conclusion that those individuals—one of whom was Charles William Eliot (1834–1926), the powerful president of Harvard University from 1869 to 1908, who opposed Dewey's theory of progressive education—did not have an opportunity to fully understand John Locke's theory. The learning process that Locke discussed so well is quite similar to Plato's concept of becoming. In his theory Plato concluded that complex or difficult concepts can be simplified by many generalizations that are meaningful to new learning experiences.[6] Once the learner makes a sensible connection between generations and the new concept he is learning, his learning problems are solved. He can now enjoy the next phase of his learning activity.

In his interpretation of the theories of the ancient Greek masters to suit conditions that existed in the New World, Locke provided a bridge to both worlds. He redefined his theoretical concepts by developing a clear picture of the order of the mental function that leads to learning. That order included two elements. The first element is the mental perception that he equated with conditions created by environmental factors leading to formulation and retention of new ideas. The second element of that order is the gaining of new experiences leading to other new experiences. While he was a student at Oxford University Locke deeply admired John Owen, the famous dean of Christ Church College. At that time Owen was one of the individuals who pleaded for religious tolerance. Locke accepted the message of religious tolerance in a much broader sense than Owen himself.

Locke regarded tolerance, not on religious, but also political, economic, and other aspects of national life as important to the development of society itself. It was from this broader perspective that Locke began to develop his theory. Owen was quite pleased to see that one of his students was able to see beyond the extent to which he was advocating tolerance. Locke argued that tolerance was as critical in other areas of national life as religion. Tolerance required the recognition of the independence of the human being to conceptualize and to express new ideas about the direction society was taking in its development. It also demands that all people have freedom to perceive and articulate new ideas and put them into the context of new situations. Locke's ability to function as a bridge of ideas between the ancient world and the New World places him in a category of his own in terms of influence on the evolution of the theory of education in the New World and beyond.

THE INFLUENCE OF THE RENAISSANCE

It is important to remember that while John Locke, Rene Descartes, Adam Smith, and other thinkers of their time were developing their theories, the Renaissance[7] was at the height of its development and influence. It was a period of remarkable accomplishments in important areas of human life. It was also a period of adventure and curiosity. People wanted to know about their world. The great explorers came during this period. Christopher Columbus discovered the New World in 1492. John Cabot (1450–1498) explored North America in 1497. Francis Drake (1540–1596) was the first Englishman to sail around the world. Jacques Cartier (1491–1557) was a French sailor whose daring explorations were the basis of the French claim to Canada. These men accomplished more than establishing a knowledge about distant lands; they also came to acquire the basic skills that were needed for successful navigation, knowledge of weather conditions, knowledge of people in the areas they reached. The opinions they formed about them would later prove crucial to the study of the human condition in general.

The Renaissance is also known for its unique accomplishments in literature. William Shakespeare (1564–1616) and Christopher Marlowe (1564–1593) distinguished themselves as brilliant dramatists and playwrights. Both men expressed the spirit of the Renaissance in plays that were performed at the Globe Theater in London. Many writers of the Renaissance, such as Cardinal Pietro Bembo (1470–1547), who wrote *On the Mother Tongue*, used the vernacular, rather than Latin, to communicate their ideas with the people. Nicolo Machiavelli (1469–1527) left a masterpiece on the use of political power. His *The Prince* (1532) gives Machiavelli the credit to be known as the father of modern political science. Ludovico Aristo (1474–1533) popularized Italian painting in his work, *Roland Insane*. Miguel de Cervantes (1547–1616) of Spain wrote *Don Quixote*, one of the greatest novels ever written. The book ridiculed the knights of the Middle Ages for their lack of proper knowledge of the needs of society and individuals. John Colet (1467–1510) founded St. Paul's School in London to generate new ideas and methods of articulating issues of the day. Colet was unique in his approach to education as he encouraged students to apply logic in seeking solutions to problems of learning.

There were other thinkers of the Renaissance who provided a new framework for the evolution of theory of both society and education. Sir Thomas Moore (1478–1535) gave the world some of the best ideas coming out of the Renaissance. His *Utopia*, which is based on Plato's *Republic*, is a classic discussion of the role of individuals in creating a harmonious society. The invention of the printing press by Johannes Gutenberg (1395–1463) in 1440 greatly facilitated the distribution of literary materials and boosted the acquisition of learning and knowledge. The curiosity that was part of the Renaissance now found expression in the literature that was readily available. Writers published materials on all subjects of learning. Many thinkers engaged in research to bring to the attention of those who sought knowledge new theories that could be formulated from what was studied. For those who were interested in the search for knowledge the invention of the printing press provided an incentive that was not available in the past.

Various forms of art, painting, sculpture, and architecture exemplify the great creative minds of the Renaissance. Painters, sculptors, and architects worked to perfect the techniques of their chosen art forms. They sought to bring out harmony and beauty in their work. In 1506 Rome replaced Florence as the eternal city. Michelangelo (1475–1564) stands out as the leading artist of the time. He achieved greatness as a painter, sculptor, and architect. His remarkable skill as a painter may be seen in the Sistine Chapel in the Vatican. Examples of his famous sculpture include the *Pieta* in St. Peter's Church and *David* in the Horeuce Academy.

Leonardo da Vinci (1452–1519), who was Michelangelo's closest rival in the arts, is best known for his paintings of the priceless *Mona Lisa* and the *Last Supper*. Da Vinci also gained fame as an accomplished architect, engineer, musician, and sculptor. He also published books on anatomy, mathematics, and astronomy. Raphael (1483–1520) worked architectural plans for St. Peter's Church. He also painted frescoes for the Vatican, including the famous *School of Athens*. Raphael's many beautiful paintings of the *Madonna and Child* show perfect balanced symmetry previously unknown in art. Many other artists helped make the Renaissance the period of the most creative age in human history. Such artists as Giovanni Bellini (1430–1516) and Titian (1477–1570) used the combination of colors to paint a world of beauty and reality.

The Renaissance also provided the individual an intellectual environment for the emergence of new forms of trade and commerce in which the ability to rationalize became the hallmark of success. Major ports along the

Mediterranean Sea included Venice,[8] the center of one of Shakespeare's most important plays, *The Merchant of Venice*, Genoa, Pisa, and Marseilles. The Hanseatic League, a powerful organization of German cities sought to control most of the trade with the New World. The founding of such organizations as the Dutch East India Company and the English East India Company was intended to facilitate trade with distant lands as a result of the knowledge that was being slowly obtained as a result of voyages of discovery, as well as to enhance trade in Europe. The Medici family of bankers exerted commercial and economic influence, not only in Italy, but also in Europe as a whole.

There were individuals who distinguished themselves in the study of astronomy. For these individuals a study of the heavenly bodies became an obsession in the quest for knowledge about the universe. The knowledge they obtained from their studies and the theories they formulated made a major contribution to the advancement of learning in general. Among these individuals was Nicolaus Copernicus (1474–1543), an astronomer of Prussian and Polish descent who founded present-day astronomy using his theory that Earth is a moving planet. This theory proved to be a major discovery in the quest for knowledge about the world. It changed forever the way people sought to relate themselves to their world. The superstition that had existed for hundreds of years that if one continued to sail in a straight line, one would suddenly fall into a bottomless pit and the fear that it generated had disappeared. Instead, a new theory came into being that if one continued to sail in a straight line one would eventually return to where one started but from a different direction. Copernicus's theory became a touchstone that opened up human minds to new endeavors in their search for knowledge.

During Copernicus's time astronomers sought to understand the world and scientific phenomenon by accepting and applying the theory that Claudius Ptolemy had espoused in Alexandria, Egypt, in A.D. 150.[9] Ptolemy was one of the astronomers who rejected the theory that Earth moved around the Sun. However, Ptolemy concluded that Earth was round and that the gravity of Earth was the center of the universe. But he was in error when he said that both the Sun and the Moon revolved around Earth at various rates of speed. Considering the methods used to obtain knowledge and the knowledge of science that the Egyptians had mastered so well, the inaccuracies that are evident in Ptolemy's theory are surprising. However, one must give the Egyptians credit for endeavoring to discover all they could about the world.

Because Copernicus doubted Ptolemy's theory, he studied the relationships between the Sun, the Moon, and Earth in an effort to offer a more realistic theory. He finally felt that he had sufficient information and knowledge to state his own theory that Earth moved rapidly around the Sun and that man does not see this motion because he travels with Earth. Copernicus also reached the conclusion that what man sees in the sky is affected by Earth's motion. He suggested that real motion in the sky must be separated from apparent motions. Copernicus empirically applied his theory in his masterpiece, *Concerning the Revolution of the Celestial Spheres*, which was published in 1543. In this book Copernicus demonstrated how Earth's motions could be used to explain the motions of other bodies in the sky.

Copernicus's work was so important that another leading Renaissance scholar and astronomer, Galileo Galilei (1564–1642), utilized it as a basis of promoting the further study of astronomy. Galilei made the first practical use of the telescope to discover the theory of the pendulum. He is also credited with discovering the famous theory of falling bodies. Galilei invented a hydrostatic balance that is now used in physics to assist draftsmen in seeking improvement in the effectiveness of the telescope. Galilei made his first important scientific contribution at the age of twenty while he was still a university student. His aim was always seeking new areas of excellence in learning and discovery. He formulated his theory of the pendulum by watching and observing a great lamp swing from the ceiling of the cathedral in Pisa, his birth place. In 1632 Galilei published his masterpiece, *A Dialogue on the Two Principal Systems of the World*, in which he disputed much of the information that the church was trying to have people accept about the world in order to accept its religious teachings.

Any person who formulated and enunciated a theory that was contrary to the official teaching of the Catholic Church ran the risk of severe reprisal. From the time of Emperor Constantine (306–337), the teachings of the Catholic Church were regarded as the foundation of law and order. Any theory that contradicted the official church teaching was considered as heresy, which was considered a serious offense against the church and state. For several centuries Constantine and those who followed him as rulers tried to stamp out all forms of heresy. A tribunal to stamp out heresy was established in 1229 with the official title of Congregation of the Holy Office.[10] Over a period of time the tribunal became known as the Inquisition and continued to function until 1834. As soon as Galilei published his theory he was summoned before the Inquisition to answer charges of heresy. During the long trial Galilei proved empirically the accuracy of his theory, but the Inquisition forced him to renounce it because it was contrary to the official teaching of the church. When Galilei said that Earth continued to revolve around the Sun, the Inquisition placed him under house arrest for a long time.

The legacy of the Renaissance to the evolution of theory of education in the New World was more profoundly felt in religious education than in any other area since the days of the Reformation. While he was performing his duty of teaching, Martin Luther (1483–1546), a devout and dedicated monk, confronted an issue that had been a central tenet in the theology of the Catholic Church—that the righteous live by faith. Luther eventually came to formulate his own theology that faith justified man before God. The promotion of this theology became Luther's mission. But since it was outside the official teaching of the Catholic Church, Luther's new theology was considered a heresy. He had to renounce it or go before the Inquisition.

But, having spent years studying and formulating it Luther could not give up the conviction that was now part of his life. Luther also began to question the system of indulgences that Pope Leo X (1475–1521) authorized for some work of piety, charity, or a gift of money.[11] Luther argued that the practice of letters of indulgences was contrary to the teaching of the Catholic Church and that it must be discontinued immediately. When the church leadership refused, a major crisis began to unfold. Luther must have forgotten that Pope Leo X was a member of the powerful Medici family that controlled financial institutions in Italy. He thought of developing the church in terms of financial investment as a form of development.

From the time Luther was appointed priest in 1507 he and Leo X disagreed on every aspect of theology. In 1517 Luther decided that he could no longer subscribe to a religious organization he now believed posed a potential for conflict. In that year he published a statement known as the Ninety-five Thesis. He used the invention of the printing press to carry his views all over Europe. Although few people understood what the message of the thesis was, they fully understood that money offered for indulgences went beyond the practice of supporting the church and that people all over Europe were collecting large sums of money in the name of the Catholic Church. Luther's study of the Bible and the history of the Catholic Church led him to the conclusion that there was something wrong with the leadership of Pope Leo X, and he began to distance himself more from his reign. Pope Leo X viewed Luther's actions as heresy making him subject to trial by the Inquisition.

The conflict between Luther and the Catholic Church edged close to a crisis in 1519 when he and Johann Eck engaged in a public debate at Leipzig. In 1520 Luther made his views known in three publications, *An Address to the Christians of the German Nation*, *The Babylonian Captivity of the Church*, and *The Liberty of Christian Church*. As a result Luther was excommunicated. Luther burned the letter of excommunication in public to show the extent of the conflict between him and the church leadership. The great schism that had lasted from 1278 to 1417 was now entering a new and decisive phase. The reformation was gathering momentum. The conflict that came out of it was resolved by the Treaty of Westphalia in 1648 following the Thirty Years' War that ravaged Europe from 1618 to 1648.[12] What this crisis shows is that once people have attained a level of thinking that makes a difference in their lives, it becomes part of their lives, they cannot give it up without losing themselves to the opposition elements that seek to neutralize them. The spirit of struggle evident in this drama found itself in the New World where the odds were much greater than in Europe.

The crisis that emerged between Luther and the leadership of the Catholic Church can be regarded as minor when compared to the one that emerged between Henry VIII (1491–1547) of Britain and Pope Clement VII (1478–1534), who was on the throne from 1523 until his death in 1534. This crisis helped promote the Reformation faster than any other factor at that time. Like Pope Leo X, Pope Clement VII was a member of the Medici family, but he was ill-suited to exercise proper leadership of the Catholic Church during a period of great difficulties. When Henry VIII ascended the British throne in 1509, his first official act was to marry his brother's widow, Catherine of Aragon, who bore him five children. Only one, Mary, who later became queen, lived to adulthood. But Henry wanted a son, so he turned his attention to a maid of honor at the royal court, Anne Boleyn.

When Henry married Catherine, Thomas Cardinal Wolsey, his chief minister, asked the pope to annul the marriage arguing that it was wrong for Henry to marry his brother's widow. Clement refused, and Henry immediately dismissed Wolsey for failing to fulfill his duty. But because Catherine could not give him the son he wanted, Henry sought to marry Anne Boleyn. But Clement refused to allow Henry to divorce Catherine to marry Anne. After a period of intense negotiation Henry reached a fateful conclusion and that was that the pope had no authority over him. He disregarded the pope's opposition to his intended marriage to Anne, whom he actually married in 1532. At Henry's insistence the British Parliament passed two pieces of legislation in 1534 making the break with the Catholic Church complete. Henry proclaimed himself the head of the Church of England, a practice that is still followed to this day. That is why Queen Elizabeth is head of the Church of England today. Henry also took the title Defender of the Faith to strengthen his new position. Henry appointed Thomas Cranmer (1489–1556) the first Archbishop of Canterbury. Cranmer had been quite active in promoting reformation in Britain because he did not fully support the theology of the Catholic Church. He therefore played a crucial role in making the reign of Henry VIII quite successful.

A question must now be asked: What are the implications of these few examples of accomplishments of the Renaissance to the evolvement of a theory of education in colonial America and beyond? John D. Pulliam and James van Patten provide some elements of an answer when they write:

The Renaissance, or rebirth of learning, began in the 1200's and lasted through the Reformation of the 1500's. There are many aspects of this movement which had influence in American development. Classicism protested against the narrow religious nature of education of the Middle Ages. Desiderius Erasmus (1466–1536) made editions of the New Testament and criticized the ignorance of the clergy and the injustice of society. The Renaissance replaced a religious point of view with a secular one making man, rather than God, the focal point with reference to art, literature, and the government. Renaissance emphasis on the development of the individual helped to purge ignorance and encourage education. Significant and new inventions made rapid progress in learning possible.[13]

Erasmus made two observations that had a profound influence on the evolution of a theory of education in the New World. The first observation was his view that the clergy was poorly educated. This is the reason why, during the colonial period, emphasis was placed on educating the clergy so they could exercise an appropriate leadership role. Erasmus's second observation was that society lacked justice. Erasmus must have seen the action of the Inquisition, the conflict that emerged between Pope Leo X and Martin Luther and between Pope Clement VII and Henry VIII, and the practice of the letters of indulgences.

These developments had a tremendous influence on the evolution of the theory of education in colonial America. Pulliam and van Patten go on to conclude that as the Renaissance spread all over Europe the desire for knowledge, facilitated by the invention of the printing press in 1440, led to an intellectual revolution that had a profound influence on the development of the New World. There, the growth of population was matched by the growth of the organized community. The growth of the organized community was made possible by the quest for meaningful education making the mobility of scholars and scholarship quite possible. The mobility of scholars and scholarship became the prerequisite of the development and stability of society itself.[14] In the relationship that emerged between the search for a new social system and the quest for education lay the elements of the evolution of a theory of education pertinent to new conditions.

There are two other important implications of the Renaissance on the evolution of a theory of education in the New World. The first implication is that the concept of freedom of exploration took some critical dimension, not only in Europe, but also in the New World. Freedom of human thought and process led to the process of formulating theories about pursuit in science, the economy, politics and society, and education in a manner that had not been attempted in the past. The process of inquiry into various aspects of human endeavor now acquired new and powerful dimensions. Individuals like Galileo Galilei, Nicolaus Copernicus, and Martin Luther made this endeavor at the peril of their own lives. But as the pressure of demanding freedom increased, church leaders slowly relented their control of all aspects of human intellectual activity to allow the human spirit to explore new areas of human effort. In this important evolution the elements of a secular society were being put in place. In the New World, while religion still exerted a major influence on the development of education, the secular component of academic pursuit could no longer be suppressed in the way it was during the Middle Ages.

The second implication that the Renaissance had on the evolution of a theory of education in the New World is in the area of seeking a functional balance between the instruction in religion and in secular subjects. Beginning with John Calvin's publication of *Institutes of the Christian Religion* in 1536, a book that refuted some of the basic theological aspects of the Catholic Church, the practice of religion required a much broader freedom to understand secular issues related to human life. Increasingly, biblical scholars were realizing that human life and society did not consist of religion alone. This is why, as he became increasingly dissatisfied with the theology of the Catholic Church, Calvin began to study alternative theology that included the formulation of a secular theory to address other important aspects of human existence and experience. By the time Martin Luther espoused new theology, the quest for religious freedom could no longer be isolated from freedom to engage in secular activity.

This development was a reality that the Catholic Church knew it could no longer control. As much as Pope Leo X and Pope Clement VII wanted to exercise control on the activity of the human mind in the way the church leaders had done in the past, they knew that they were fighting a lost cause. They were increasingly becoming aware that any effort to restrict the quest for human freedom in a larger context would have an adverse effect on their power. The flow of new ideas that began as part of the learning process generated by the spirit of the Renaissance became the hallmark of human endeavor in all aspects of life. Curiosity and the desire for knowledge in all aspects of human life provided an environment in which people began to search for education in more meaningful ways than they had done in the past.

Writing in 1641 on the general subject of learning as a human endeavor, Rene Descartes asked, "Is it improper to conclude that physics, astronomy, medicine, and all the other disciplines that are dependent upon the consideration of composite study be related to the study of arithmetic, geometry, and other such disciplines?"[15] Descartes went on to state his theoretical perspective that human endeavor and success are not limited to a few individuals or a few areas, but are related to a wide range of areas that included religious and secular areas. This is necessary to give society a complete and functional balance in society. Descartes suggested that the quest for knowledge is part of being human and that it is a continuous process because society is in a continuous process of change. Even if human beings commit errors in the process of learning, those who seek knowledge must continue their efforts because knowledge is not absolute, it is only relative.[16]

In the preface to Descartes, Donald A. Cresse discusses the problems that thinkers of the Renaissance encountered in their quest to acquire knowledge saying of Descartes himself, "Throughout the early part of his life, Descartes was plagued by a sense of impotence and frustration about the task he had set about to accomplish: a new and stable base for all knowledge. He had the pragmatic vision, but he seemed to despair of being able to work it out in detail."[17] These are among the problems that Renaissance thinkers encountered in their struggle to bring new meaning of knowledge to a rapidly changing world. Scholars in the New World would later struggle to solve the same problems. Given the greatness of the human spirit there was every indication that these problems would be solved. The Renaissance had provided the tools, now the emerging society had to do the job.

THEORY IN NEW ENGLAND

In accordance with the new spirit of human endeavor made possible by the Renaissance, the beginning of organized society in the New World demanded a corresponding evolution of a new theory to guide its development. That evolution was related to three areas: politics and society, the economy, and education. This study is concerned primarily with the evolution of the theory of education. The ideas that came out of the Renaissance helped create an environment that was conducive to making new efforts to continue the course that it had charted. It is important to remember that the evolution of the theory of education in the New World closely resembled the development and character of society in Europe. The stagnation that came with the fall of the Roman Empire came to an end with the revitalization of human intellect beginning with the Renaissance.[18]

The rejuvenation of interest in ancient classical literature meant that the human being of the Renaissance was quite capable of comprehending the need to articulate new perceptions about the nature of society. While the Renaissance replaced religion as the modus vivendi in Europe, in the New World religion was beginning to have a serious impact on the thought process. While Europe was becoming increasingly secular, the New World was becoming increasingly religious. The publication of Francis Bacon's (1561–1626) *Novum Organum* in 1620 provided the climate of the publication of *The Advancement of Learning* in 1605. In both publications Bacon advanced an impressive argument in favor of a secular thought process to off-set what was regarded as the powerful influence of religion. The ideas that Francis Bacon expressed, and even the modified theology of John Calvin himself, had little appeal to the Puritans.

However, removed from Europe and struggling to tame the wilderness, the colonies in the New World depended on religion to give them a sense of future, especially for those in New England and the Middle Atlantic region. John D. Pulliam discusses the implications of this trend of thought saying, "English colonists who wanted to change or purify the Anglican Church became known as Puritans and were very independent in the settlement of New England."[19] This line of thinking became the foundation on which the evolution of a theory of education was built. That theory could not be divorced from the Puritan perception of society as a form of Calvinist theology. For this reason religion exerted an important influence on education based upon the theory derived from that theology.

The evolution of theory in New England is quite evident in the legislation that was passed early during the initial stages of its settlement. On October 28, 1636, the Massachusetts legislature enacted legislation creating Harvard College, the first college in the New World, and appropriated 400 pounds sterling for its initial support. This was done for the sole purpose of training ministers who were needed to serve the Puritan community.[20] In taking this action the Massachusetts legislature was trying to implement the theory that the founder of Harvard, John Harvard (1607–1638) had enunciated as a religious minister and philanthropist—that religion must form the basis of meaningful life because religion was the basis of morality, and any society without either has nothing to build itself upon.

This view was expressed by a leading member of the Puritan community in 1643 when Harvard was struggling to raise funds to support itself. The member made an impassioned appeal for funds saying that God had carried them safely to New England, and that they had built homes, provided necessities for their livelihood and to worship God, that one of the next things they longed for and looked after was to promote learning and develop it for future generations fearing to leave an uneducated ministry to the churches when current ministers would no longer be there. As much as God motivated Harvard to give his state to educational facilities,[21] it was now their turn to give generously to the college. The member argued that the college had the function of educating people in the promotion of religious and moral values to safeguard society, and it was in the best interest of the community as a whole to support the college with their money. Harvard himself so believed in this college that he gave 400 volumes and nearly 800 pounds sterling to the college that carried his name.

The fact that Harvard College was founded only sixteen years after the Puritans landed at Plymouth indicates the extent of the influence that they exerted on the process of defining the direction the evolution of theory was going to take to direct the development of society. In 1638, to emphasize the European traditions in the kind of education that Harvard College was to give, Newtowne, where it was located, was renamed Cambridge after Cambridge University in Britain, which John Harvard and many other colonists had attended. Harvard College opened its doors to students in the summer of 1638, the year that its founder died. Immediately Harvard College utilized the theory of education that had been formulated during the founding of universities in Europe during the Middle Ages. The basic approach to theory adopted by instructors at Harvard College was directed at religious and moral development of students as a viable basis for their intellectual development. This theoretical perception reflected the main components of a theory that was operating in universities in Europe at that time.[22]

Among the major components of that theory was the old belief utilized by the ancient Greek masters that the teacher represented the parent in his relationships with the student. The Romans utilized the same concept known as *loco parentis*.[23] Utilizing this central tenet of theory, school officials at Harvard required instructors to place students into groups under the responsibility of an instructor who ensured that each student received proper instruction that enabled him to acquire proper religious and moral values that were expected by society. Parents placed their complete confidence in the ability of instructors to represent them in the education of their children. This practice has existed to this day. For example, in 1988 one parent stated her view that once she took her child to school she no longer had a role to play, as the teacher assumed total responsibility of the child's education because by virtue of her position the teacher represented the parent.[24]

The excitement that the Puritans experienced in the founding of Harvard College was muted in that same year, 1636, by an aspect of the practice of religion that left a scar on their image of the kind of society they were trying to build on the foundation of Puritan theology. The arrest and trial of Anne Hutchinson (1591–1643) for heresy shows the extent of intolerance that was part of the Puritan belief system. Hutchinson was found guilty and banished from Massachusetts in 1637 raising serious questions about the theology that they were using in building a new society. Hutchinson's fate was similar to that of John Huss (1369–1415), the Bohemian religious reformer who had questioned some traditional teachings of the Catholic Church. Hutchinson had questioned the central tenet of the Puritan theology regarding the role of the individual in society, especially the component that stated that children were little devils who must be restrained by force, if necessary, to make them conform to the standards required of everyone by society.[25] For the Puritans, Hutchinson's fate substantiated the wisdom of their theology. For non-Puritans, it signaled the emergence of a new form of religious persecution. This tragic development placed New England in a state of uncertainty about the role of religion in society and about the future. The demise of John Huss and Anne Hutchinson, more than 200 years apart, shows the extent of intolerance exercised by the church.

In 1642, wishing to convince the Puritans that their future was secure, the Massachusetts legislature passed legislation requiring parents and guardians to ensure that their children attended school for the sole purpose of receiving instruction in religious and moral values as the most valuable basis of a meaningful life in society. Gerald L. Gutek suggests that understanding and practicing religious and moral values was considered essential to understanding the law of Puritan Massachusetts.[26] There is no doubt that in formulating the principles that led to this legislation the legislature was enunciating its basic theory of education. The similarity of this legislation to the British Poor Law of 1601 is striking.

The British law made two provisions that would influence the legislation in Massachusetts of 1642. The first provision was that taxes be raised from property owners to support the instruction of children of the poor. The second provision was that all children of the poor be apprenticed to a trade. In enacting its own legislation on similar lines the Massachusetts legislature was motivated by theoretical consideration that the ignorant people would easily fall victim to evil forces that would drain them of their religious and moral values, depleting the human resources that society needed to ensure its progress. The passage of the legislation of 1642 was the result of the belief in a theory that the state had responsibility in guiding the development of education as a condition of ensuring the development of society. From this legislation parents and guardians knew what their responsibility was in the education of their children.

However, nearly seventy years later, Jonathan Edwards recaptured the theoretical importance for the instruction of children. He was moved to remind his society of the value of that instruction saying, "Let me, therefore, once more, before I finally cease to speak for this congregation, repeat earnestly to press the counsel which I have often urged upon heads of families have, while I was their pastor, to great painfulness in teaching, warning, and directing their children, bringing them up in the nurture and admonition of the Lord, beginning early when there is yet opportunity."[27] Believing that its legislative action was yielding tangible benefits to society, the Massachusetts legislature passed new legislation in 1647, the famous "Old Deluder Satan Law." This legislation called for two major requirements that had not been enacted before. The first requirement was that communities of fifty or more families organize for purposes of hiring a teacher to instruct children in reading, writing, and arithmetic. The second provision was that communities of one hundred or more families also employ a teacher of Latin to prepare students for entrance into college.

The enactment of this legislation clearly shows the theoretical consideration behind it. The argument that was made for introducing it was a compelling one, that as it was the chief aim of the Old Deluder Satan to keep human beings[28] from the knowledge of the Bible by keeping them ignorant, so it was by providing them with knowledge that they would escape the power of temptation. It was therefore required that every district in any jurisdiction with fifty or more families must appoint a teacher.[29] One reaches four conclusions regarding the formulation and application of the Puritan theory of education. The first conclusion is that the state felt that it had an obligation to require education for all students. That requirement was based on its theory of education. There was no input by the community and parents to the structure of that theory. The second conclusion is that the state could formulate its theory on the role of the community to control the conduct of education in accordance with its requirements. The third conclusion is that the state could establish conditions by which civil authorities could supervise education. The fourth conclusion is that public funds could be used to support education.[30]

The evolution of a theory of education in New England was intended to address three levels of education: elementary education, secondary education, and higher education. The focus of elementary education was to ensure basic literacy—especially reading, writing, and arithmetic. These were considered the touchstone of the success of education at all levels. The curriculum at the elementary level was structured so as to ensure a proper sequential progress in learning. The learning process itself began with the letters of the alphabet, then syllables, words, then sentences. From there the students were introduced to some basic elements of Puritan theology and the Lord's Prayer. The most important text was the famous *New England Primer*, which appeared for the first time in 1690. It was so popular that it was called the Little Bible of New England.

That the primer was a factual reflection of the Puritans is shown in that it contained as a form of instructional materials, "An Alphabet of Lessons for Youth," "The Lord's Prayer," "The Dutiful Child's Promises," "The Creed," "The Ten Commandments," and "The Names and Order of the Books of the Old and New Testament." These were all part of the syllabus students at the elementary level were expected to learn.[31] The teacher, usually a ministerial student, required students to learn by imposing strict discipline that was prescribed by a theory enunciated by the Puritan authorities. Among the elements of Puritan theory that the primer contained were little statements like, "In Dam's fall we sinned all," "Thy life to mend this book attend," and "The cat doth play, and after slay."[32]

The Puritans regarded secondary education as being synonymous with the Latin Grammar school. Only sons of the social, religious, and political elite of New England attended these schools. The students who attended these schools were made to understand that they would one day exercise responsibility in their society as social, political, and religious leaders and that they would be considered a failure if they failed to measure up to this expectation. This means that Puritan society defined success and failure for the students before their education at the secondary level even began. As the name implied, the Latin Grammar school offered instruction in Latin, Hebrew, Greek, and English. Instruction material came from the works of Cicero, Livy, Caesar, Virgil, Plato, Aristotle, and Herodotus. The study of these authors was considered the hallmark of an educated person because it emphasized moral, social, and religious values. The study of utilitarian subjects, such as science, history, modern languages, mathematics, and geography, was considered important only as they would appear to supplement the traditional study of the classical languages.

The Puritan theory of higher education was rooted in the faith of the colonists in the Calvinist theology of the importance of the Bible as a major instructional material to ensure that religious values were taught to college students. Calvinist theology was taken for granted. An individual who, after attending college, was unable to espouse all of Calvinist theology was considered to have missed an important aspect of his higher education. He was therefore considered to be less effective as a minister or leader in society. His place is society was therefore relegated to a level less than his level of education. This is why students took their college studies seriously; they did not want to be considered to have failed to comprehend the essential elements of the work that formed a major part of the thrust of their contribution to society.

As the Puritans saw things, the salvation of the human soul was the major function of the body. Man was created not to indulge in worldly pleasure, but to prepare the soul for eternal life.[33] In spite of the doctrine of predestination, the Puritans believed that man can increase his chances of the salvation of his soul by an intense study of the Scriptures. Conditions of admission into college were quite strict. For example, entrance into Harvard College was based on the consideration that when any scholar was able to understand Tully[34] or some other prominent Latin writer and make true Latin in classical verse and prose and prove able to decline correctly the nouns and verbs in Greek, then he may be admitted into college. But no claim would be made to admission before these qualifications were met.[35] Gerald L. Gutek concludes that the curriculum closely reflected that of the European colleges of that time: first year: Latin, Greek, logic, Hebrew, and rhetoric; second year: Greek, Hebrew, logic, philosophy; third year: philosophy, metaphysics, moral philosophy; fourth year: Latin, Greek, logic, philosophy.[36] Lloyd Duck suggests that most colleges that were established after Harvard had the same objective of training ministers and other religious leaders. This is true of Yale (1701), Dartmouth (1769), and Brown (1764).[37]

THEORY IN THE MIDDLE ATLANTIC COLONIES

The evolution of a theory of education in the Middle Atlantic colonies reflected its cosmopolitan structure. The major colonies of this region—New York, New Jersey, Delaware, and Pennsylvania—did not embrace a single religious faith or theology as New England did. In this development the Middle Atlantic colonies became a pluralistic society in which the concept of religious pluralism was quite evident in the diverse sects that became part of the region. Among these religious sects were Anglicans, Roman Catholics, Jews, Lutherans, Dutch Reformed, and Presbyterians.[38] The surprising thing about this region was its religious tolerance. People of different faiths lived with each other happily and cooperated in building their region. There were no cases similar to that of Anne Hutchinson. This diversity was taken into account in developing a theory of education. Each religious group designed its own educational system to reflect its religious beliefs.

The existence and development of the various languages in the region added an imperative condition for the evolution of a theory formulated to address the need for education among members of these sects to serve as ministers and leaders in the community. Because of the agricultural potential of the region the students were encouraged to think in terms of acquiring a broad education that would have them embrace both academic education based on elements of liberal studies and vocational studies. Students were expected to gain considerable knowledge of agriculture. Due to adverse traditions that included religion and language, there was no single trend for the evolution of an education that would be applicable to the region as a whole. While this allowed the development of free enterprise, it also made it hard to formulate theory leading to programs that would give coherence to the development of formal education. The result was that the region failed to find common ground on which to build a strong system of education.

However, the recognition of the need to share in the struggle in seeking improvement in the educational system gave credence to efforts that were being directed at seeking improvement in education itself. In New York, known as New Amsterdam before 1664, the Dutch Reformed Church exercised considerable influence on a theory of education, but not in the same way as the Puritans did in New England. The Dutch West India Company supported the development of education because its officials believed that education of the people was essential to the services they would render for the benefit of society. At the same time the English established the charity schools that were supported by the Anglican Church.[39] It is important to remember that this support was based on the theory that poor people needed education in order to help them become useful members of their society. In New England the Puritans' involvement in the pauper schools was based on the belief that the poor needed education in order to fight the "Old Deluder Satan."

In Pennsylvania the evolution of theory followed the pattern that was being developed in New York. However, Quakers, Presbyterians, and German Lutherans each developed a system of education that was intended to serve their own interests. The Quakers went out of their way to reject the harsh corporal punishment that the Puritans applied to their educational process as part of conditioning children to the demands of adults. The Quakers believed that children were innocent creatures of God, beautiful, and quite able to learn if the right approach was made. The Quakers also believed that children were better able to learn from love shown by adults rather than from fear of corporal punishment. They also operated under the theoretical belief that children were different and that each child had special needs that must be fulfilled, not by applying methods that controlled their thoughts and emotions, but by those that sought to promote freedom of expression as part of the learning process.

Although differences in theoretical approaches to education were quite pronounced between Puritans and Quakers, the evolution of theory in other religious groups in the Middle Atlantic region was somewhere in line with that pursued by the Quakers. They subscribed to the theoretical approach that severe discipline for children, such as corporal punishment, was detrimental to their educational interests and should be avoided at all costs. It would seem that Puritans were the only religious group to believe that severe discipline was a necessary condition for learning.

Like New England, the evolution of a theory of higher education in the Middle Atlantic region was directed at producing ministers of religion. Some colleges that were founded late during the colonial period focused mainly on this purpose. For example, Princeton was founded in 1746 by the Presbyterian Church as the College of New Jersey to train ministers. Rutgers was founded in 1766 as Queen's College by the Dutch Reformed Church for the same purpose. The founding of these colleges coincided with the period of religious revival known as the Great Awakening.[40] One must understand that the Great Awakening was more than a religious revival. It was also a period known as the Age of Reason or the Enlightenment. During this time the need to learn, to acquire knowledge on a variety of subjects became part of being human. The acquisition of knowledge was considered critical to the advancement of both the individual and society. Many colleges in the Middle Atlantic region operated under the theoretical principle that, "A man who knew English would not surreptitiously spread that commercial language, and certainly he would not favor loosening church ties with Holland."[41] Although the British were doing this to justify their exposure of New Amsterdam, they knew that the promotion of education among all people became the national asset that any group of people needed to ensure its own development.

For the Middle Atlantic colonies, teachers came from the ranks of the ministers. These teachers were taught religious subjects that adequately prepared them to function effectively. In the Dutch Reformed schools great emphasis was placed on learning essential concepts properly. School activities began with a prayer and the reading of Scriptures. In many cases boys and girls attended the same school.[42] This was done to promote understanding between them. The sectarian character of education in the Middle Atlantic region made it difficult to create a common school system until the days of Horace Mann.

THEORY IN THE SOUTH

In the South the evolution of theory took the shape of the need to develop agriculture. The basic unit of society was the plantation, and plantation owners represented a class of land owners who had the political and economic power needed to direct the development of society. For the South formal education was less important than the acquisition of knowledge about specific aspects of agriculture. The little formal education that was available was extended to members of the elite to prepare men to become gentlemen who understood duty and chivalry in its finest traditions.[43] Duty and chivalry were exercised in the interest of the people. Training was also provided in practical knowledge of management of the plantation. Men were also expected to develop an ability in oratory or making speeches. Ability in oratory was considered an important quality of leadership in the community.

Writers from the South have often compared social and economic conditions in the South to those that existed in ancient Athens where society was strictly stratified. Some of these writers have expressed concern about the lack of formal education and the results of failure to see their society from a broader perspective. For example, in 1941 Wilbur Joseph Cash (1901–1941), a journalist from South Carolina, described the problems that the South was facing in its failure to see itself as needing fundamental change in its attitudes saying that violence, intolerance, and aversion to new ideas, an inability to engage in analysis, a tendency to act from emotion rather than from rationality, a sense of individualism and a narrow idea of social responsibility, an attachment to racial values and an inclination to justify something wrong in the name of any values, and a lack of realism had been the characteristic vices of the past. In spite of efforts to change things, these characteristics remained as of that time.[44]

This is a serious indictment of a society by one of its own. In giving this graphic description of conditions in the South, Cash was suggesting elements of a new theory, which, if applied, would enable its members to see the extent of the problems it was facing and to do something to solve them. The beginning of the civil rights movement in December 1957 demonstrates the extent of these problems.

An important characteristic of the South was that it blended the ideas of the members of the aristocracy with elements of democracy to create a social system that not only recognized leaders who became statesmen, but also recognized other people as less than human. The institution of slavery represented this class of people. This is how George Washington, Thomas Jefferson, James Madison, and James Monroe came to national prominence. All of them became leaders in a far larger area than the South. These men also acquired an ability for oratory and thus were able to put forth their ideas and shape the future of the colonies and the country as a whole. For example, on December 7, 1796, President George Washington, who served from 1789 to 1797, made an impassioned appeal to the Congress to establish a national university saying: "The Assembly to which I address myself, is too enlightened not to be fully sensible how much a flourishing state of the arts and science contributes to national prosperity and reputation."[45] Washington argued that the country contained many fine, highly respected institutions of learning. But the financial resources on which to build them were far too small to attract prominent scholars in the different fields of learning. He concluded that only the federal government had such resources. In 1810 James Madison made the same appeal.

However, the evolution of a theory of formal education in the South was of far less importance than in the other two regions. The reason for this lack of interest in the formal development of education was that the South wasunable to see the end of the institution of slavery. Since 1516—when

King Charles I of Spain gave the colonists permission, known as *assiento*, to import slaves—the number of slaves shipped to the New World dramatically increased when twenty Africans, three of them women, arrived in Jamestown. From that time to Emancipation slavery played a major role in sustaining institutions in the South. Every other move was related to slavery. Therefore, there was a lack of theory because the need for formal education was not as profoundly felt as it was in the other two regions. The lack of emphasis on the role of religion meant there was little emphasis placed on moral values. The problems that were experienced in society arose primarily from the lack of formal institutional structures that were considered essential to transmitting a new social code.[46] In this context the evolution of theory took a back seat to other matters.

SUMMARY AND CONCLUSION

The discussion in this chapter leads to two conclusions. The first is that as the New World began to develop, it utilized theories formulated during the Renaissance by thinkers in Europe to provide an adequate basis for that development. The utilization of the theories of John Locke enabled the colonists to try something that had meaning for their struggle for development. Locke's theories were more applicable to conditions that existed in the New World because colonists were developing a new society different from the one in Europe. The evolution of theory to address problems of society could not be separated from the evolution of theory to address the kind of education that they needed to maximize their developmental efforts.

The second conclusion is that as the three regions of the New World began the task of development they adopted different theories they believed were relevant to their needs. New England opted for the strict interpretation of Calvin's theology, the Middle Atlantic colonies chose to utilize various religious theories and theology to address their specific needs. The South did not define its theory in a way the other two regions did. This means that the South remained in a state of underdevelopment for years to come. As a result, the South experienced serious social problems until the twentieth century. This chapter has presented evidence to suggest that as long as the society of the South was structured on the institution of slavery, it was not possible for its members to see the future without it. Slavery was an intimate part of the political, social, and economic system. This inhibited its ability to initiate the evolution of a theory of education that would promote the development of education as a condition of other forms of its development.

NOTES

1. Lloyd Duck, *Understanding American Education: Its Past, Practices, and Promise* (Burke, VT: Chetelaine, 1996), p. 49.

2. Ibid., p. 50.

3. John Dewey, *Experience and Education* (New York: Macmillan, 1938), p. 27.

4. Gerald L. Gutek, *Historical and Philosophical Foundations of Education: A Biographical Introduction*, 2nd ed. (New York: Merrill, 1991), p. 19.

5. Ibid., p. 104.

6. Ibid., p. 106.

7. The Renaissance, known also as the period of Great Re-awakening, is believed to have started about 1300 and lasted until about 1700. It was a period of rebirth of the process of thinking and revitalization of ancient and classical literature. It was the beginning of the scientific or logical approach to problems of human existence. The Renaissance was the bridge between the medieval period and the modern age.

8. Founded in A.D. 452, Venice is often called the Queen of the Adriatic because no other city is quite like it. It is not built on solid ground. Instead it lies on a cluster of small mud islands at the head of the Adriatic Sea. It has canals for streets and gondolas, or flat-bottomed boats, for taxicabs. The Piazza of St. Mark has an old clock tower built in 1496. The Crusades stopped at Venice on their way to the Holy Land.

9. Historians are not sure about when Ptolemy was born and when he died, or about his early life. Some estimates say that he was born around A.D. 80, and was about seventy-one years old when he died.

10. Certain groups existed whose views did not correspond with the official teaching of the Catholic Church. Among them were the Albigenses and the Waldenses. These two groups were the primary targets of the Inquisition. But as time went on the number of individuals who disagreed with the teaching of the Catholic Church steadily increased making it difficult to stamp out these heretics.

11. One condition of gaining indulgences was money offerings toward building St. Peter's Church. Luther and an increasing number of individuals began to think that the practice was not right and represented corruption.

12. Lynn Miller, *The Global Order:Values and Power in International Politics* (Boulder, CO: Westview Press, 1994), p. 43.

13. John D. Pulliam and James van Patten, *History of Education in America*, 6th ed. (Englewood Cliffs, NJ: Merrill, 1995), p. 7.

14. Ibid., p. 8.

15. Rene Descartes, *Meditations on the First Philosophy*, trans. Donald A. Cress (Indianapolis, IN: Hackett Publishing Company, 1993), p. 15.

16. Ibid., p. 37.

17. Ibid., p. vii.

18. John D. Pulliam, *History of Education in America*, 5th ed. (New York: Merrill, 1991), p. 7.

19. Ibid., p. 10.

20. Duck, *Understanding American Education*, p. 61.

21. Richard Hofstadter and Wilson Smith, *American Higher Education: A Documentary History* (Chicago: University of Chicago Press, 1968), p. 6.

22. Duck, *Understanding American Education*, p. 62.

23. Ibid., p. 63.

24. Barbara Walters, "Americas Kids: Why they Flunk," an ABC-TV documentary, 1988.

25. Duck, *Understanding American Education*, p. 63.

26. Gutek, *An Historical Introduction to American Education*, p. 5.

27. H. Norman Gardiner, ed., *Selected Sermons of Jonathan Edwards* (New York: Macmillan Publishing Company, 1904), p. 148.

28. The definition of men here is literary, meaning male human beings because women were not considered in the same light as men until ratification of the Nineteenth Amendment in 1920. However, the Bible refers to man as the universal human being. Perhaps this is what was meant by men.

29. Gutek, *An Historical Introduction to American Education*, p. 6.

30. Ibid., p. 7.

31. Ibid., p. 6.

32. Ibid., p. 17.

33. S. Alexander Rippa, *Education in a Free Society: An American History*, 6th ed. (New York: Longman, 1988), p. 18.

34. Some scholars think that Tully was Servius Tullius (578–532 B.C.), the seventh legendary king of Rome, who initiated social reform and passed laws that were intended to serve the interests of all people.

35. Hofstadter and Smith, *American Higher Education*, p. 8.

36. Gutek, *An Historical Introduction to American Education*, p. 139.

37. Duck, *Understanding American Education*, p. 87.

38. Gutek, *An Historical Introduction to American Education*, p. 11.

39. Ibid., p. 12.

40. Duck, *Understanding American Education*, p. 123.

41. Ibid., p. 122.

42. Ibid., p. 123.

43. Gutek, *An Historical Introduction to American Education*, p. 9.

44. Wilbur Joseph Cash, *The Mind of the South* (New York: Alfred A. Knopf, 1941), p. 429.

45. Hofstadter and Smith, *American Higher Education*, p. 158.

46. Gutek, *An Historical Introduction to American Education*, p. 9.

3

Theory During the Revolutionary Period

> Knowledge is in every country the surest basis of public happiness. To
> the security of a free Constitution it contributes in various ways.
> —George Washington, 1790

THE INFLUENCE OF THE AGE OF REASON

The American Revolution[1] was a result of developments that had been taking place since the Renaissance. The leaders of the Revolution, George
Washington, Thomas Jefferson, Benjamin Franklin, and many others, were
the product of these developments.[2] These men lived during a period of time
known as the Age of Reason, or the Enlightenment,[3] when man glorified the
acquisition and application of reason as the most important mental skill
they needed not just to lead a successful life, but also to influence society.
The renewed interest in intellectual activity that came with the Renaissance
gave people an opportunity to plan their own development. This development was evident in the literature that began to appear with the Renaissance
and carried on into the Age of Reason.

The Age of Reason was different from the Renaissance in one important
respect—it produced a group of thinkers, artists, writers, and scholars who
modeled their works after those of ancient Greek masters. In the process
they attained a new level of clarity of both perception and articulation unknown in the past.[4] The literature that came out of the Age of Reason was
far more powerful than that of earlier times in addressing critical issues.
These neoclassicists totally rejected the notion that there was only one way
of assessing the impact of religion, social events, and the political thought
process. They even rejected the traditional authority that the church had exerted over many years. They rejected the thinking that a government in Europe can continue to impose its own wishes on an unwilling people who
were struggling for a new identity. They turned to the application of logic

and reason as a scientific approach to all issues. They advanced their belief that obedience to reason and logic would hold society together.

As the society of the Age of Reason increased its knowledge of science, its members applied logic to comprehend all natural phenomena to the extent that their belief in religion decreased because it had not conformed to that logic. They began to believe that man, rather than God, exercised the major responsibility in shaping the character of society. The emerging thinking was that, if society went wrong, then man, not God, must accept blame. This meant that God gave man power to make decisions and choices and that God did not impose these on man. In this regard the Age of Reason went much further than the Renaissance in opening new ways of encouraging all forms of human endeavor. It was a new era of thought process.

People of the Age of Reason learned about this endeavor from the literature that came out of the late sixteenth and early seventeenth centuries. Below are cited a few examples of how this literature gave new meaning to the Age of Reason and the influence it had on people's ability to utilize reason to solve the problems of society. Christopher Marlowe (1564–1593) might have acquired a literary stature equal to that of William Shakespeare had he not been killed at the age of twenty-nine. In his *Tamburlaine the Great* and *The Tragical History of Doctor Faustus* Marlowe utilized blank verse to describe social and political issues in a way that ordinary people could understand. Ben Jonson (1573–1637), a close friend of Shakespeare, insisted on following classical forms of ancient drama in order to remind his readers of the importance of their contribution to the thought process of his time.

Among the great writers of the period just before the Age of Reason were John Donne (1571–1631) and John Milton (1608–1674). Donne wrote on themes that were deeply religious to address social responsibility. His *For Whom the Bell Tolls* is a classic presentation of his view that human beings can play a role in seeking societal improvement by showing concern for the welfare of others. In the same way, Milton turned a personal disaster he encountered in 1652, when he became blind, into something positive by writing his masterpiece, *Paradise Lost*. This work was not only inspired by poetic beauty, but also by an intense desire to address issues that Milton felt needed to be addressed. The message that both Donne and Milton were trying to send was quite consistent with the spirit of the Age of Reason and that was that human beings were quite capable of resolving problems, whether social or personal, by applying reason. Both men argued that problems confront human beings to test their willpower, and the ability to resolve them demonstrate man's superiority over adversity. This level of thinking was new and represented a new approach to social issues.

A group of thinkers and writers, who became known as Puritans, include Andrew Marvell (1621–1678), Robert Herrick (1591–1674), John Suckling (1609–1643), Edmund Waller (1606–1687), and John Bunyan (1620–1688).

These men addressed religious, social, scientific, and political issues in ways that had not been done in the past. Their approach challenged the reading public to rise to the occasion to prepare themselves to understand these issues. To get the message they were carrying, the people needed a new level of knowledge, an ability to interpret their message in a manner that enabled them to be involved in the affairs of society. Bunyan's *Pilgrim's Progress* became one of the most popular and widely read books of all time. These authors also addressed religious, social, and political issues in satirical ways that brought their work to the attention of readers. While satire can be humorous, it can also be quite serious in bringing issues to the attention of the people. They ridiculed the notion that only certain people must have power to influence society.

Among those who utilized satire to carry their message to the people was Jonathan Swift (1667–1745). Swift was at his best in his *A Tale of A Tub*, which attacked social institutions of his day. In *A Modest Proposal* Swift perfected the essay as a form of literary success. Another great writer of that time was Alexander Pope (1685–1744), who wrote poetry that was critical of the rising middle class. Pope also wrote philosophical essays that had the potential to change the ways people perceived their role in society. Pope's *Essay on Man* is a classic discussion of the positive and negative attributes of the human being. Pope was quite successful in transmitting his message to society that its development was vested in the intellectual potential of all the people and that single human beings possessed all the ability society needed to ensure its advancement.

The novel, as we know it today, had its beginnings during the Age of Reason. Daniel Defoe (1660–1731) made the greatest contribution to its development. He wrote such challenging and realistic works as *Robinson Crusoe* and *Moll Flanders*. Defoe's works are connected episodes and, while they have no central plot, they persistently address issues of great social importance. If there is any one aspect of the literature of the Age of Reason that motivated people to acquire education, it was the evolution of the novel. People wanted to read and enjoy the thoughts that authors were projecting in a beautiful flow of a language they understood.

Scholars consider Samuel Richardson (1689–1761) one of the best novelists of this period. His *Pamela* is a book about the experiences of a servant girl who described them to her parents. From reading this book thinkers of the Age of Reason began to see their society from a broader perspective, enabling them to articulate new theories about education and society in general. In *Tom Jones* Henry Fielding (1707–1754) added great dimensions to the literature of the period. At the end of the seventeenth century English writers began to pour out tales of horror contained in literature known as Gothic novels to suggest what was wrong with society and what must be done to correct it. One of the most famous examples of this form of literature was *Frankenstein* written by Mary Wollstonecraft Shelley (1797–1851).

It is clear that this form of literature was intended to address the social horrors that had not been addressed in the past. Because this literature was
quite sophisticated and required ability to interpret, people felt that they
needed more education to understand it. The Age of Reason was making an
increasing impact on the need for a higher intellectual level to enable people
to understand their society.

THOMAS PAINE: MESSENGER OF COMMON SENSE AS THEORY OF CHANGE

Among those who made the best contribution to the evolution of theory
during the Age of Reason was Thomas Paine (1737–1809). A vintage agita-
tor, Paine had a tremendous influence on the evolution of theory of religion,
politics, and education that led to the American Revolution.[5] History has
recognized Paine as an Englishman by birth, a Frenchman by decree, and an
American by adoption. Paine exerted influence on events leading to the Revolution by the power of his ideas and personality. However, as is often the
case with influential and controversial figures, Paine was greatly admired by
some and intensely disliked by others.[6] Historians recognize Paine as the
consummate American patriot who did so much for his adopted country
and asked nothing in return.

Because his family was poor, Paine left school at the age of thirteen to help
them survive. At the age of nineteen he went to sea for a brief period of time.
He did not think that he wanted to be a sailor for the rest of his life. He
therefore resigned and was employed as a customs collector in London. But
he was soon discharged because he was critical of the way customs officials
seemed to exploit the people. When his first wife died Paine married a
woman with whom he had little in common. After he was separated from
her, he was alone for an extended period of time, which he needed to sort
out the priorities in his life. Slowly he began to learn new principles that he
understood as essential to success in life. He began to rebuild his life in an
impressive manner. His confidence in himself dramatically increased enabling him to see issues in society from a much broader perspective.

In 1774, at the age of thirty-seven, Paine met a powerful and influential
American patriot, Benjamin Franklin, who was in London at the time.
Franklin succeeded in persuading Paine to immigrate to America where he
played his role in the Revolution and left his place in history. Thus, the two
men began a relationship that would have a profound impact on the course
of events in the thirteen colonies. Paine arrived in America with letters of
recommendation that Franklin had written testifying to his literary potential
and sharp mind. Paine was immediately hired as a contributing editor of the
Pennsylvania Gazette, which Franklin had founded in 1729.

Immediately Paine began to express his views in a way that pleased his
readers. His reputation as a thinker was rapidly rising. He addressed such is-

sues as the need for political freedom and independence. He was at his best in articulating his theory of education, arguing that education was the salvation of a people struggling for development and that everyone must take it seriously. Paine was so successful in his literary efforts that in 1776, the year that Adam Smith published *Wealth of Nations*, he published *Common Sense*, the work that left his name engraved in the annals of the evolution of theory in colonial America. Although he was fourteen years younger than Smith, Paine achieved instant celebrity status. The publication of these two books in the same year permanently altered the way people were thinking about the future. For Britain the publication of these two books created conditions they would no longer be able to control.

The process of the Revolution had reached a level where there was no turning back, and both books had done it. In his newly found role Paine had become the messenger of the theory of change. *Common Sense* had the same impact on the political thought process as *Wealth of Nations* had on economic ideas. In addition to promoting political independence *Common Sense* was also a powerful statement on how to build a new nation based on ideals that were central to its development, stability, and happiness. Some say that Thomas Jefferson got his concept of the pursuit of happiness from the ideas of Thomas Paine. However, it is not surprising that George Washington, Thomas Jefferson, and other leaders in colonial America read the two books with intense interest. Franklin took great pride in the fact that he had influenced the content of *Common Sense*. The book had a powerful influence in the manner in which it projected the future of the colonies, arguing that if people in the colonies applied common sense in their approach to issues, then reason would prevail to enable them to chart a new course of development consistent with their goals and objectives. The acquisition of education would greatly help in meeting these objectives.

The publication of *Common Sense* was raising Paine's fortunes more rapidly than he had imagined. In December 1776, encouraged by the success of *Common Sense*, Paine began publishing a series of pamphlets entitled *The Crisis*. The first of these allowed Paine to state his political and educational theory. He argued that the political crisis that the colonies were experiencing was a test of human endurance and that tyranny was very much like evil, it would not easily be defeated. But with education and the fortification of the ideals of freedom, those struggling against it would prevail. When hostilities broke out between the colonists and Britain, Washington ordered that the pamphlet be read aloud to his soldiers to motivate them to fight for the cause. Indeed, Paine's works offered encouragement to the Continental army during the darkest days of the Revolutionary War. Paine himself served as a soldier in 1776, but in 1777 he was appointed secretary to the congressional committee on foreign affairs. His honesty in trying to express the questionable financial transactions of Silas Deane (1737–1789),[7] an American commissioner sent to France to buy war materials and promote the ideas of the

Revolution, became so controversial that he was forced to resign in embarrassment and shame for trying to tarnish the reputation of a loyal patriot.

The loss of employment created serious financial problems for Paine. He was forced to depend on charity and friends to maintain himself financially. He was then appointed clerk of the Pennsylvania Assembly, but gave most of his earnings to the Revolutionary War efforts. Although the Pennsylvania legislature gave him $2,500 and New York gave him a house in New Rochelle and the Continental Congress voted to give him $3,000, Paine soon became poor again because he did not seem able to manage his financial affairs in the same way he was able to manage the promotion of his social and political agenda.[8] Paine felt that he was being betrayed by a society he tried to serve to the best of his ability and to whose cause he was fully committed. He simply did not know what to do. He was more able to deal with his financial problems than with those who tried to discredit him for questioning Silas Deane. He considered going back to Britain, but he knew he had closed the door to that possibility by the expression of his ideas.

In desperation Paine left for France in 1787, but he soon went to Britain. While there he published his famous book, *The Rights of Man*, in 1792. The book was a response to Edmund Burke (1729–1797),[9] who had criticized the direction that the French Revolution had been taking in 1789 when it broke out. Indeed, Burke had argued that some individuals outside France, and these obviously included Paine, had no business interfering in an internal matter, and that the revolution itself failed to apply reason to shape the future that would hold meaning for the life of the people. Burke concluded that the number of deaths the revolution was causing betrayed its purpose. Once again, Paine felt that he was a target of criticism by those he thought should understand his motives. Paine defended his actions in both colonial America and in France as arising from a conviction that he was doing the right thing.

The publication of *The Rights of Man* suffered a severe setback when the government of William Pitt (1759–1806)[10] suppressed the book because France and Britain were in a state of war. Paine was even arrested and tried for treason because, while he was in America, he had engaged in activities that were considered a betrayal of British interests. In December 1792 he was banished from Britain. Paine was a man without a country. In desperation he returned to France, which accepted him in appreciation of his support in the revolution, but he did not enjoy the same rights as the French people. He lived the rest of his life as an exile. He did not feel comfortable returning to America because of his loss of respect as a result of his role in the Silas Deane affair. He was not wanted in Britain, and he was tolerated in France.

But, with all this adversity, Paine remained true to his principles and ideals; he never compromised them. He had persistently advanced his theory that the people in any society must reserve the right to replace any government that did not meet the needs of its people with one of their choice. He argued also that one of these needs was education and that it was critical that the government formulate an educational policy that, when implemented, would result in giving the people the kind of education that would help them meet their needs. In the people's ability to meet their needs, the government stood to benefit more than inform of service and participation in national events. This is the environment that set a country on the highway to national development. Paine's position had a special appeal to the revolutionary leaders in both America and France. In August 1792 the French National Assembly extended citizenship to Paine, but he could not support the bloodshed and violence that came with the revolution. In this position Paine was, in effect, agreeing with Edmund Burke's criticism of the senseless violence that came with the revolution, especially the arbitrary executions that were carried out by the use of the guillotine.[11]

As a result of his opposition to the brutality and violence associated with the revolution, Paine was once more out of favor with the leaders of the French Revolution. He was stripped of his French citizenship and imprisoned for ten months. The American minister to France, James Monroe (1758–1831),[12] claimed him as an American and succeeded in securing his release from prison. While he was in prison Paine wrote *Age of Reason*, in which he stated his belief in religion, democracy, and education. The book was inspired by his observations in France during the revolution in which error ruled supreme and the application of reason was void of any meaning. He argued that when the revolution was over, the French people faced the same enormous task that the Americans faced after their own revolution, restructuring the educational system so that they could begin to build a new and vibrant society in which application of reason, not violence, would rule supreme.

In 1802 President Thomas Jefferson arranged for Paine's return to the United States where Paine continued to work on his theory of society, politics, and education. He was remembered for promoting democracy and education as two pillars that sustained the development of any society. For many years Paine's theories became the foundation on which the development of both education and democracy were built. For a man who went through periods of serious personal difficulties to leave a legacy that has lasted this long is a testimony to his conviction of the rightness of his cause. The United States and Europe could no longer remain the same. When he died in 1809, Paine was remembered as one of the principal founders of democracy and the initiator of the evolution of the theory of education in the United States.

THE INFLUENCE OF BENJAMIN FRANKLIN

One cannot have a complete picture of the evolution of the theory of education during the American Revolutionary period without studying the contributions of Benjamin Franklin, Samuel Johnson (1709–1784), Jean-Jacques

Rousseau (1712–1778), and Thomas Jefferson.[13] Of all the people who exerted influence on the evolution of theory during this period Benjamin Franklin stands apart as a giant. During his long and productive life Franklin made a list of impressive accomplishments that included statesmanship, soap-making, book-printing, gardening, and writing. He was an inventor of the effective heating stove and many other instruments. As a statesman Franklin was in the front line of men who helped lay the foundations upon which the United States was built into a great nation. He was the only man to sign all four key documents in American history—the Declaration of Independence, the Treaty of Alliance with France, the Treaty of Peace with Britain, and the Constitution of the United States.

Franklin's service as American minister to France helped direct the course of the Revolutionary War in a way that made a difference in the outcome. Franklin could very well be considered the most able and successful diplomat that the United States has ever sent abroad, as the saying goes, to lie for his country. Thomas Jefferson, thirty-seven years younger, called him the greatest man of his age, a revered sage whose knowledge of the issues was unquestionable. His dedication to the independence and development of the country was total and without any reservation, just like that of Paul Revere (1735–1818).[14] This is why he was profoundly disturbed by the action of individuals like Benedict Arnold (1741–1801)[15] who betrayed their cause and the country.

Franklin attended school in Boston for two years and proved himself an excellent student in reading, writing, and arithmetic. But at the age of ten he left school to help his father meet the needs of his family. Believing that the doors of learning and education are never closed, he continued his education on his own, teaching himself many things that would later prove crucial to his own life and the country. He relentlessly worked on his own style of writing using a volume of the British journal, *The Spectator*, as a model. As a result his prose became clear, simple to follow, and effective. Franklin was on his way to becoming the great man that he eventually was, and to make a contribution to the evolution of the theory of education during his time and beyond.

Franklin also taught himself the basic principles of algebra, geometry, navigation, logic, grammar, and natural and physical sciences. He studied French, German, Italian, Spanish, and Latin. This was a feat accomplished by few people of his time. He read widely, including John Bunyan's *Pilgrim's Progress*, Plutarch's *Lives*, Cotton Mather's *Essay to Do Good*, and Daniel Defoe's *Robinson Crusoe*. In this endeavor Franklin became one of the best educated persons of his time. For this reason he made an outstanding contribution to the evolution of the theory of education. Gerald L. Gutek acknowledges the accomplishments of this remarkable man saying, that in addition to his accomplishments in science and an impressive record of service to the nation, Franklin was also interested in the development of good education to serve the needs of an emerging society. He concludes that Franklin's educational ideas included two basic components of study. The first component was the humanistic element, and the second was the utilitarian component. He suggests that these functions still presented challenges to educational administrators of the day.[16]

An operational principle that Franklin used in formulating his theory is that education in America must be so designed as to allow equal opportunity to all students. In order to meet this objective, education must be related to the new level of nationalism to make national development possible.[17] He concluded this nationalism was needed in order to eliminate the colonial practices that had inhibited the ability of individuals to gain the kind of education needed to make a viable contribution to the development of a new nation. He stressed the importance of developing a scientific approach to the development of both society and education, and he endeavored to gain the essential components of the kind of education that he was now promoting.

In 1749, taking his major theoretical perspective into consideration, Franklin suggested the components of a curriculum that, in effect, constituted a new program of study that would include English grammar, Latin, science, history, vocational courses, and trades. He felt that instead of perpetuating the old classical curriculum, his suggested curriculum would be broad enough to cover the educational interests of all students. He also suggested that each school have a library that carried books, journals, magazines, and other educational materials on a broad range of subjects. His proposal for a utilitarian curriculum included shipbuilding, engraving, painting, printing, carpentry, carving, cabinet making, and agriculture.[18]

Franklin's success in publishing *Poor Richard's Almanac* from 1733 to 1758 came primarily from his ability to articulate issues that were important to readers. Supplemented by wit, common sense, and wisdom the almanac carried sayings that Franklin scattered through each issue to challenge the mind of the reader to think independently in terms of new ways of perceiving issues. The following are only a few examples of sayings that made the almanac popular: "A penny saved is a penny earned," a saying one sees on television commercials today; "Early to bed, early to rise makes a man healthy," "God helps those who help themselves," "A rising tide lifts all the boats," a favorite of President John F. Kennedy (1917–1963); "A small leak will sink a great ship," "Little strokes fell great oaks."[19] Gerald L. Gutek has captured the essence of the message the almanac was carrying for its readers saying that *Poor Richard's Almanac* advanced interesting ideas on common sense and a viable philosophy.[20] Gutek concludes that the instructions from poor Richard represented the practical and utilitarian side of education, such as hard work and thrift that became major characteritics of the rising American middle class that included merchants, entrepreneurs, and tradesmen. The spirit of entrepreneurship was based on a sophisticated drive for success anchored in the search for a new level of knowledge. Those who read the almanac knew that it was the product of a mind that was well-read and knew the trials of being human in a rapidly changing world. This gave a new impetus to the quest for a new meaning of education. To promote his theory of what society needed to do, Franklin established the first weekly subscription library in Philadelphia. The members of the library contributed money to buy books and then used them free of charge. The original collection of these books still exists. The circulation of books facilitated the quest for knowledge and education in a manner that highlighted Franklin's wisdom.

In addition to carrying out successful experiments with electricity, Franklin carried out major assignments on behalf of the people. For example, in 1753 the Pennsylvania legislature sent him to London to represent it in a dispute over tax laws that Britain was enacting to control economic and political activity in the colonies. He spoke eloquently and argued forcefully against demanding the payment of taxes without representation. He also took part in the fight against the infamous Stamp Act of 1766. At that time relationships between Britain and the colonies were deteriorating rapidly with little hope that they would be restored. Although he knew that the conflict between the two sides had reached a point of no return, Franklin made a gallant effort to enable the British to see that the crisis was being caused by the application of its laws to control the colonies.

On his return to America, Franklin argued that the colonies must unite to maximize their defenses and protect their economic survival. In 1754 he presented a plan of union at a conference held in Albany, New York, and attended by seven colonies. There he argued in favor of a uniform system of education to help create a new level of uniquely American nationalism and consciousness. He argued that this would also reduce conflict between the colonies caused by competition that the British government would exploit for its own benefit. It is from this line of thinking that the first seven presidents of the United States advocated a national system of education even though the Constitution of the United States had delegated education as a responsibility of the states.

It is important to remember that, in the evolution of the theory of education in America, Franklin's initiative was in response to the trends of thought made possible by the Age of Reason and directed at the political revolutionary tendencies that were resulting from the view held by the colonists that Britain was acting out of malice. This means that the colonists and Britain interpreted the conflict that was growing between them from two opposing perspectives. Once this trend of thinking was set in motion it could not be reversed. It is equally important to recognize that Franklin's placing an emphasis on the need for balance between scientific and utilitarian components of the curriculum was a departure from the curriculum that had been inherited from Europe at the beginning of the colonial period.[21]

Franklin succeeded in convincing his fellow compatriots to recognize that change in the educational system from the one initiated at the beginning of the colonial system to a new system must be initiated for the purpose of change in the political, economic, and social system. They knew that, since Britain was not willing to accept that kind of change, a political revolution was the only means of bringing it about. Therefore, the seeds of a revolution were planted as soon as the British Parliament enacted the Navigation Act in 1764 to regulate colonial shipping activity. The seeds germinated in 1765 when the British Parliament enacted the infamous Stamp Act to generate revenue by requiring the colonists to buy stamps and place them on various documents.

The plant gained strength when a disturbance broke out in Boston on March 5, 1770, and British troops opened fire, killing three men and wounding eight more.[22] The plant of the revolution grew even stronger when the British Parliament enacted the Tea Act in 1773. The formation of the Continental Congress in September 1774 to organize an official response to these events demonstrated to the colonists that a major military conflict with Britain was inevitable. The knowledge that the acceptance of his educational proposals would result in creating a comprehensive system of education was a gratifying experience for a revered sage. Franklin knew that it would provide students with a curriculum that would meet their needs as well as those of a nation soon to be born.

THE INFLUENCE OF SAMUEL JOHNSON

Although he lived all his life in Britain, Samuel Johnson[23] had a profound influence on the evolution of the theory of education in America. Johnson dominated the intellectual activity during the second half of the eighteenth century by the quality of his ideas. He also manifested extraordinary personality in his writings. His literary accomplishments influenced almost every major writer of his day and beyond. Among his most outstanding literary achievements were his *Dictionary of the English Language* (1755) and *The Lives of the Poets* (1789), a critique of fifty-two famous English poets. It is quite possible that Noah Webster (1758–1843), an American educator who became famous for publishing *An American Dictionary of the English Language* in 1828, had read Johnson's work.[24] Webster published the first dictionary in 1806, but it was less successful than Johnson's. Today *Webster's International Dictionary* is used in educational institutions across the world, thanks to the example that Samuel Johnson set in 1755. Johnson also wrote essays and plays.

Today most of our knowledge of Johnson's works comes from his fascinating biography, *The Life of Samuel Johnson* written by his close friend, James Boswell (1740–1795). It is a fascinating account of the man who believed in the power of ideas. Among those ideas was his belief that the human urge to be free cannot be restricted or controlled, and that, by his very nature, a human being is quite capable of comprehending the issues that society faces.

This comprehension is the result of the mental and intellectual freedom that education makes possible. Johnson advanced a theory that was already in place during his time—that with proper education every human being is quite capable of making a viable contribution to society. Therefore the challenge of society is to design education so that it allows every student an opportunity to contribute to the welfare of society by meeting his own needs first. The search for solutions to the problems of society cannot be limited to the powerful; opportunity must be extended to all by allowing them an opportunity to acquire knowledge of the issues. Johnson regarded this basic concept as the foundation of all successful educational endeavors.

Johnson began to formulate his theory of education in 1735 in a private school that he and his wife founded from the 800 pounds sterling ($4,000) that she brought as dowry. In order to involve more people in the evolution of his theory, Johnson gathered around him a circle of friends consisting of British intellectual thinkers. Among them was Oliver Goldsmith (1730–1774, of Anglo-Irish descent), who wrote various forms of literature. One of Goldsmith's most famous works is *The Vicar of Wakefield*, a powerful novel about how religious leaders played a role in seeking solutions to social problems. Goldsmith also wrote *The Deserted Village*, a poem about deteriorating social conditions that forced many people to seek refuge in places other than Britain.

Richard Sheridan (1751–1816) was another member of Johnson's inner circle of thinkers and friends. Sheridan won fame for writing three satirical comedies: *The Rivals*, *The School for Scandal*, and *The Critic*. All three were regarded as highly successful in addressing critical social issues, including the availability of educational opportunity. Sheridan decried the system of patronage and class privilege that existed in his society. He argued that, as long as these conditions existed, society would continue to decline until it reached a point where it would be difficult to rebuild. He warned his fellow countrymen that, if conditions continued to deteriorate, their society would face the same fate as the Roman Empire.

Edmund Burke, a leading statesman, essayist, and social critic, was another member of Johnson's circle of friends. Burke's most important contribution to the evolution of theory was his view that for evil to continue in society all it required was for good people to do nothing. *A Philosophical Inquiry into the Origins of Our Ideas of the Sublime and Beautiful* (1750) has been recognized as an authoritative discussion of theory on social issues. He called for a broader, more adequate education to ensure that all people were better informed and equipped to combat evil. Burke expressed his opinion that society has a responsibility to provide opportunities for the advancement of the individual as an essential prerequisite to the advancement of society. He argued that no society would develop if people remained in a state of underdevelopment. In the twentieth century Burke has been quoted by religious leaders, politicians, civic leaders, and scholars.

Historian Edward Gibbon (1737–1794) was also a member of Johnson's inner circle of friends and intellectual associates. Gibbon spent twenty years writing his monumental work, a six-volume study that he began in 1776 and completed in 1788, *History of the Decline and Fall of the Roman Empire*, which was hailed as a masterpiece even by those who disagreed with parts of it. This was an impressive study of a society that had lost its proper focus and values. Like other members of the group, Gibbon believed that education was the salvation of a society. He argued that the reason why the Roman Empire fell was that it was neglecting the education of the people depending, instead, on military power alone. The free flow of new ideas, represented by an adequate education, had been repressed.

Gibbon also argued that the leaders of the Roman Empire had forgotten that military power alone was insufficient to sustain the vibrancy of society. This is the position that Sheridan took, and Gibbon was happy to know that he had a faithful ally in the promotion of a line of thinking he believed would benefit society. Gibbon saw a clear relationship between the role of the teacher and that of the student in the new development of education. He explained that relationship saying, "Every man who rises above the common level has received two forms of education. The first is from his teacher, and the second, more personal and more important, is from himself."[25]

The influence that Johnson and his associates exerted on the evolution of the theory of education was quite profound both in Europe and in America. However, they were the last great neoclassical thinkers and intellectuals of the Age of Reason. In an intellectual revolt that rejected the classical rules of writing, a new breed of thinkers stressed the importance of feeling, rather than reason and restraint. They argued everyone must be free to think and write as he pleased. This quest for a new definition of freedom was not limited to literature. It also extended to other areas of human endeavor, such as political thought, economic revival, social transformation, and educational theory. There is no question that these developments combined to create the climate that led to the Revolution.

THE INFLUENCE OF JEAN-JACQUES ROUSSEAU

Jean-Jacques Rousseau was a French thinker and writer, who was a member of the group of political, philosophical, and educational leaders whose views inspired the evolution of theory that was directed at the search for solutions to problems of learning. Born of Huguenot parents, his mother died in childbirth. When he was sixteen years old Rousseau ran away from the engraver he was apprenticed to and went to Savoy where he became friendly with Madame de Warens, a wealthy widow. He began to learn to write and formulate ideas that showed off his bright mind. He went to Paris where he learned to refine his writing. With increased confidence in his ability to write Rousseau moved to Paris where, through interactions with other writers, he gained new levels of articulation of theory and ideas. He immediately began to write two books that left his mark on the evolution of theory.

These two books were published the same year—1762. The first book was *Emile*, a novel about the educational development of a young man. In it Rousseau discussed his theory of the kind of education he believed all young people should receive—education that gives the learner confidence in his ability not only to learn, but also to initiate action in a new area of endeavor. Once confidence in learning becomes a part of a student's effort, it will extend to other areas of achievement. But for the student to accomplish this objective society must create an environment that enables the student to learn. The second book was *The Social Contract*, in which he discussed an ideal society, a utopia. Rousseau argued that might never makes right and that people have a duty to obey only legitimate governments.

Like other influential figures of the Enlightenment, Rousseau endeavored to discover the applicability of the laws of nature to the human condition. He concluded that the arbitrary social boundaries created in society so as to place people into a stratification was contrary to the application of the laws of nature and must be eliminated to ensure human development.[26] Rousseau criticized the traditional educational system as being based on too much verbalism, which was based on an assumption that education entailed the mastery of bodies of literature demonstrating the need to comprehend the essential concepts contained within. Through *Emile* Rousseau addressed the inadequacy of the existing system of education and presented his own theory of education. In it he criticized what he regarded as unrealistic education, that which did not address the needs of students or those of society.

In presenting this theory Rousseau outlined three components that he considered essential to the application and success of the learning process. (1) Nature is a great educator because it teaches through the senses to grasp the laws that operate in the world. If a human being is unable to learn from nature, how can he learn to understand the laws of society? Rousseau suggested that in order to learn what man must know to function in society, he must learn from the laws of nature first. (2) Teaching and learning must be adapted to the stages of development of the student. As the child grows, his capacity to learn also increases. Unless the educational process takes these stages of development into account, the learning process has little meaning to the student. (3) Teaching must be related to the student's experience so that he can deduce the meaningful relationships that exist between the concepts that he is learning and new concepts he is yet to learn.[27]

Rousseau identified five stages in the development of the child that, he argues, both society and the teacher must recognize in order for education to have meaning. These are infancy, childhood, boyhood, adolescence, and youth. He suggested that for each stage there must be an appropriate set of learning activities designed to promote further learning. Rousseau explained his position: The development of a human being was the major thrust for education. He concluded that childhood had its place in the scheme of human life and activity. Therefore it was important to view man as man and a child as a developing human being known as child.[28] Recognizing the fact that adults were once children, Rousseau rejected the Puritans' interpretation of Calvin's theology that children are little devils unable to adjust to the demands of society without strict discipline. He also rejected their view that children were conceived in sin, arguing, instead, that they represented perfection in creation. Society must assume the responsibility of teaching them well.

Rousseau was convinced that the child was innocent and naturally good at birth. If society was able to construct an ideal environment, then the child would transform that innocence into learning what is good in society. He would never be exposed to an environment that would be conducive to negative behavior. The child's expression of happiness and unhappiness arises from his consciousness of the environment in which he lives. Rousseau concluded the presentation of his theory by relating Emile's education to a broader world environment. His extensive travels during which he meets various people from different cultural backgrounds, his ability to learn languages other than his own, as well as his study of natural history all combine to form the natural curriculum that gives him a complete education. Rousseau warned that any other approach to education would yield little benefit to either the student or society.

THE INFLUENCE OF THOMAS JEFFERSON

The last of the examples of thinkers of the Age of Reason (to be included in this study)—whose influence on the evolution of educational theory was profoundly felt in America—is Thomas Jefferson (1743–1826). Born into a prosperous plantation family in Albemarle County, Virginia, Jefferson had an opportunity for formal education early in his life. He attended both English Grammar and Latin Grammar schools when he was nine years old. In 1760, when he was sixteen years old Jefferson entered the College of William and Mary in Williamsburg, which had a population of about 1,000. There Jefferson met two men who would have a profound influence on his mind. The first man was William Small (1734–1775), a professor at the school, and the second man was George Wythe (1726–1806), one of the most learned judges in the community. In 1765 Wythe wrote the original Virginia protest against the Stamp Act, which the British Parliament enacted in that year. Small, Wythe, and Jefferson entered into a relationship that lasted for the rest of their lives.

After graduation from college in 1762, Jefferson studied law with George Wythe. He was admitted to the bar in 1767 and began the practice of law with great success until public service began to take all his time. In 1772 he married Martha Wayles Skelton (1748–1782), a widow and daughter of

John Wayles, a prominent lawyer who lived in Richmond. They had one son and five daughters, but only two children lived to maturity: Martha (1772–1836) and Mary (1778–1804). When his wife died in 1782 after ten years of marriage, Jefferson raised his two daughters and never remarried.

Jefferson was elected to the Virginia House of Burgesses in 1769 and served until 1775. He proved to be an articulate thinker and writer. Soon after the Revolutionary War began, Jefferson was asked to write the Declaration of Independence. The state of Virginia elected him governor for one year in 1779. But the state suffered severely from the effects of the Revolutionary War during that year. After serving a term as secretary of state beginning in 1774, Jefferson was elected president of the United States and served from 1801 to 1809.

Jefferson left his greatest mark on the theory of education. In 1779 he introduced into the Virginia legislature a "Bill for the More General Diffusion of Knowledge," which he based on three theoretical considerations. (1) Democracy demanded educated citizens to function efficiently. He argued that without education it would be difficult to sustain democracy. (2) The best form of education was secular and political, rather than religious. Jefferson did not discount the importance of religion, but, as a product and spokesman of the Age of Reason, when there was more emphasis on application of reason to the human condition, he saw society evolving around secular principles guided by reason. He concluded that education was critically important to strengthen that reason so that it would continue to serve the needs of society. (3) Control of education should be placed under the authority of the state government because it was in a position to understand the needs of the people better than any other agency.

It is important to remember that the educational theories of the figures of the Age of Reason placed emphasis on secular education rather than on religious education as was the case during the colonial period. To emphasize the secular character of education Jefferson concluded, every student would be given an opportunity to continue his education, including through the grammar school in his district. From that point on the student would have an opportunity for further education in boarding school, and his expenses would be paid "with a compensation to the master or usher of his tuition at the rate of twenty dollars by the year."[29]

The ideas and theories of the individuals discussed in this chapter show that the Age of Reason produced people whose line of thinking was radically different from thinkers of earlier times, both in America and in Europe. S. Alexander Rippa concludes, "From the mid-eighteenth century to the eve of the Revolutionary War the ideological foundations of American life were profoundly affected by a changing intellectual climate in Europe."[30] Rippa goes on to add that in subtle and various ways the constant flow of new ideas coming out of the Age of Reason rapidly found their way into the American colonies from Europe. These ideas and theories had a profound impact on the thought process of the people in the colonies in that they radically altered superstitions and practices that controlled human life for centuries.[31] New perceptions began to emerge during this age that had not existed in the past in relation to how people valued their world, the universe, and religion. The entire social, economic, and political system was being revised in ways that demanded radical change, and this development had a special application to the colonies.

During this period science and mathematics had new applications to the social and political character of society. For example, the discoveries that Isaac Newton (1642–1727) made in astronomy and mathematics had a direct influence on society. Newton began to carry out experiments when he was sixteen years old, and before he was thirty years old he discovered the now famous binomial theorem and system of tangents. In 1687 Newton enunciated a most important theory—that every particle of matter is attracted by or gravitates to every other particle inversely proportional to the squares of their distances.[32] The application of this theory was profoundly felt on society as thinkers of this age saw its implications to political systems. The world of the past had been replaced by a new one with an entirely new set of dynamics. The theory of every particle being attracted to another particle had profound implications on those dynamics.

THE ELEMENTS AND EVOLUTION OF NEW THEORY

As the ideas arising out of the Age of Reason continued to grow they began to initiate new thought processes among the colonists. Slowly, but steadily, concepts of space and time helped set the colonies apart from Britain. The values that were part of life in the colonies relative to their relations with Britain began to lose their influence. The colonists found that industry, thrift, and courage brought greater rewards in America than in Britain. They did not have to depend on control from Britain to lead a productive life. They began to believe that the future would be better without Britain's influence. They were self-reliant and self-sufficient. Those who lived in rural areas had gained experience in producing a sufficient amount of food. They were quite contented with their lives. Those who lived in urban areas earned good income. What was the reason for maintaining a relationship with Britain? By the time of the Boston Massacre in March 1770, a decision had been reached to seek political independence from Britain.

To this equation of rapidly deteriorating relationships between the colonists and Britain must be added the variable of King George III (1738–1820), who was on the British throne from 1760 to 1820. When he succeeded his grandfather, George II in 1760, George III faced political problems that no previous monarch had ever faced. Several revolutions affected every aspect of British life. The French Revolution threatened to reduce the standard of living in Britain as the British people were asked to make sacrifices to contain forces that were hostile to their life style. The continuing conflict between the British government and the colonists finally cost the British their colonies at a time when economic and industrial production was expected to improve the standard of living for all people. The advent of the Industrial Revolution created a new society and more than doubled the British population. This compounded the economic and social problems that the people were already experiencing.

Although Britain acquired new colonies, such as in India, to replace the loss of colonies in the United States, it took Britain quite some time to establish itself in these new colonies. The Act of Union, passed in 1800, brought Ireland into the kingdom, which then became known as the United Kingdom of Great Britain and Ireland. But nationalist sentiments in Ireland made it difficult to keep the kingdom together. George III, hardworking and proud, tried to reduce the power of the Whig aristocrats who had held political power since the days of Queen Anne. Under the strain of responsibility, George III became emotionally disturbed, losing his ability to think rationally. By 1811 he was considered insane and was forced to relinquish responsibility to his son, George IV (1762–1830), who acted as regent until he became king in 1820 following his father's death. The American colonists exploited the situation to their fullest advantage. The crisis between Britain and the colonists reached a breaking point with the Boston Tea Party on December 16, 1773.

Soon after the Declaration of Independence was signed on July 4, 1776, elements of a new theory were emerging to influence the direction the new nation was taking. Under the Articles of Confederation one of the major actions taken by the administration was to encourage settlement in the Northwest Territory. The Continental Congress passed the Northwest Territory Ordinance in 1785 to make provision for the development of education as an incentive for those who were considering settling in the territory.[33] In the same way, the ordinance of 1787 had the same effect. Gerald L. Gutek concludes that this action was taken on the theoretical assumption that education was "necessary to good government and the happiness of mankind."[34] Indeed, in this approach the new nation was setting the stage for the evolution of a new theory. At its inception, the federal government expressed serious need for that evolution.

While the federal congress set aside land for the purpose of developing education, as evident in ordinances of 1785 and 1787, it refrained from making specific requirements about the utilization of any financial resources arising from the use of the land. But it is quite clear that it considered investing those funds in the development of education as the direction to take. When the U.S. Constitution was ratified in 1789, it delegated education to the states. However, the first six presidents recognized the need to establish a national university to coordinate all educational efforts across the country.[35] This is why, on January 8, 1790, President George Washington appealed to

Congress to open a national university saying, "Knowledge is in every country the surest basis of public happiness. In one in which the measures of government receive their impression so immediately from the sense of the community as in ours, it is proportionally essential."[36] The president concluded that the security of a free country depended on education and that it was important to convince those who were educated to serve the needs of their country. There is no question that Washington was putting in place elements of a new theoretical perspective he felt were greatly needed to map out the future of a new nation. As the new society became more fully established and its stability was ensured, the need to strengthen the educational system became more profoundly felt. The evolution of a new theory would give greater meaning to a new educational endeavor. It is quite surprising that Washington, and the next five presidents, would still make an appeal for a national university system when the Constitution delegated all education to the states.

The belief in a scientific approach to all social problems required a reexamination of old theoretical perspectives. This reexamination was demanded by new perspectives brought about by the Age of Reason. The application of logic and reason demanded the formulation of a corresponding theory to address all areas of human endeavor. President Washington took these perspectives into consideration in his address to Congress. As the benefits of the Age of Reason and of the Revolution became evident, many individuals became more involved in articulating theories they believed would promote both the new nation and the educational system. One such individual was Benjamin Rush (1745–1813), a patriot and nationalist who received his medical degree from the University of Edinburgh in 1768. Rush was an uncompromising believer in good education for all Americans. In 1798 Rush added a critical dimension of a new theoretical perspective saying that he viewed education—especially for youth—to be absolutely essential. Rush concluded, "Our schools, by producing one general and uniform system of education, will render the mass of the people more homogeneous."[37] Indeed, Rush was projecting a theoretical perspective that was needed to address the educational process beyond the Revolution.

SUMMARY AND CONCLUSION

The discussion in this chapter leads to two conclusions. The first is that from the beginning of the Age of Reason, through the times of Thomas Paine, to those of Benjamin Rush, the evolution of educational theory took on powerful and progressive dimensions that eventually led to the Revolution. Once the elements of this revolution were in place, they in turn set the evolution of the theory in motion. These two developments had a symbiotic relationship: Each was crucial to the success of the other. When both were put in motion they would not be halted or slowed down, they had to run their course. The second conclusion is that, once the elements of the thought processes were in place, the Age of Reason raised human consciousness to a level never attained in the past. This in turn elevated social institutions to a level where they served human needs more efficiently than in the past. American society became what it did because of the role individuals played. The evolution of the theory of education made it possible for these individuals to play that role well.

NOTES

1. Instead of discussing the Revolution as an event that took place at a specific time, this chapter refers to it as a period of time beginning with the Boston Massacre in March 1770 and followed by the action that the Continental Congress took in September 1774 to defend American rights not to import goods from Britain as of December 1, 1774. The Revolution officially ended with the signing of the peace treaty in Ghent on April 19, 1783, thus making it possible for the last British troops to evacuate New York on November 25 of that year. Therefore, one can say that the Revolutionary period lasted from 1770 to 1783.

2. Gerald L. Gutek, *An Historical Introduction to American Education* (Prospect Heights, IL: Waveland Press, 1991), p. 23.

3. Historians seem to agree that the Enlightenment began about 1600 and lasted until about 1800. This was a period of time when many people worshipped reason. Some people even raised altars to the Goddess of Reason to have more influence on political, social, and economic developments.

4. Gutek, *An Historical Introduction to American Education*, p. 24.

5. John D. Pulliam and James van Patten, *History of Education in America*, 6th ed. (Englewood Cliffs, NJ: Merrill, 1995), p. 42.

6. Ibid., p. 43.

7. Silas Deane was an American patriot and diplomat who was prominent in events leading to the Revolutionary War. In March 1776 the Continental Congress sent him to France to buy war supplies. Deane was recalled in 1778 to give an account of his financial transactions. But no evidence of wrong-doing was found, making Paine's charges unfounded. This discredited him so badly that his reputation was damaged, and he was therefore forced to resign in disgrace.

8. This fact brought discredit to Paine when he made charges against Silas Deane.

9. Edmund Burke, a social reformer of major proportions, is credited with the statement, "For evil to continue, all it requires is for good people to do nothing." This view of the action that Burke urged is quite typical of the thought process of the Age of Reason.

10. There were two members of the Pitt family who served as prime ministers, father and son—William Pitt Sr., who served from 1766 to 1768, and William Pitt Jr., who served from 1782 to 1792.

11. Indeed, the guillotine was used for the first time in 1792. It was named after its inventor, Joseph Guillotine (1738–1814), a medical doctor who argued that persons condemned to death could be executed mercifully and painlessly by using the guillotine. Like proponents of the death penalty today, Guillotine did not know, or

refused to accept the fact, that there is no such a thing as merciful and painless death by any method of execution.

12. James Monroe served as the fifth president of the United States from 1817 to 1825. He is the author of the famous Monroe Doctrine proclaimed on December 2, 1823, stating that European nations could not seek colonial empires in the Western Hemisphere. The doctrine came out of the conditions of war that existed in Europe during the time of Napoleon.

13. This presentation is being done according to the order of their birth to put events surrounding them in their proper chronological order.

14. Paul Revere, the son of French Huguenot parents, played a major role in promoting the Revolution. He participated in the Boston Tea Party on December 16, 1773. Revere rode two hours from Boston to Lexington on April 18, 1775, to warn the patriots about British military intentions, making it possible for them to take precautionary measures to defend themselves and their cause.

15. History says that Arnold distinguished himself as a soldier and military leader at the beginning of the Revolutionary War. But, in 1777, when Congress appointed five new major generals, all of them younger than Arnold, he became disillusioned with the system of promotion even though George Washington persuaded him to stay on. In 1780 he turned into a traitor and betrayed the revolutionary cause.

16. Gutek, *An Historical Introduction to American Education*, p. 31.

17. Ibid., p. 33.

18. Ibid.

19. Ibid., p. 30.

20. Ibid., p. 31.

21. Ibid., p. 34.

22. To maximize their publicity against the British, the colonists called this incident the Boston Massacre by which it is still known.

23. Not to be confused with Samuel William Johnson (1727–1819), an American political and educational leader and a conservative who took no part in the Revolutionary War. He was elected to the Continental Congress from Connecticut in 1784 and served until 1787 and in the U.S. Senate from 1789 to 1791. Also not to be confused with Samuel Johnson (1696–1772), a graduate and tutor at Yale College and the first president of King's College (Columbia) from 1754 to 1763.

24. Johnson published his famous dictionary in 1775, three years before Webster was born. The title of the dictionary suggests an American counterpart to Johnson's work.

25. Quoted in William van Til, *Education: A Beginning* (Boston: Houghton Mifflin Company, 1974), p. 414.

26. Gutek, *An Historical Introduction to American Education*, p. 236.

27. Ibid., p. 237.

28. Ibid., p. 236.

29. Thomas Jefferson, "A Bill for the More General Diffusion of Knowledge," 1779. Quoted in Gutek, *An Historical Introduction to American Education*, p. 52.

30. S. Alexander Rippa, *Education in a Free Society: An American History*, 6th ed. (White Plains, NY: Longman, 1988), p. 43.

31. Ibid., p. 44.

32. Ibid., p. 45.

33. Barnes's Historical Series, *A Brief History of the United States* (New York: American Book Company, 1885), p. 104.

34. Gutek, *An Historical Introduction to American Education*, p. 24.

35. Richard Hofstadter and Wilson Smith, *American Higher Education: A Documentary History* (Chicago: University of Chicago Press, 1968), p. 157.

36. Ibid., p. 178.

37. Ibid., p. 170.

4

Theory During the Common School Movement

> The only efficient way to produce individuality and harmony of natural feeling and character is to bring our children into the same schools and have them educated together.
>
> —Calvin E. Stowe, 1836

THEORY FOR A NATION IN TRANSITION

The signing of the peace treaty in Ghent on April 19, 1783, signaled the end of the Revolutionary period and the beginning of the era of national development. It was also a period of reconstruction and the resetting of national programs. Although the ideas of seeking reform in education began during the colonial period—when Massachusetts passed legislation in 1642 and 1647—they began to take shape only after the Revolutionary War. The change in the political status of the country required a corresponding change in the educational system. In order to accomplish this objective the new nation needed to follow the provisions of the U.S. Constitution closely.

Those who were motivated to seek reform were guided by a vision of the future and by the knowledge that the Constitution was not as rigid as to preclude new efforts to bring about meaningful change in the various national institutions, including developing a new theory of education. The fact that the Constitution allowed room for amendments to address issues that did not exist at the time it was completed suggests a degree of flexibility. Those who sought reform were not directly guided by provisions of the Constitution, but by their observations of the nature of change they envisioned.

In the 200 years that the Constitution has been in effect, there have been twenty-six amendments to the original document, suggesting the conclusion that it can, indeed, accommodate change to bring about improvement. The last of these amendments, giving those eighteen years of age the right to vote, was ratified by the states on July 5, 1971.[1] Richard M. Nixon was the first president to benefit from it, just as Warren G. Harding was the first to benefit from the Nineteenth Amendment of 1920 giving women the right to vote. The forty-five years from 1783 to 1828 were a period of transition in the development of the United States. This transition actually began with the adoption of the Articles of Confederation in 1781. This was the agreement under which the thirteen colonies established a government of the United States independent from and outside British control, continuing use of the name that had been used in the Declaration of Independence.

The articles served as the basis of law for the new nation until the present U.S. Constitution went into effect in 1789 when George Washington was elected president.[2] The articles reflected the distrust that many colonists had for a powerful central government, as well as proving to Britain that the new nation was quite capable of conducting government business on a higher leveling. Thus, the Articles of Confederation carried a psychological boost, not only among members of the government, but also among members of the public in recognizing both their right and responsibility in playing a major role in shaping the future of the country by their involvement in the democratic process. For the first time in their lives the people began to feel that both the country and the government belonged to them. They took to heart Jefferson's idea that government could be instituted with the concern of the governed, a totally different practice from British political influences. With these developments, confidence in the future began to grow. The process of transition was in place—all that was needed was to let it run its course.

Beginning in 1786 there was an increasing demand that the articles be revised to suit new conditions. This demand came from the thinking that the people and their government intended to conduct the business of running the country by constitutional means. Under these conditions no man was likely to emerge as king or tyrant. The principles of democratic behavior were fully established for the present and for the future. One can see that the foundation of democracy in the United States was built out of the Articles of Confederation. By the time Washington was elected president of the constitutional convention in 1787, confidence in the future had grown to unprecedented levels. This confidence was evident in some events that began to take place in Europe and the United States. The end of the monarchy in France in 1799 stressed the need to institute other forms of government. The action taken by the British Parliament in passing the Canada Constitution Act in 1791 suggested to the United States that its neighbor would not be under the direct rule of the monarchy. Canadians were quite free to pursue a national agenda that was consistent with the wishes of the people. Britain did not rush to impose conditions in Canada that were likely to lead to another revolution.

In the United States a number of events were taking place that indicated that the future was going to be different from the past. For example, as soon as he was inaugurated in 1789, President Washington signed the first act passed by Congress concerning the administration of oaths. In the same year Congress established the Department of Foreign Affairs, now the State Department. In 1790 Washington approved plans for a new capital city to be named after him. In that same year the Supreme Court held its first session headed by Chief Justice John Jay (1745–1829),[3] who served from 1790 to 1795. Also in 1790 the first national census was taken showing that there were 3.9 million people in the country. On December 15, 1791, the Bill of Rights became law. In 1793 the cotton gin brought sweeping changes to the economy of the South. The gin enhanced the production of cotton and increased the use and value of slave labor. In 1794 , after two years of construction, the first toll road was completed and opened extending sixty-two miles from Philadelphia to Lancaster, Pennsylvania, at a cost of $465,000.

By the time of Washington's death in 1799,[4] Americans could look to the future with a new level of confidence and a higher sense of belonging. By the time that John Adams (1735–1821)[5] succeeded Washington in 1787, the population stood at 4.9 million people. Two new states were admitted into the union, Mississippi in 1798 and Indiana in 1800. In that same year, 1800, the Library of Congress was established and Congress appropriated $5,000 to buy books and other educational materials. Also in 1800 the city government was moved to its present site of Washington, D.C., and the White House became the official residence of the president. Adams was the first president to live in the White House.[6] In 1803, during the presidency of Thomas Jefferson, John Dalton (1766–1844), a British chemist and teacher, proposed his atomic theory of matter. In the same year the United States purchased Louisiana for $15 million. Also in the same year, Chief Justice John Marshall (1755–1835) established the Supreme Court's power of judicial review.

There were other important developments that took place during this period of transition. In 1808 Congress prohibited the importation of slaves from Africa. Britain had taken such action in 1807. In 1805 Lewis and Clark reached the Pacific coast. During the presidency of James Madison (1751–1836) from 1807 to 1817 the confidence that Americans had found and felt for the future was dealt a severe setback in the War of 1812 with Britain. However, confidence quickly returned in 1814, when a peace treaty was signed between the two countries. This confidence was shown in 1816 when the first savings bank was founded in Philadelphia. The presidency of John Quincy Adams (1767–1845) from 1825 to 1829 witnessed other important developments. One of the most important was the organization of a women's labor union in 1825, setting the stage for the Seneca Falls conference in 1848. From that point on, women began to demand equal rights using their pursuit of education to demand equal treatment with men. In 1828 the first passenger railroad company began laying tracks from Baltimore.

ANDREW JACKSON AND THE ERA
OF THE COMMON MAN

These unprecedented developments lead to two important conclusions. The first is that they proved to Americans that the concept of social and political change became a central tenet of the development of the nation. This kind of change began to unfold with differences that emerged between the thirteen colonies and Britain. The road to revolution was mapped out because it was virtually impossible to resolve or reconcile these differences. The second conclusion is that by the time of the presidential elections in 1828, the concept of change had become more inclusive than was originally initiated before the Revolution. Change included the nature of relationships between people as the evolution of national institutions demanded more involvement from the people than they had in the past. This involvement was demanded by the inception of democracy. Above all else, this change demanded fundamental reform of the system of education. This reform was paramount to every other change that was taking place.

There is no question that these developments demonstrated the changes of that period of transition that began in 1783 and, by 1828, poised the country for the thrust of educational reform. It was not possible that education would remain the same before and after the Revolution while every other aspect of national life was going through change. Therefore, Americans understood the developments of this transition as providing an opportunity to bring change to national leadership as a condition of initiating reform in education. The election of Andrew Jackson (1767–1845) in 1828 as president of the United States suggests the beginning of a new period beyond the transitional phase. The fact that Jackson took tremendous pride in being the first president to be born in a log cabin in North Carolina shows the extent to which the United States was experiencing change in its political thought processes. His election was a recognition of his dedication to the promotion of social equality as a critical factor of national development; it also symbolized the new direction that he would chart for the development of his nation.

Jackson's background shows that, by the time of his election, he had gained tremendous experience in the dynamics of social change. After teaching school for a short period of time he went to Salisbury in North Carolina in 1784 to begin his law studies under Spruce Macey. With a mind able to learn fast, Jackson soon established a reputation as one of the most articulate lawyers in town. Although professional standards for lawyers were not as high as they are today, Jackson set for himself strict standards that made him very popular. He always remembered how he endured poverty in his early life, and, so, understood the poverty of the people he associated with.

He was determined to enter public life so that he could make a difference in the lives of the people who were making an effort to improve the conditions that controlled their lives.

His first opportunity came in 1788 when John McNairy, senior judge of the Cumberland superior court, appointed him solicitor for a region that is now part of Tennessee. The two men had studied law together and had become close friends. On his way to Nashville, Jackson stopped in Jonesborough (now Jonesboro) to take part in a civil suit. He accused the opposing lawyer (Aaron Burr) of taking illegal fees and challenged him to a duel, a system that people in those days, including lawyers, used to settle disputes.[7] The argument ended with both men firing their pistols. Hamilton later died of his wounds. Jackson had made his point—challenging those in positions of power not to exploit the powerless and the weak. Jackson went to serve with distinction as U.S. senator in 1787 and as judge until 1804.

In seeking to appreciate Jackson's commitment to reform one must understand three characteristics that distinguished him from national leaders of the past. The first was his unwavering commitment to reform. As his administration took office in March 1829 he remarked to Martin van Buren (1782–1862),[8] who was to serve as his secretary of state, that the administration must not disappoint the people in their expectation of reform. Among the reforms he intended to initiate was to end the practice of apprenticeship to wealthy individuals. Instead, he proposed to have people go through formal training to acquire the professional training they needed. The second characteristic was his belief in the potential of all people to make a viable contribution to society. Jackson advanced his theory that, to enable them to do this, he felt that they should have an education that was different from the education people received in the past. This is why the reform of education was necessary. The third characteristic was his belief that the reform of education was the principal component of the reformation of society.

Because of his commitment to the principle of social equality, it is not surprising that Jackson's term of office from 1829 to 1837 is appropriately known as the Jacksonian era, or the age of the common man. A discussion of the reform movement in the United States must, of necessity, begin with the election of Andrew Jackson. Jackson's social reform rightly earned him a place in history as the leader of Jacksonian democracy. His legal training under Spruce Macey, a wealthy attorney, helped him understand the social implications of the position he held.

Jackson served with distinction during the War of 1812. Tragic as this war was, it gave Jackson an opportunity to understand the need for social reform to serve the needs of the people. His defeat by John Quincy Adams in the presidential elections of 1824 was a form of education that he needed to plan efficiently for the elections of 1828, in which he defeated Adams. On March 4, 1829, Jackson traveled from his home in Tennessee to Washington, D.C., to take the oath of president. His inauguration was a cause for national celebration. Supporters, friends, and admirers from all over the country followed him to Washington because they saw him as a representative of their own aspirations. The age of the common man was now theirs.[9]

Jackson's inauguration brought thousands of people to Washington, D.C. The city was jammed with enthusiastic supporters who wanted to be part of this rare opportunity to celebrate an important event that they believed represented their cause. Daniel Webster reacted, "A monstrous crowd of people is in the city. I never saw anything like it before. They really seem to think that the country is rescued from some dreadful danger."[10] As he walked from his hotel to the inauguration ceremonies, thousands cheered him. This imposing figure, a proud man just under sixty years old, impressed the crowds by his personal appearance and dress. His black suit, his articulate disposition, his face mellow with experience and knowledge, his silver-white hair neatly pushed back, Jackson dominated the inauguration with the poignancy of his composure and thought. Those who could not get closer did everything possible to catch a glimpse of their idol running through the streets to a new national destination. The entire ceremony brought the decorum of the past at the White House to an end.[11] To the people Jackson represented change—the future belonged to them because he was the transition.

In his inaugural address Jackson was to the point. He reminded his audience that the U.S. Constitution must be respected by all, balanced with states rights, and he promised the people that his administration would pursue a policy of innovative approach based on the equality of all people. As soon as the inauguration was over, Jackson made his way down to unpaved Pennsylvania Avenue, mounted his horse, and headed for the White House. Carriages, wagons, and thousands of people on foot followed close behind to participate in a lavish reception of cake, ice cream, and orange punch that had been prepared for them in advance. This was the first time such a reception was opened to members of the public and the first time most had been inside the White House. This symbolized the beginning of a new era.

As soon as the inauguration ceremonies were over, Jackson began to concentrate on the formulation of his theory to address the enormous task of reforming education. Acutely aware of his background as the first president born in a log cabin, Jackson fully identified himself with the aspirations of the common man. His social reform permanently transformed the United States from an aristocratic society into a state in which the concept of democratic values and principles had practical meaning to the struggling masses. His administration was based on his conviction that educational development based on equality ensured national development. He outlined five basic reasons to explain his thrust for educational reform. He believed that education: (1) improves social institutions and their functions so that they serve the needs of the people; (2) is an instrument with which to sharpen individual perceptions of self and society; (3) creates a social environment and conditions in which individuals see themselves within a larger context of collective principles and values; (4) helps develop talent vested in individuals to serve their needs and those of society; and (5) makes democratic values more viable.[12]

In an effort to implement these principles, Jackson operated under a basic theoretical belief that equality of educational opportunity was the hub on which the vehicle of social justice, stability, and development would run. He also believed that, in a society in which slavery and other social inequalities were the order of the day, this line of thinking had a special appeal to the masses of deprived people who were struggling for improvement in their lives. By demonstrating sensitivity to the plight of the masses, Jackson charted a new course. A critical component of his philosophy of education was his view that, in order to improve democratic values, the educational system must be reformed because society is viable only as its people participate in its operations.

FACTORS INFLUENCING THE REFORM MOVEMENT

The major influence of the Jacksonian era is the creation of a new level of consciousness that gave a clear portrait of the flaws of the social and economic system that Jackson believed well-planned and coordinated educational reform could adequately address. In spite of the efforts of the delegates to the constitutional convention to create a political system that represented the interests of the people, economic and political power was still in the hands of the elite and the privileged. Jackson embraced the thinking that the practice of democracy was enhanced, and operated at its best, when the largest number of people participated in the political and educational process. He was aware that of the 12,866,020 in the United States in 1832 only 1,217,691 people cast their ballots in the popular presidential election: 687,502 for him and 530,189 for Henry Clay (1777–1852), his opponent.[13] He concluded that if democracy was to be enhanced more people must participate in the election process. Jackson saw the election of 1832 as a demonstration of the need for basic reform in education to help people understand the importance of their role in the political process in order to make it more representative.

Henry Clay presents a fascinating dimension in the history of U.S. politics relative to Andrew Jackson. Born in Virginia and son of a Baptist minister, Clay studied law and was admitted to the Virginia bar in 1797. He was elected to the U.S. House of Representatives in 1811, and, on the first day of the session, was elected Speaker of the House. He would be elected five other times. He came to national prominence during the War of 1812 and served as secretary of state under John Quincy Adams. No man wanted to be president of the United States more than Clay. After serving on the commission to negotiate the terms of the peace treaty of Ghent, Clay felt that he was ready to run for president. Although he ran five times, he failed to attract the support of the majority of voters. By the presidential election of 1832 Jackson was so popular that Clay did not have a chance.

One must see Jackson's efforts at reform from a much broader perspective. One can say that the factors that influenced the reform movement had their origins in the events that took place over an extended period of time, beginning with the colonial period. S. Alexander Rippa has taken the position that the introduction of slavery in 1619 carried implications for the future of the country in far more serious ways than the colonists were able to see. Rippa suggested, "The most important and probably the most enduring effect of the slave system was the repression of creative thought."[14] The concept of creative thought was synonymous with freedom of expression, a battle cry from the colonial period to the Revolution.

During the colonial period, creative thought could not be exercised by one group of people if another group was denied it. Such was the effect of slavery on the colonial society. Slavery inhibited the ability of the revolutionary leaders to seek an end to it. They did not know that, while the thirteen colonies obtained political freedom from Britain, they could not be free as long as African Americans were still enslaved. Rippa concludes that the repression of the thought process was far more pervasive as it was applied to limit thought among slaves. The continuation of slavery after the Revolution proved to successive leaders that it had to free America of a scourge that had inhibited its ability to reform. This is why President Abraham Lincoln could no longer avoid the issue of slavery.

It is a widely held view that continuation of slavery beyond the Revolution denied the country an opportunity for development. Since slavery affected the economic, social, and political activity in the country, it was not possible to envisage meaningful reform within the confines of slavery. Rippa also suggests that by not even addressing slavery, the American society of the revolutionary period was weakening the resources that it needed to ensure its own advancement.[15] The failure of the delegates to the constitutional convention to take decisive action to end slavery created serious problems for the future. By the time the reform movement began it was clear to those who were part of it that slavery had to come to an end if the direction of national development was to have a new meaning for their struggle.

By the time Jackson took the oath of office in 1829 the West was still a frontier. The increasing influence of industry was felt more on the mode of production than on the styles of life. This was becoming evident as the number of people who were migrating from Europe increased significantly for the first time in the history of the country. There was also new thinking that slavery was a handicap to reform. This view was being held by an increasing number of immigrants who were more comfortable than their predecessors in practicing cultural diversity as the frontier continued to expand, which led to a corresponding viewpoint that slave labor must be supplemented with paid labor. The issue was where to draw the line. This situation meant that those who needed better paying employment opportunities needed better education to perform the skilled jobs that slaves could not perform. This was an important factor of educational reform.[16] Robert E. Potter goes on to conclude that the average working day in 1830 was thirteen hours, six days a week; it was quite clear that the emergence of the factory was having a more profoundly negative effect on human relationships than in the past. The advent of the Industrial Revolution placed more emphasis on material benefit than on human relationships. This situation demanded a fundamental change in values in order to ensure that national developmental programs did not become the victims of greed. This was the major concern that Karl Marx and Friedrich Engels expressed in 1848, until the reform movement was initiated. With child labor laws the educational process was losing its proper influence, and, as a result, new thinking was evolving to address the problems of child labor and the need for better education. Changing labor laws to reduce the number of hours children were working would mean that children would spend more time in school. This would be a real investment in the future.[17]

As the number of immigrants continued to increase, especially after 1820, those who came brought with them their customs, languages, and cultural practices. The perceived danger was that this would reduce the country to fragmented units and communities that had no common affiliation to the values of the United States. It was feared that immigrants were losing an opportunity to form common bonds that would help identify themselves with the ideals that made the United States what it was. The ideals of George Washington, John Adams, Benjamin Franklin, Thomas Jefferson, and James Madison were being substituted for the fragmented values of immigrants to the extent that a national identity was difficult to carve. Because many of the immigrants were from the lower economic classes, the tired and huddled masses of Europe, they were uneducated and did not understand their responsibility in a democratic system.[18] Reform of education would usher these immigrants into a new stream of thinking and activities that would give them a new agenda. Thirty percent of the inhabitants of New York and Boston were immigrants by 1845.[19]

There is no question that the recognition that children and immigrants needed education more than they needed employment became a major factor that influenced the reform movement. It was clear, during the great potato disaster in Ireland, that the natural increase in population combined with the rapid increase in the number of immigrants emphasized the fact that the existing educational system was no longer sufficient to meet the needs of the rapidly growing population. In his study, *Western Literary Institutions* in 1836, Calvin Stowe put this need in the context of the need for fundamental reform saying, "Unless we educate our immigrants, they will be our ruin. It is no longer a mere question of benevolence of duty, or of enlightened self-interest, but the intellectual and religious training of our foreign population which has become essential to our own survival and safety as a nation."[20] Stowe concluded that it was not ignorant and uneducated foreigners that the danger to the country came from, but rather a lack of vision and foresight about the educational needs of the counry. Of course, Stowe was talking about white children. It was not possible to include slave children in his call for reform to bring about a different kind of education. It was for others to promote reform to enable black children to acquire the kind of education they saw as the salvation of a nation.

Joel Spring suggests that three theoretical perspectives emerged at the initial stage of the common school movement that later had a profound impact on efforts to create common schools. The first perspective was that children from a variety of religious, ethnic, economic, and social backgrounds educated in the same schools would gain common political and social values that would help eliminate conflict. The belief that using education would eliminate social evils and build a new political foundation became a central tenet of the reform movement.[21] Social values would not be assumed, they had to be learned, not in the same old ways practiced during the prerevolutionary period, but in an environment that permitted reform of the school system.

The second theoretical perspective was the belief that schools must become the channel for transmitting knowledge about the structure and functions of the U.S. government and the role of the people. It was also felt that, as the schools during the colonial period were used to promote religion as an essential component of society, schools of the reform movement must be utilized to promote secular values as an essential component of an emerging society.[22] But for the schools of this period to fulfill this new national objective they required fundamental reform. Thinkers of the postrevolutionary period advocated the emergence of an educational system that would provide the kind of citizens who understood their responsibility in a democratic society. The thrust for the common school movement was considered to be the means to this development.

The third theoretical perspective that Joel Spring outlines as a critical factor of the reform movement is the need to create state agencies to ensure the efficient operation of the school along secular lines. In 1642 and 1647 Massachusetts had opposed legislation to require communities to organize for the purpose of running schools. But during the reform movement there was a need to create state agencies that would place the schools on a system that was intended to operate in a way that would meet the needs of all students. Although the state of New York was the first to create the position of state superintendent of schools in 1812,[23] there was a need to do more because, by 1830, the position of state superintendent was no longer sufficient to see to the growing educational needs of the students. Nevertheless, the act of creating a state position such as the state superintendent of schools was a long jump from practices of the past into the thrust for reform in the early nineteenth century.

One must remain aware of the fact that these three theoretical perspectives of the reform movement combined with other important factors to demand action on this critical national frontier. Those who opposed the common schools argued that their advent would take away the spirit of private enterprise that was central to the pioneering spirit of the colonial period. They argued also that this fact was recognized by the Supreme Court's ruling in the *Dartmouth College* case in 1819. They also argued that education as it was envisaged by the proponents of the common schools could not possibly be provided to all students on the basis of total equality. To the extent that practical realities have inhibited the evolution of a practice that would make this possible even today, this aspect of the argument had some merit. But it was not a sufficient reason to reject efforts toward accomplishing equality of opportunity through the reform movement.

The liberals argued that for education to serve the purpose for which it was created it must be available to all students on the basis of equality for democracy to be strengthened. In 1830 John R. Commons recalled the line of development the debate was taking saying, "It is a lamentable fact that persons destitute of education are ignorant of the loss they sustain, and hence, fail to avert the evil from their off springs."[24] In his study, *Public Education in the United States: A Study and Interpretation of American Educational History* (1919), Ellwood P. Cubberley (1868–1941), who served as professor of education at Stanford University from 1898 to 1917, and as dean of the College of Education there from 1917 to 1933, discussed the common school movement in the context of the views held by conservatives and liberals. Cubberley concluded that the conservatives were motivated by greed for power while the liberals were motivated by the common good of the country. He saw the conflict between "public men of large vision" and "politicians of small vision"[25] as a struggle for control, not only of the educational system, but the political process itself.

Cubberley reached the conclusion that the reform movement was based on the clear theoretical principle that in a democratic society the concept of equality was an underlying consideration that could not be compromised and that American society would rapidly degenerate if reform was not initiated. He went on to suggest that the essential operative concept of reform was that the state needed to assume its constitutional responsibility of providing education to all its citizens on the basis of equality. The conditions of the times would indicate that failure to initiate such a reform would leave the United States unsure of its future and unable to chart the course of its development. With a rapid increase in the number of immigrants arriving in the United States, a stage would be set for major conflict to emerge and paralyze the efforts of the country to ensure its development. Cubberley suggested a compelling argument in favor of the kind of reform that was being initiated saying, "A state which has the right to hang has the responsibility to educate as an inherent right to self-determination and improvement."[26]

No less important to the reform movement was the need to improve the curriculum. From the days of the Old Deluder Satan legislation to the Age of Reason the curriculum had been slow to accommodate the demands of new conditions. John D. Pulliam and James van Patten note that by 1825 these changing conditions made it possible to introduce a curriculum to include more than just religious courses, such as the study of history and geography.[27] This new effort of trying to bring about change in the curriculum was based on a theoretical assumption that a new level of study based on a new curriculum was critical to the educational endeavor of students to help them adjust to life under new social conditions in a country that was rapidly changing. But innovative as this effort was in 1825, it did not translate into the thrust for the kind of reform that was expected. But the curriculum change of 1825 proved to be the kind of experiment that was needed to test the direction that the reform movement would take.

This experiment did much to alert the country of the need to reform the existing system of education. For example, it understood the need to examine the benefits of the pauper schools that had been initiated during the colonial period. A conclusion was reached that the pauper schools had run their course and that there was now need for a new system of education. Gerald L. Gutek suggests that at the same time the Sunday schools were steadily declining in popularity, American society was increasingly becoming secular.[28] Although the Sunday schools were not particularly associated with specific religious organizations the very name itself had, by the time of the reform movement, invoked questionable motives on their part.

A major factor of the reform movement was the question of how to finance education in the event that the reform movement was successful. In 1830 the Workingman's Society of Philadelphia complained severely that the state of Pennsylvania had failed to develop an educational system that gave every student an opportunity to gain an education and that efforts must now be initiated to bring universal education about at no cost to the parents of students. The Workingman's Society concluded, "Thousands of students are now suffering the consequences of this disregard to the public welfare on the part of our rulers."[29] The working men of Boston adopted a similar line of argument when they stated (also in 1830) that elected representatives had a responsibility to express the feelings and views of the people and also had a duty to respect the popular opinion to express such. The working men of Boston concluded that the establishment of a liberal system of education available to all students would ensure national independence.[30]

These two statements, issued by two powerful workers organizations, were directed at an aspect of the reform movement that politicians were afraid to address: financial support of education from public funds. The reason for this argument was the theory expressed by many that the schools must be free from the taint and stigma associated with the plight of charity schools, which were exclusively for the children of poor families. Any change had to include the fundamental thinking that "public education ought to be equal, public, and open to all, and the best which can be defined."[31] Robert E. Potter quotes John R. Commons as taking these views and expressing them in a clearer manner than had been done in the past saying, "Every citizen ought to contribute his fair share towards expenses for education. It is the most important branch of legislation, much more important than the criminal law, as prevention is better than cure."[32] Today, paying property tax has been pretty much accepted as the most effective method of ensuring financial support for public schools even though some controversy has arisen over the question of the distribution of those funds.

This position opened the first serious debate about the method of financing education after the reform movement was successful. The conservatives argued that those who were pushing school reform were forcing their position on a national issue that infringed upon the concept of free enterprise. They also argued that to expect everyone to pay a tax to support schools would be unfair to those who did not have children in school. But those who argued in favor of reform were of the opinion that education carried much value, even for those who did not have children in school. Among those who took this line of argument was Ralph Waldo Emerson (1803–1883),[33] who made a considerable contribution to the debate on the reform movement.

Emerson argued that the reform movement was an imperative condition of the development of the United States and that every student possessed an intellect that could only be developed through education for the benefit of the country. Without equality of educational opportunity it would be impossible to develop this intellect.[34] Emerson concluded that any person who was concerned with issues, persons, or places, could not see the problem of existence in its proper perspective. He suggested that intellect separated outstanding men from ordinary men, and that education could make all men outstanding. That was how society could benefit from education extended to all stduents on the basis of equality.[35] Emerson concluded that just as the success of the student lies in the school's respect of the student, the success of education lies in society's respect of its goal to educate all students on the basis of equality.

Apart from the arguments against or in favor of reform, there were other factors that seemed to promote reform. By 1830 the primary schools were reasonably well organized. Teachers were better trained than in the past. The establishment of the normal school was making a difference in the manner in which they approached their responsibility. The United States was overcoming the effects of the War of 1812 and was looking to the future with renewed confidence. The Industrial Revolution was placing considerable demands on the mode of production, and this required better trained workers. The demographic shift from rural to urban was a phenomenon that required knowledge of emerging issues in society. The institution of slavery was being questioned more forcefully since Congress took action in

1808 to stop the shipment of slaves from Africa. These were among the major factors that influenced the reform movement.

LEADERS OF THE REFORM MOVEMENT

When the thrust for reform was finally made it was the result of the thinking of earlier individuals who had a vision of the future they simply could not repress or give up. These individuals were many and came forward to offer their ideas of reform from different backgrounds and viewpoints. This section presents only five examples of individuals whose ideas can be considered pertinent to the reform movement. The actual leaders of reform paid tribute to the work that these pioneers did to lay the foundation of a major national movement that has had so much meaning to Americans today. It must be remembered, however, that the ideas of reform began to emerge more strongly during the Age of Reason, the period of the great intellectual awakening that changed the way people viewed their society and conditions that controlled human life.

The first example is Robert Owen (1771–1858). In 1960 Harold Silver gave an impressive account of Owen's theory and the impact that its evolution had on the reform movement. Silver concluded that Owen began to develop his theory in Britain where he had considerable trouble having it accepted. The frustration that many innovative thinkers experienced with their ideas is the main reason why many of them left Britain and came to the New World. Owen was a British industrialist whose ideas were at the same level as those of Edmund Burke. Owen believed that society would benefit by reforming education to make it come into line with current social trends.[36] Owen argued that society had no choice but to reform education because the modern world was rapidly changing in terms of industrial development, population increase, trade between nations, and relationships between members of the community, all of which combined to create new conditions that only reform of education could address as a response.

Owen came to the United States in 1825 to promote his ideas of school reform, especially for young children. He was one of those individuals who believed that introducing children from two to six years old to the learning environment would later help eliminate problems associated with learning such as discipline and building self-confidence. Owen advanced his theory that if children were trained in physical and motor coordination, moral values and basic skills, intellectual response to environmental factors would later come naturally.[37] But to have education function to fulfill this objective would demand reform in which teachers would be trained in new methods of instruction including methods of assessing children's needs. Owen also concluded that the existing school system must be reformed to accommodate this trend of thinking.

The second example of an individual who pioneered the evolution of the theory of reform in education was Joseph Lancaster (1778–1838), a Quaker school master who came to the United States from Britain in 1818. Lancaster is best known for his Lancasterian system of education in which he used carefully selected students for further training so that they, in turn, would help other students. In this manner the number of students who were able to teach increased rapidly. Robert E. Potter comments on Joseph Lancaster, saying that he developed many teaching strategies which he believed, when properly utilized, would help improve the quality of education but were not expensive.[38]

Another individual who pioneered reform in education was Andrew Bell (1753–1832), an Anglican clergyman who invented an inexpensive method of teaching large numbers of students in Madras, India. In 1797 Bell returned to Britain where his ideas found an ardent supporter in Joseph Lancaster. Bell's ideas were adopted in the United States as a basis to promote reform in education as a necessary condition of national development. This call for reform was based on a theoretical argument that a nation could not develop with only a small percentage of its population educated. Living in the age that he did, Bell was not reviving the theology of the Puritans, he was only trying to think of reform within the spirit of the Age of Reason. Bell did not even mention region as a focus of his efforts, but he was trying to promote a secular education consistent with the demands of the time in which he lived.

William Maclure (1763–1840) also pioneered reform in education. In 1820 Maclure expressed his ideas of reform in his book, *Opinions on Various Subjects*, in which he argued for education reform to address the need for workers to gain new and meaningful educational experiences. Maclure urged communities to provide facilities so that workers could learn to improve their skills and level of productivity.[39] He advanced his theoretical argument that failure to initiate reform would place the United States at a disadvantage in its efforts to gain skills needed to carry out trade and commerce in the changing world. Indeed, by the time of his death in 1840, Maclure had watched the development of the Industrial Revolution and the impact it was having on society. It took nearly twenty years for some of Maclure's ideas to catch on in the reform movement.

The fifth example is James G. Carter (1795–1849) who pioneered reform in education by enunciating theory. Carter had worked his way through Harvard by teaching school in Massachusetts. He was deeply concerned about schools' poor conditions in the state and was appalled that little had changed since he was a student. In 1826 he published his *Essays Upon Popular Education* in which he criticized the lack of democratic principles in the manner in which the schools were operated. He also decried the lack of reform in education itself.[40] Carter called for fundamental reform in education, arguing that its absence inflicted a great injury to the efforts the students were making in acquiring an education. He argued that such reform would give the United States an opportunity to see itself better in the context of developments that were taking place in the world. Perception of self was a critical factor in the development of the country.

THE THRUST FOR REFORM

When the work of these pioneers was fully recognized, a number of individuals came forth to provide leadership in putting these theories into effect. These individuals combined these theories and the legacy of the Jacksonian era to create a new national consciousness that suggested some glaring weaknesses in the American system, both social and educational, as well as the need to initiate fundamental reform. Because political and economic power was still the privilege of a few, these individuals felt that continuing this practice would inhibit the thinking that democracy was at its best when the largest number of people possible participated in political and economic systems. The exclusivity of the political process generated new fears that America was becoming an aristocratic society as had existed in Europe. With the increase in population from 5,308,000 in 1800 to 12,866,000 in 1830, poverty and other social dysfunctions were on the rise, putting the value of social institutions into doubt.[41]

Beginning in 1837, the year that Jackson completed his second term of office, these are some of the realities that the leaders of the reform movement took action on to make reform effective. But the question is: What type of reform was envisaged in education? From that time to the end of the nineteenth century, American education was based on three basic theoretical assumptions. (1) Education must be the duty of the state and a right for the people. Even though the U.S. Constitution delegated education as a local responsibility, it was evident that the federal level had an important role to play in its development. (2) Because the exclusive charity schools embodied elements of an aristocratic society, there was a need to dissolve them in favor of creating common schools. (3) There must be a better way of financing education than was the case at the time.

These three assumptions also brought three individuals who championed the cause of reform perhaps more than others. They were Horace Mann (1796–1859) of Massachusetts, Henry Barnard (1811–1900) of Connecticut, and William Torey Harris (1835–1909) of Missouri. These men came into the arena of educational reform to chart a new course. Mann so believed in educational reform that he gave up his law practice to become secretary of the Massachusetts Board of Education. In thirteen years, from 1835 to 1848, Mann championed the cause of educational reform, in a way that reflected the ideas of Andrew Jackson, for the improvement of American society through educational development. The success of Mann's efforts must be seen in the context of the strategy he utilized to accomplish the objectives he had identified. First, he persuaded the business community to become involved in seeking reforms in education because he convinced them that better educated workers were more productive. Edmund Dwight (1780–1849), a leading industrialist who had nominated Mann for the position of secretary of the Massachusetts Board of Education, played a leading role in creating a new consciousness among members of the business community about the need to support the reform movement.

Second, Mann also persuaded workers to support the idea of common schools because they would generate a new awareness of equality, not only in education but also in society as a whole.[42] But Mann and Barnard's influence was felt more profoundly in the structural form of the school system they advocated based on the theoretical arguments for reform that had been made by leading pioneers before them. Major revision of the curriculum, introducing common schools, training of teachers, tax support of education, more effective administrative systems, involvement of the community and parents, and the use of technology—all combined to form a central element of the thrust for educational reform that is evident in the American educational system today.

The mass migration of Irish to the United States, beginning in 1837 and coinciding with the beginning of the reform movement, added a new dimension that enabled Americans to see the need to transform their society through transforming the school system. In the same year, Mann succeeded in persuading the Massachusetts legislature to create a State Board of Education, and he accepted the position of secretary. In 1838 Mann outlined his theory of the work he intended to carry out to fulfill his responsibility saying, "The theory of our laws and institutions is, first, that in every district there should be a free district school, sufficiently safe, and sufficiently good for all children within its territory where they may be well instructed in the rudiments of knowledge and imbued with the principles of duty."[43] Mann was successful in his efforts. From 1837 to the beginning of the Civil War, the United States had come to accept reform of education in the way pioneers and leaders had advocated. The enactment of the Land Grant Act in 1861, forming the state university system, underscored the federal role in the development of education as a response to the call for reform.

Henry Barnard deserves as much credit as Horace Mann for his efforts in promoting the reform of education. Barnard also deserves credit as one of the most committed and effective leaders of the reform movement in Connecticut. A former teacher, Barnard worked relentlessly to reform the school system by various means. In 1838 he was elected to the legislature and immediately began the task of reform that was directed at improving the curriculum, school facilities, teacher preparation, conditions that controlled teachers, unifying school districts, ensuring financial support of the schools, initiating community and parental involvement, ensuring an effective system of administration, and hiring more female teachers.[44] By the time of his death in 1900 the educational system in Connecticut had gone through a transformation that made it one of the best in the country, as it was in Massachusetts under the influence of Horace Mann. Officials in education came from all over the country to learn what Mann and Barnard were doing to create such a high reputation for education in their states.

William Torey Harris did in Missouri what Barnard and Mann did in Connecticut and Massachusetts. Conditions of the times demanded action to give an effect push to the ideas of reform. A very successful superintendent of schools in St. Louis from 1867 to 1880 and U.S. commissioner for education from 1898 to 1906, Harris carried out his duty under the theoretical influence of the belief that the school had a responsibility to teach students to exercise the power of utilizing reason in both their learning activities and role in society. To accomplish this objective Harris argued that the educational system must be reformed to include more courses to allow students to choose subjects according to their interests. The curriculum must be revised from time to time to make sure that it was responding to the needs of the students. He suggested that a good curriculum must include language, sciences, social studies, mathematics, and literature.[45] By the time of his death in 1909 the United States had embraced the thinking of these three men as a basis for the genuine reform that they were trying to accomplish.

SUMMARY AND CONCLUSION

This chapter has focused on two components of the evolution of the theory of reform of education, which cover the period of transition from 1783 to 1828, during which time important conceptual elements fell in place to enable those who had a vision to launch the campaign for reform. The second period, from 1828 to 1837, produced a number of pioneers in the reform movement. Their work was crucial to the success of the reform movement when it was finally initiated in 1837. One can say that the success that Horace Mann, Henry Barnard, and William Torey Harris achieved was a result of the work that was done by earlier thinkers who had a vision of the future. The legacy that these thinkers left is that they refused to give up that vision. It was the legacy that the Jacksonian era had passed on.

It is difficult to specify the exact date when the reform movement was completed. In effect, it was never completed because reform is still going on to this day. But it is often suggested that the reform movement was disrupted by the outbreak of the Civil War. At the same time, the conclusion of the Civil War made it possible to introduce an important component of the reform movement—the emancipation of slaves and the beginning of a new system of education that had never been in place. Horace Mann had hoped that the success of the reform movement would bring slavery to an end without resorting to a major conflict. Events did not turn out that way. However, the Civil War was a blessing in disguise. The reform movement resumed during Reconstruction and is still in process today. There are important issues that can only be addressed by formulating new theories of reform. These issues include: how to resolve the problems of drugs and violence in school, equitable financial distribution for school districts, making the curriculum relevant to the needs of students, equitable representation on the school board, etc. The process of reform never comes to an end because conditions in society keep changing.

NOTES

1. Pathfinder Publications. *The Constitution of the United States with the Declaration of Independence* (Boston: Pathfinder Publications, 1973), p. 8.

2. Ibid., p. xi.

3. John Jay was a distinguished statesman who, with Benjamin Franklin and John Adams, negotiated the terms of the peace treaty with Britain bringing the Revolutionary War to an end. He also helped Alexander Hamilton and James Madison get the Constitution ratified. He contributed significantly to *The Federalist*. He graduated from King's College (now Columbia University) in 1764 and was admitted to the bar in 1768. He was named secretary of foreign affairs from 1784 to 1790, when President Washington named him Chief Justice of the Supreme Court.

4. When Washington died on December 14, 1799, Napoleon Bonaparte (1767–1821) ordered France to observe ten days of mourning to honor the man he respected tremendously. In the United States men and women wore mourning clothes for months.

5. The reader will remember that John Adams and Thomas Jefferson died on the same day, July 4, 1826.

6. The White House got its present name during the presidency of Theodore Roosevelt (1857–1919) from 1901 to 1909. It had been known as the Executive Mansion since 1818.

7. In 1804 Alexander Hamilton (1755–1804) became involved in a political dispute with Aaron Burr (1756–1836), then vice-president to Thomas Jefferson, an old political rival in New York politics and in their practice of law. Burr challenged him to a duel. The two men fought on July 11, 1804.

8. Martin van Buren served as the eighth president of the United States from 1837 to 1821. He also served as U.S. senator from New York beginning in 1821, and as governor in 1828 when Jackson named him U.S. secretary of state.

9. S. Alexander Rippa, *Education in a Free Society: An American History*, 6th ed. (White Plains, NY: Longman, 1988), p. 79.

10. Ibid., p. 80. Indeed, the first six presidents were all members of the aristocracy. Jackson was the first president the people genuinely believed represented them and understood their needs.

11. Ibid., p. 81.

12. Dickson A. Mungazi, *Educational Policy and National Character: Africa, Japan, the United States, and the Soviet Union* (Westport, CT: Praeger, 1993), p. 33.

13. Robert E. Potter, *The Stream of American Education* (New York: American Book Company, 1967), p. 186.

14. Rippa, *Education in a Free Society: An American History*, p. 15.

15. Ibid., p. 84.

16. Ibid., p. 190.

17. Ibid., p. 171.

18. Ibid., p. 192.

19. Ibid., p. 191.

20. Calvin E. Stowe, *Western Literary Institutions*, 1836. Quoted in Potter, *The Stream of American Education*, p. 192.

21. Joel Spring, *The American School, 1642–1985* (White Plains, NY: Longman, 1986), p. 71.

22. Ibid., p. 72.

23. Ibid., p. 70.

24. John R. Commons, address to the City and County Convention in New York, July 10, 1830. Quoted in Potter, *The Stream of American Education*, p. 193.

25. Ellwood Cubberley, *Public Education in the United States: A Study and Interpretation of American Educational History* (Boston: Houghton Mifflin, 1919), p. 165.

26. Ibid., p. 166.

27. John Pulliam and James van Patten, *History of Education in America*, 6th ed. (Englewood Cliffs, NJ: Merrill, 1995), p. 65.

28. Gerald L. Gutek, *An Historical Introduction to American Education* (Prospect Heights, IL: Waveland Press, 1991), p. 57.

29. John R. Commons, *A Documentary History of American Industrial Society*, 1910. Quoted in Potter, *The Stream of American Education*, p. 192.

30. Ibid., p. 195.

31. Ibid., p. 192.

32. Ibid., p. 195.

33. Emerson, who had studied the traditional curriculum of Latin, Greek, English, and history, served as a teacher from 1819 to 1823. He, therefore, knew what the issues in the debate about reform were.

34. Ralph Waldo Emerson, *Essays and Poems* (London: J. M. Dent, 1906), p. 157.

35. Ibid., p. 158.

36. Harold Silver, *Robert Owen on Education* (New York: Cambridge University Press, 1960), p. 110.

37. Ibid., p. 111.

38. Potter, *The Stream of American Education*, p. 146.

39. William Maclure, *Opinions on Various Subjects* (New Harmony, IN: School Press, 1820), p. 66.

40. James G. Carter, *Essays upon Popular Education* (Boston: Bowles and Dearborn, 1828), p. 42.

41. David Nasaw, *Schooled to Order: A Social History of Public Schooling in the United States* (New York: Oxford University Press, 1979), p. 29.

42. Ibid., p. 481.

43. Gerald L. Gutek, *Historical Foundations of Education: A Biological Introduction* (Upper Saddle River, NJ: Merrill, 1991), p. 206.

44. Potter, *The Stream of American Education*, p. 198.

45. Ibid., p. 278.

5

The Theory of Secondary, Higher, and Teacher Education

> A teaching profession cannot be established on a basis which only covers the work of the common schools. The knowledge that is to be conveyed to the child is not all that is required on the part of the teacher.
> —Andrew Traper, 1890

THEORY OF LATIN GRAMMAR SCHOOL

The evolution of the theory of secondary education was a much slower process than that of the common school movement. When John Eliot (1604–1690), who had graduated from Jesus College, Cambridge, in 1621, arrived in Boston in 1633 he shared some ideas about how education in the New World could be improved. He succeeded in persuading the authorities to pass legislation to direct the course of education. The result was that the Massachusetts General Court passed legislation in 1642 and 1647 along the lines that Eliot had suggested. As unique, exciting, and innovative as these two pieces of legislation were, they were overshadowed by more pressing needs to survive in the hostile wilderness. Although their impact was considerable, they did not form a sustainable pattern of development until after the Revolutionary War. Although the colonial society did what it considered necessary to promote primary education and higher education, there was little that was done to promote the development of secondary education.

Primary education was developed during the colonial period because it was considered essential to reading, writing, arithmetic, and moral and religious values. Higher education was developed because it was considered essential to the training of individuals to enter the ministry and become preachers and leaders in the community. But there was no immediate purpose for the development of secondary education. During the colonial period the Latin Grammar school was the equivalent of high school. However, the Latin Grammar school did not meet the needs of individuals and society in the same way that primary education and higher education did in their struggle for development.[1] The Latin Grammar school did not fit into the natural progression of education because it was irrelevant to higher education. It was considered part of one's intellectual development, but it lacked the utilitarian function that was associated with both primary education and higher education.

However, recognizing that the kind of education that must come between elementary school and higher education was missing, colonial society neglected to develop the Latin Grammar school exclusively to prepare students for college. This is why higher fees were charged for attending the Latin Grammar school than was normal. John D. Pulliam suggests that the Latin Grammar school was slowly but steadily increasing in popularity as an important level of education.[2] As colonial society continued to develop, the need for education at the Latin Grammar school level began to increase. It slowly became recognized as forming an important bridge between elementary school and higher education. Officials in institutions of higher learning were now beginning to require at least exposure to the experiences in the Latin Grammar school before students were allowed to seek admission there. Prospective students in higher education made an effort to be admitted into the Latin Grammar school to gain confidence in their ability to pursue courses in institutions of higher education. Those who set their sights to respectable careers as preachers and speakers wanted to make sure that the road to these careers passed through the Latin Grammar school.

Although the Latin Grammar School had been in operation in Maryland since 1767, Benjamin Franklin proposed the establishment of an English academy in 1749 to provide for a preparatory education suited to the needs of those students who wanted to go to college.[3] What Franklin had in mind was a combination of education that sought a balance between academic education and vocational training for the development of the country. This balance was not in the minds of many students or those who were promoting education in the Latin Grammar school. The theory of the academy did not appeal to many people at that point because they saw the Latin Grammar school as having more quality and purpose as long as it was directed toward college entrance. Franklin was operating at a much higher level of thinking than those who did not understand the purpose of an academy. They thought that it was a form of manual training.

In order to provide a form of education beyond the elementary level, and different from what Franklin had in mind, a number of model schools appeared. The models were usually conducted by one teacher who would handle several grades each with a few students taking a variety of subjects.[4] Franklin wanted to see the evolution of a system of education at the Latin Grammar school that was comprehensive and inclusive enough to cover areas of study now associated with secondary education. These areas included modern languages, navigation, bookkeeping, history, geography, various arts, sciences, and mathematics. Franklin concluded that the courses offered in the Latin Grammar school were too narrow to prepare students for the kind of lives they would lead.

Although these courses were offered in areas of high population, such as Philadelphia, New York, and Charleston, they were sporadic in the quality of instruction they actually gave. Because they were not considered full academic preparation for college entrance they were not destined to last a long time. From 1667 to the beginning of the Revolution, the Latin Grammar school enjoyed a considerable degree of popularity, attracting a wide range of students who thought these schools were the best preparation for college and gave them an opportunity to exercise some influence in society. Until 1776 enrollment in both the Latin Grammar school and college increased considerably.[5] Toward the end of the Revolution, when colonists became convinced that they were going to win, there was renewed interest in the Latin Grammar school. In 1780 Andover Academy in Massachusetts was chartered, and in 1781 Exeter in New Hampshire was also chartered.[6]

For the Exeter school, gifts from the Phillips family in 1778 made it possible to create a constitution for its operation. The theoretical reasons for the school were quite typical of the time: "To lay the foundation of instructing youth not only in English and Latin Grammar, writing, arithmetic, and the success wherein they are commonly taught, but also especially to teach them the great end and real business of living."[7] The first major purpose of the school was to teach piety and virtue. The second purpose was to teach English, Latin, Greek, writing, arithmetic, music, geometry, logic, geography, and other liberal studies. There is no question that the leaders of education in 1781 were thinking of the evolution of the theory of secondary education as a product of vision needed to plan the future. However, developments began to dictate an alternative line of thinking about the Latin Grammar school. The signing of the Treaty of Ghent in 1783 demanded a reexamination of the importance of a purely academic education at the secondary level. In spite of the advent of the Age of Reason, which placed emphasis on the development of human intellect as the best form of national investment, the future of the Latin Grammar school was in doubt. The slow development of industry influenced Franklin to formulate a new theory of the Latin Grammar school and vocational training. He succeeded in formulating a theory that made it possible for the development of academic education and vocational training to take their course side by side.

In 1821 the Latin Grammar school had increased in popularity to the extent that Boston opened in that year the famous English Classical School, which was renamed the English High School in 1824.[8] Boys as young as twelve years old were admitted if they passed entrance examinations. The school was exclusively for children of wealthy families, and children of poor families had no chance of being admitted. This was one factor that later promoted the campaign for the common school. The curriculum included such subjects as English language, history, geography, mathematics, philosophy, and physical science. By 1827 the school was so successful that Massachusetts passed legislation requiring communities of 4,000 inhabitants or more to build a high school for purposes of instructing the youth in these subjects.

In 1826 Boston opened a high school for girls. But parents and members of the community complained about the high cost of sending students to these schools and protested against higher taxes to support them. It was ironic that when these students applied for admission many of them were turned down because the school did not have sufficient funds to operate. Within a short period of time the school was closed, giving proponents of the reform movement yet another reason to demonstrate the need for reform. By the time of the presidential elections in 1828, Andrew Jackson, like Bill Clinton in the presidential elections of 1996, clearly understood the importance of education in the struggle for national development. Jackson's opponent, the flamboyant Henry Clay, as a member of the aristocracy, did not seem to understand the critical nature of the issue.

In 1855 Boston opened another school for girls that included a component for teacher training. All students had to meet entrance qualifications and were required to take specified courses without any opportunity for electives.[9] Theodore R. Sizer concludes that in the same year, there were 262,096 students in 6,185 high schools.[10] Slowly the Latin Grammar school was being replaced by the high school. By the time the reform movement was underway, the Latin Grammar school was on its way out and the high school was on its way in.

THE PHENOMENON OF THE ACADEMY

Beginning in 1845 the popularity of the Latin Grammar school was declining for a number of reasons. The curriculum, emphasizing mastery of the grammatical structure of the classical languages, had become too mechanical. The use of the classical languages as a means of communication was eroding away in favor of the vernacular languages, a trend that began during the Renaissance. Latin had lost much of the humanism that was its distinctive feature before the Renaissance. The use of Latin was now considered too narrow to offer the broadly based education that was necessary in the nineteenth century.

This development meant that, during the twenty years from 1841 to the beginning of the Civil War, the Latin Grammar school was no longer considered a viable form of education beyond the primary level. Its place was being taken by the academy, which Franklin originally proposed in 1749. The advent of the Industrial Revolution in the nineteenth century minimized the importance of academic education in favor of technical education. Although many people decried the demise of the Latin Grammar school,[11] it had to give way to new demands. The academy provided an opportunity for a functional balance between academic education and the vocational training that was considered essential to securing employment. The academy also provided the social and economic environment that students needed to make the adjustment to a changing society.

Beginning in 1840 there developed a new phenomenon in the United States, the belief that the Latin Grammar schools were promoting elitist attitudes that did not contribute to the general faith in the possibility of improving human life through participation in common goals. It was also believed that through their liberal approach to education the academies could become the means by which these common goals could be fulfilled. The application of open enrollment and nonstructured curriculum were both associated with the ideals of the common man that became a central tenet of Andrew Jackson's agenda. The academies also represented the concept of free enterprise, what Gerald L. Gutek called a new frontier for the individual.[12] The academies were believed to be the channel through which social mobility was possible on the basis of equality.

Although the academies lacked formal structure, they were believed to have the capacity to meet the educational needs of all students beyond the primary level. They became the means by which a civilization could prosper by developing a new social entity and industrial identity. The added advantage of the academies was that they provided an individual student an opportunity to set his own goals and live his own unique dreams. While the curriculum in the academies captured the elements of the Latin Grammar school, they were also broad enough to accommodate the varying interests of students as a reflection of the interests of the nation.

THE EVOLUTION OF THE THEORY OF HIGH SCHOOL

But as Rome grew and fell, so the days of the popularity of the academies were numbered. During the Civil War the academies fell into the background as efforts were being directed at winning the war. During Reconstruction interest in education beyond the primary school was considered important for a number of reasons. It was considered a bridge to professional training associated with college education. It was considered a part of the natural progression to college from the primary school. It was viewed as an important acquisition, and anyone who did not have it was regarded as having missed something important in his life. As a result of the reform movement the primary schools were doing well, and it was natural to see a good transition from primary school to high school. To have this happen, the high school had to do well also so that there was a logical and smooth connection from primary school to college.

The twenty years from 1870 to 1890 witnessed a rapid development of the reform of high school. Although elements began to form before 1820, it was in 1821 that Boston opened the English Classical School. But it was not until 1870 that the high school began to form its present character. In 1964

Edward Krug stated that the U.S. commissioner of education for the year 1889–1890 reported that there were 2,526 public high schools with a total enrollment of 202,063 students compared to 94,391 students enrolled in 1,632 academies.[13] This shows that the high school was developing rapidly as the academy was declining. One reason that contributed to this phenomenon was that the Industrial Revolution led to mass production of materials while it created an expanding base for taxation that was needed to support the schools.

It must be remembered that the establishment of the modern high school was the result of the reform movement. Although taxation to support the schools was a controversial issue, it had been adopted in varying degrees by 1870. Although a set of theories had evolved over a period of time to support taxation for the schools, there were still those who were opposed to paying taxes because they did not have children in school. This is why in 1872 three members of School District Number 1 in Kalamazoo, Michigan, sued the school to stop collecting taxes to finance the high schools.[14] The argument made by the individuals was as old as the reform itself, that forcing people who did not have children in school to pay taxes was a violation of the principle of fairness. However, writing the opinion of the Michigan Supreme Court, Justice Thomas M. Cookey (1824–1898) argued that taxation was necessary to ensure the adequate instruction of all students and to provide a "link between the ordinary common school and the state university."[15]

The decision of the Michigan Supreme Court was needed to end the controversy over taxation to support public high schools. Although the controversy came to an end, the development of public high schools lacked unity and conformity until 1892 when the National Education Association (NEA) appointed a committee consisting of ten members to study the situation and make recommendations for improvement regarding a course of study to be offered, teaching methods, testing procedures, promotion of students, and what was needed to study to qualify for college entrance. The chairman of the committee was the powerful Charles W. Eliot, president of Harvard University, from 1869 to 1908. Other committee members were William Torey Harris, U.S. commissioner of education, four college presidents, a college professor, a headmaster of a private school, a headmaster of a girl's school, and a principal of a boy's high school.

That the committee took its assignment seriously is shown by its report. The committee recommended that the early introduction of the student to the fundamentals was critical to educational success in the high school. Students preparing to go to college must be introduced to the required courses early in their high school studies. These courses were Latin, social studies, modern languages, English, literature, sciences, and mathematics. High school students must be taught by the same methods so that there was consistency in how they learned. Eight years of primary schooling and four years of high school would be required to prepare students for success in college. Colleges must set admission standards consistent with their expectations of the academic work the student was capable of accomplishing. This admission criteria should be the same for all colleges.

This report contained everything that Eliot wanted to see in high school. Since his appointment as president of Harvard in 1869 he was worried by what he saw as a lack of structure and uniformity in the curriculum of the high school. Now he was finally given the opportunity to design it in the way he considered necessary. From that time to 1918, high school education was based on the Eliot model.[16] He was the most influential leader in the development of education at both the high school and college level. For high schools across the country this report served as the guide, for college Harvard served as a model, and Eliot took credit for both developments. Any high school that ignored or failed to implement this model was not considered to offer higher education to its students; any college that did not follow the Harvard model was considered to lack the essential components of a good college education.

The election of Grover Cleveland (1837–1908)[17] as president of the United States in 1892 considerably increased the strength of the high school because Cleveland, a moderately liberal Democrat, believed in education as a critical factor of national development. This is why, in 1895, he encouraged colleges to refine their admission criteria to be consistent with high schools to ensure that the instruction they were offering would be consistent with those criteria. He wanted to see a close working relationship develop between colleges and high schools in order to provide quality education, which he said was essential to the success of the United States. In 1899 the NEA established its own college entrance requirements in order to strengthen the high school. In 1902 a committee on unit courses recommended fifteen units of work for graduation from high school. A unit was defined as a course of study covering an academic year of not less than thirty-five weeks taught in four or five periods of at least forty-five minutes per week.[18]

The evolution of the theory of high school took a major turn in 1918 when the NEA named the Committee for the Reorganization of Secondary Education chaired by Clarence Kingsley to study and recommend new course offerings. The committee issued the famous Seven Cardinal Principles of Secondary Education listing seven objectives its members thought must be included in the curriculum. These were: promotion of health, ensuring command of the fundamental processes, teaching the importance of worthy home membership, training for a vocation, teaching responsibilities of a citizen, appreciating profitable use of leisure, and understanding the importance of ethical character.[19] In 1974 William Van Til explained the theoretical significance of this development saying, "Stress on the seven cardinal principles strengthened the curriculum claims of such high school subjects as industrial arts, home economics, music, fine arts, physical education, and business education. Emphasis on the new subjects encouraged the development of a more unitary social studies program for citizenship, rather than completely separate history, geography, economics, etc."[20]

The implementation of these objectives as an interpretation and application of theory was so successful that twenty years later, in 1938, the NEA appointed a new committee, the Education Policies Commission, to delineate categories of educational objectives in high schools. Taking the Seven Cardinal Principles of Secondary Education as its guide, the Educational Policies Commission utilized its own theory to place its own objectives into four categories. These are: self-actualization, human relationships, economic competence, and civic responsibility. In 1961 both the Seven Cardinal Principles of Secondary Education and the objectives of the Educational Policies Commission were affirmed as a proper educational program. From that time the character of high school has taken the line of development that it has to this day.

Recognition that the curriculum determines the success or failure of the educational process has been a factor that has influenced efforts to improve the high school. The National Defense Education Act of 1958, the Civil Rights Act of 1964, the Elementary and Secondary Education Act of 1965, and the Education Consolidation and Employment Act of 1981 all represent an effort to reform the high school and reverse the declining interest in education among students. By the beginning of 1981 the United States was emerging from the social traumas of the 1970s and wanted education to help reset the national agenda and priorities. Title IX of 1971, the Higher Education Act of 1972, and *Roe v. Wade* of 1973 added a new level of urgency as a call to reform the curriculum. This is why in 1983, the National Commission on Excellence in Education issued a grim report about the declining quality of high school education and the need to improve the situation. In this context the reform movement has been in the process of changing.[21]

THE EVOLUTION OF THE THEORY
OF HIGHER EDUCATION

The institution of higher education had its origins during the colonial period. Today there are three important characteristics associated with higher education. These are teaching, scholarship, and service to the profession. These three characteristics distinguished the university from other institutions of higher learning. During the colonial period the development of the institution of higher learning followed the patterns of two influential universities in Britain: Cambridge University founded in 1284 and Oxford University founded in 1167. Since the Middle Ages these two universities admitted students from prominent families because, as Gerald L. Gutek says, that higher education in Great Britain had been for years provided, not on the basis of equality, but on consideration of social class.[22]

The pattern of universities in Western Europe followed that which was used in opening universities in Spain and in Italy. The essential characteristic of their structure is that the curriculum was liberal arts, which was believed to provide individuals an opportunity to exercise influence in society especially as members of the clergy. Upon completion of their liberal studies Medieval students went on to specialize in one of the areas of the professions that included theology, medicine, or law. Later political science, sociology, business, and economics were added to the list of professions that one could study. Thomas Aquinas (1125–1274) and Peter Abelard (1079–1142) provided the theoretical framework for the curriculum that was adopted in these universities. These two thinkers were religious men who had studied theology, but operated by a theoretical belief that a religious person must also have a functional knowledge of other important areas of human endeavor. This thinking was the basis of liberal studies as we know it today. Aberlard, a French philosopher, began his work as a teacher in 1113. Students came to him from all over Europe because he was very good. Aquinas was an Italian biblical scholar who believed that education must be inclusive, meaning that it must entail a study of a wide range of courses to complete one's education.

The need to preserve the religious traditions of European universities combined with the need to have a broadly based education to form the reliable theoretical foundation of institutions of higher learning in colonial America. The oldest colleges were founded on the theoretical considerations arising out of this line of thinking. This is why, in October 1636, the Puritans of New England exerted great pressure in designing the charter for Harvard College and proposed the same type of curriculum that was offered in European universities at the time. This was the only way for them to make the claim that they were offering an education of the same quality as that which was being attained in colleges in Europe. The College of William and Mary in Virginia was founded in 1693 under similar conditions. The College of New Jersey in 1742 and Princeton in 1746 were founded under similar theoretical considerations.[23]

An interesting feature of the colleges of the colonial period was the curriculum. Although these colleges operated under their own particular principles, regulations and requirements that made them unique, they all functioned under traditions that were considered to uphold standards that were similar to those in colleges and universities in Europe. This is how they hoped to receive the recognition that they needed to build their reputations. There were two considerations that were central in their operations. The first was that students must meet the requirements of the Latin Grammar school. This requirement was made because mastery of Latin, Hebrew, and Greek, the classical languages, were considered the hallmark of an educated individual. Any college that did not offer these languages was considered to lack quality in its course offerings.

The second consideration was the kind of curriculum they offered. Frederick Rudolph outlined the typical curriculum of the college in the colonial society as follows:

First Year: Latin, Greek, logic, Hebrew, and rhetoric

Second Year: Hebrew, Greek, natural philosophy, logic

Third Year: Metaphysics, moral philosophy, natural philosophy

Fourth Year: Metaphysics, Latin, Greek, and natural philosophy

Source: Frederick Rudolph, *The American College and University: A History* (New York: Alfred A. Knopf, 1962), p. 26.

While the presidential election campaign was going on in 1828, controversy was rapidly developing about the need to maintain this curriculum in colleges. In that year the Yale Corporation and some members of the faculty at Yale College produced a document severely criticizing the retention of what they called the dead languages curriculum and advocated a more inclusive curriculum. Jeremiah Day (1773–1867), president of Yale College, and James L. Kingsley (1778–1852),[24] professor at Yale from 1801 to 1851, responded by writing what has become known as the Yale Report. In it the two men defended the classical character of the curriculum and went on to outline the elements of the theory on which they based their argument, saying that they were of the opinion that their plan of education was designed to seek the improvement of education. Not only did the course of study and the methods of instruction need this improvement, but there was also a variety of instructional strategies to enhance the quality of education. They stated their belief that change, from time to time, was needed to meet the changing demands of the country so as to accommodate the methods of instruction to suit the country's fast development.[25]

After the Revolution the curriculum began to improve considerably to include physical sciences and social sciences. The age of Andrew Jackson set the stage for the emergence of the modern college. The religious revival started by John Wesley (1703–1791) and his brother, Charles Wesley (1707–1788), in the late eighteenth century swept across Europe and the United States by the first half of the nineteenth century. This revival created a new level of religious fervor unmatched by any similar revival since the days of the Crusades. The desire to know things religious and secular motivated both religious and secular leaders to encourage the people (as well as themselves) to seek a higher level from which to excel in all areas of human endeavor, including learning.

These developments constituted an environment that produced a desire among religious denominations to found their colleges. As was the case with the founding of colleges in colonial society, the fundamental purpose of the colleges founded by religious denominations was to train religious leaders who would serve the needs of the community in all aspects. In this regard the American Protestant involvement, like its European parent organization, placed a premium on educated religious leadership. However, the proliferation of religious groups created a situation in which differences of pedagogy and theology were increasingly becoming difficult to resolve. Instead of trying to seek accommodation, the Protestant organizations decided to found their own colleges. The denominational colleges became popular institutions because they were the principal means of educating the faithful who were needed to build religious institutions committed to serving the church and the community for the benefit of all.

In addition to seeking to fulfill this fundamental objective, the denominational colleges also sought to fulfill other educational needs. They sought to prepare students as teachers at the secondary level. Among the Protestant denominations that founded colleges were the Baptists, Lutherans, Methodists, Congregationalists, Presbyterians, Episcopalians, Quakers, and Mormons. Fearing to lose ground, the Catholic Church also became fully involved in founding colleges.[26] In addition to the denominational colleges, private colleges were also being founded to provide an alternative secular education that did not emphasize religious instruction. The following are only a few examples of colleges that were founded during this time:

College	Year	Denomination	Location
Albion	1835	Methodist	Albion, Michigan
Amherst	1821	Private	Amherst, Massachusetts
Centenary	1825	Methodist	Shreveport, Louisiana
Collins	1842	Private	Collins, Virginia
Fordham	1841	Catholic	New York, New York
Geneva	1848	Presbyterian	Beaver Falls, Pennsylvania
Mercer	1833	Baptist	Macon, Georgia

DARTMOUTH COLLEGE CASE: A TEST OF NEW THEORY

As the number of denominational and private colleges increased, the state governments felt isolated and removed from an important national development. They regarded the opening of these colleges as an erosion of the power they thought was theirs to exercise. Tension between the church organizations and the state legislatures was increasing rapidly. Using the U.S. Constitution to delegate education a state responsibility, the state legislatures felt compelled to displace the governing board of these colleges with state boards. In the state of New Hampshire tension between the legislature and the Congregationalists had been simmering since 1758, when a body of members of the denomination applied for permission to open a college. When the state government rejected the application, the Congregationalists gave their support to a school for Native Americans (known as Indians at the time), which had been founded by Eleazar Wheelock (1711–1779) in Lebanon, Connecticut.

In 1769 the Congregationalists decided to move the school to Hanover, New Hampshire, and renamed it Dartmouth College. The Native Americans in Connecticut had shown little interest in the white man's form of education. Immediately a controversy arose between the Congregationalists and the legislature about who must control the college. The controversy arose partly from the political rivalry that broke out between the theory espoused by the Federalists, who controlled the board of trustees and the Jeffersonian Democratic-Republicans, who controlled the state legislature. In 1816 things came to a head when the Democratic-Republicans used their majority in the legislature to try to take control of Dartmouth College and change the charter that had been granted by King George III in 1769 for a private school. The charter was to last forever.

Without warning the legislature nullified the original charter and decided to implement one of its own, arguing that higher education was too important to be delegated to religious organizations because all they were doing was perpetuating their sectarian teachings to the detriment of the real educational interests of the people of the state as a whole. To some people in the United States this argument presented a persuasive theoretical basis for the state to take over the operation of the school. They feared that allowing religious organizations to control institutions of higher learning would create elite institutions that would be exclusively for a few selected individuals. There was, therefore, considerable support for the state takeover of the school. Taking this apparent support into consideration the state supreme court ruled in favor of the takeover.

However, in the *Dartmouth College* case, the Dartmouth College Board of Trustees immediately brought suit against the legislature arguing that its action was unconstitutional and that the take-over was a seizure of what did not belong to it. Daniel Webster (1782–1852), who graduated from Dartmouth in 1806, presented the case for the Dartmouth College Board of Trustees to the U.S. Supreme Court, saying, "The twelve individuals who were trustees were possessed of all the franchises and the immunities with them. The powers and privileges which the twelve were to exercise exclusively are now to be exercised by others. The case before the Court is not of ordinary importance, nor of every day occurrence."[27] Webster argued that the results of this case would affect not just Dartmouth, but also every college and all institutions of learning in the country. He rhetorically asked if the legislature of the state of New Hamphishire should be allowed to take an institution that was not its own and turn it from its original use and convert it to a purpose that it would use at its discretion? Webster concluded that the answer was in the negative. Writing the Court's ruling on the case, Chief Justice John Marshall (1755–1835),[28] advanced a theoretical framework that has been the conventional wisdom to this day. He told the parties in the case, and the country, that the right of the trustees to exercise independent control was intended to protect both the existence of private colleges and to prevent state takeover. This independent control was meant to ensure that any control was safe-guarded by the Constitution. Concurring with Webster, Marshall stated that there was no argument whether there may be an institution founded by the legislature and placed immediately under its control.

Referring to the original charter Marshall asked a few rhetorical questions of his own to substantiate his line of thinking saying, "Is Dartmouth College such an institution? Is education altogether in the hands of the government? Does every teacher become a public officer, and do donations for the purpose of education necessarily become public property so far that the will of the legislature, not the will of the donor, becomes the law of the donation?"[29] Marshall concluded that these questions were of serious consideration to American society and deserved to be considered carefully. Marshall then concluded that the action of the state legislature in trying to take over the running of Dartmouth College constituted a violation of the Constitution of the United States and that the judgment was in favor of the Dartmouth College Board of Trustees.

There is no question that, in this ruling, Marshall was strengthening the theoretical belief that his Court put in place with its ruling in *Marbury v. Madison* in 1803 that the Supreme Court had constitutional authority to review any legislative action. There is also no question that, in its ruling in the *Dartmouth College* case, the Marshall court was enunciating a new theory. Today Dartmouth is a leading private institution of higher learning. But more important still, this decision made it possible for many denominational organizations and private bodies to open institutions of higher learning across the country. The Wesley Foundation of the Methodist Church, for example, opened Wesleyan universities all over the country. If the ruling in the *Dartmouth College* case had gone in favor of the state legislature, higher education in the United States would have never become a reality. It would have also meant that Harvard, Yale, Princeton, Stanford, Georgetown, and other leading private institutions would have experienced the same fate, or they would have never opened in the first place. The Marshall court also put in place an important principle that has had universal application, which is that the concept of free enterprise is applicable to higher education. Like other aspects of free enterprise, higher education—as a dimension of national development—was outside government control.

THE THEORY OF STATE UNIVERSITIES

In its ruling in the *Dartmouth College* case the Marshall court said something that the state governments used to believe—that they, too, could be involved in higher education. Marshall's statement—that there may have been an institution founded by government and placed completely under its direct control, the officers of such an institution would be public officers employed entirely by the government[30]—offered a suggestion, even an encouragement, that seemed an invitation to state legislatures to be involved in higher education. Taking their direction from the ordinances of 1785 and 1787, which were passed by the Continental Congress before the Constitution was ratified, state legislatures tried to put the setback they had suffered in the *Dartmouth College* case behind them, and they began to think in terms of establishing institutions of higher learning that they would control.

The critical provisions made in the ordinances of 1785 and 1787 were that the federal government granted two townships of land for purposes of establishing institutions of higher learning to each state upon being admitted into the Union. Having been admitted into the Union on March 1, 1803, as the seventeenth state, Ohio was the first to take advantage of the provisions of these ordinances to pass the Ohio Enabling Act, which made provisions for founding institutions of higher learning. The Ohio State University was established in Columbus in 1870. This began a pattern that other states followed. But, some years before, the federal government itself had ventured into higher education. For example, in 1857 it established the Columbia Institute for the Deaf, later renamed Gallaudet College, in honor of Edward Miner Gallaudet (1837–1917),[31] the founder of the school, and Howard University for Negroes in 1867 in honor of Oliver Otis Howard (1830–1909),[32] who had directed the Freedman's Bureau established to promote the development of Negroes during Reconstruction. The year 1867 was also the year that the U.S. Office of Education was established to facilitate the flow of information about what the states were doing to promote education.

In 1862, encouraged by positive developments, the U.S. Congress was ready to pass major legislation to encourage the states to make a definitive move to establish state institutions of higher learning. In 1853 the legislature of Illinois petitioned the U.S. Congress to authorize the state to establish an institution that would provide the working class an opportunity to acquire the skills they needed to function more efficiently in a world of changing technology. Nine years later, in 1862, a congressman from Vermont, Justin S. Morrill (1810–1898), seized the opportunity to introduce a bill which, if enacted, he hoped would encourage the states to establish institutions that would offer mechanical and agricultural instruction as well as scientific and classical studies. It is clear that the Morrill bill would seek to strike a functional balance between mechanical and agricultural training and academic education along the lines that Benjamin Franklin had proposed in 1749.

The enactment of the Morrill Land Grant Act of 1862 was a result of the political and legislative struggle going back to the *Dartmouth College* case. From 1857 to 1862 there had been a growing controversy about whether to continue the institution of slavery. The Lincoln-Douglas debates had alerted different factions about the consequences of ending slavery. This controversy had permeated every aspect of national life to the extent that any issue was seen in terms of whether to continue slavery. This is why, when the Morrill bill passed overwhelmingly, it was sent to President James Buchanan (1781–1868), president of the United States from 1857 to 1861, who immediately vetoed it because he thought that provisions in the bill contravened sections of the U.S. Constitution and that the bill came at a time of great controversy concerning slavery.[33] It turned out that the Morrill Land Grant Act was quite precise in its provision stating, "Be it enacted by the Senate and House of Representatives of the United States of America in Congress assembled, that there be granted to the several states, for the purposes hereinafter mentioned, an amount of public land, to be apportioned to each state a quantity equal to 30,000 acres for each Senator and Representative in Congress to which the states are respectively entitled by the apportionment under the census of 1860."[34] But Buchanan's successor, Abraham Lincoln (1809–1865), who served from 1861 to 1865, promptly signed it.

From 1862 to 1890, the application of the Morrill Land Grant Act was so successful that a second Morrill Act was passed in 1890 to provide for direct cash grants of $15,000 which would be increased yearly to a maximum of $25,000 to support the land grant colleges.[35] Thus, began the practice of state universities that are today found across the United States. The following are only a few examples of state universities and when they were founded: University of Maine, 1865; University of Virginia, 1867; University of Illinois, 1867; University of California, 1868; University of Nebraska (the author's alma mater), 1869; University of Arkansas, 1871. Today these universities compete with private institutions in the quality of their service in the three areas associated with universities: teaching, scholarship, and service.

THE EVOLUTION OF THE THEORY
OF TEACHER EDUCATION

The evolution of the theory of teacher education follows three major phases. These are normal school, teacher's college, and the professional school. From the beginning of formal education during the colonial period, the need for good teachers was profoundly felt as essential to the success of the educational process. During the colonial period the qualifications of teachers varied greatly in education, preparation, personal qualities, and character. Teachers in the lower levels were often inadequately educated and trained. The most desired qualification was their ability to operate by their religious and moral values. If they possessed rudimentary knowledge of the basic skills in reading, writing, and arithmetic, then they were considered to hold proper qualifications. Many of them were students for the ministry, and some were even bond-servants.[36]

The selection, training, and certification of teachers varied from one colony to the next. In New England the responsibility of selecting and appointing teachers fell on the shoulders of members of a committee. The town minister usually gave final approval. In the middle Atlantic colonies the church organization responsible for high school assumed the responsibility of selecting and appointing teachers. In the plantations of the South individual instructors or tutors were appointed by the families themselves. That lack of a uniform system of selecting and appointing teachers means that quality of teaching was also lacking. It also means that throughout the colonial period there was an inadequate method of training teachers.

Efforts to improve the standards in teaching were not made until after the Revolution. From 1775 to 1783 the position of both teachers and the school fell into the background. By 1830, when new efforts were being made to improve teaching, the situation had deteriorated so badly that it was almost beyond salvage. In that year Henry Edwin Dwight (1797–1832) described the deteriorating situation, saying:

The want of competent teachers is one of the principal reasons why the classics have been studied with so little enthusiasm in our country. Teaching with us, is in most instances a secondary employment, one which the graduates of our colleges embrace for a few years, and then abandon forever. . . . Their limited resources compel them to devote several years to this employment, and when they have learned a little of the art of teaching, which, in truth, is one of the most difficult arts ever acquired, they resign their places to those who are still young, and who have had less experience than themselves.[37]

Dwight seemed to know what he was talking about. He was an authority on the problems of the profession of teaching. In 1829 he published *Travels in the North of Germany* in which he expressed great admiration of the German system of education including the conditions under which teachers served. Just before his untimely death in 1832 Dwight had been invited to be professor at a university in New York City, but he declined because he wanted to devote all his efforts to the improvement of teacher education and the conditions under which they served.[38] Dwight felt that everything must be done to improve the qualifications of teachers by formal training. The idea of the normal school was born out this line of thinking. Soon Dwight was joined by those who shared his views, and the ranks of those who were demanding change and improvement began to grow rapidly.

Among those who gave Dwight unconditional support was Samuel Read Hall (1795–1877), a minister who conducted a private school for those who sought to improve their skills as teachers. Hall was so successful that in 1830 he was named head of the normal school department at Phillips Andover Academy where he specialized in training teachers in methods of teaching, school organization, principles of education, school administration, and community relationships. In 1833 he published a book, *Lectures to School Masters on Teaching*, which made him an instant national celebrity and a major figure in the profession of teaching. All over the country, normal schools were established on the model that Hall had designed.

They also came from all over the country to learn from the undisputed master. From that time to the end of the century the normal school became synonymous with teacher training.

Following the model that Hall had established, state legislatures passed laws establishing normal schools. When Horace Mann was named Secretary to the Board of Education in Massachusetts in 1837 he immediately urged the establishment of the normal schools as an important part of his campaign for reform. In that year the Massachusetts legislature passed legislation establishing three normal schools to be located at Lexington, Barre, and Bridgewater. These schools offered courses in training teachers to teach reading, writing, grammar, arithmetic, spelling, history, geography, music composition, art, mathematics, philosophy, and religion.[39]

Other states soon followed the example initiated by Massachusetts. In 1844 New York passed legislation establishing a normal school. David Perkins (1810–1848), director of the school, made a significant contribution to the improvement and effectiveness of the normal school by publishing an impressive book in 1847, *Theory and Practice of Teaching*. The book became a standard text in normal schools across the country. Although the operations of the normal schools were interrupted during the Civil War, they had become so popular that they quickly resumed their functions as soon as it was over. By 1875 the normal school had become indispensable to the profession of teaching. The two years that were spent in normal schools were very productive and helped elevate teachers to a higher level of professional skills, bringing respect to the members of the profession. Henry Edwin Dwight would have been pleased to see this development.

As progressive, popular, and important as the normal school had become, it had to give way to a new form of development beginning in 1885: the teachers college. As colleges and universities became more developed and better organized into four-year study programs, the normal school was now considered inadequate to meet the needs of the future. A four-year study to receive a degree in education became the standard procedure. Students combined an academic course of study with courses related to teaching. Increasing academic standards, high school enrollment, and population matched by increasing technology and social change combined to make two years of training in normal school inadequate. The needs of both the students and society could now be met by the four years of training obtained from teachers colleges. A degree in education, rather than a two-year certificate, was considered the standard qualification for the profession of teaching.

In a rapid fashion, universities began to establish colleges of education for the purpose of training students to be more effective as teachers. In 1873 the University of Iowa was among the first institutions of higher learning to establish a permanent Department of Education. In 1879 the University of Wisconsin did the same. In 1886 Indiana University and Cornell University established colleges of education. In order to provide a functional transition from normal school to teachers colleges, some normal schools were absorbed into teachers colleges. From 1910 to 1920 nearly twenty normal schools were converted into teachers colleges. By 1930 nearly 20 normal schools had been turned into teachers colleges.[40]

In 1900 a new trend was beginning to form. A rapidly growing number of high school students was made possible by the establishment of teachers colleges, which were becoming centers of study of education as a discipline like any other on campus. Faculty members and graduate students conducted research in various areas of education, theory, teaching and learning, psychology of education, the impact of social issues on education, and environmental factors, all becoming topics of study in colleges of education. The colleges of education were becoming centers of academic endeavor in new and unscaled ways. This kind and level of activity could not be carried on in the normal school. The colleges of education also related their activity to local elementary schools and high schools where they applied the theory they learned to the classroom in actual situations. Upon graduation the teachers from colleges of education had an opportunity to interact with experienced individuals to gain new valuable experiences. For example, at Columbia University in New York, Nicholas Murray Butler (1861–1947)[41] gave a series of lectures to over 3,000 teachers over a period of a few years.[42]

By 1950 the success of colleges of education at the undergraduate level led to the next higher step, the evolution of the graduate college of education. In this process, the graduate school became a new phenomenon, the evolution of a professional school. The professional school was different from the college of education in some important respects. Those who were part of it established a specific area of discipline or study. The professional school offered an opportunity to develop expertise in a selected area for study, such as educational leadership, educational foundations, psychology of education, student services, human relationships, etc. These professional schools offered doctoral studies in a variety of areas.

In 1890 Andrew Traper (1848–1913), superintendent of schools in New York, recognized the importance of developing a professional perspective in institutions of higher learning and called for action to give effect to it by outlining elements of the theory he was enunciating. In his book, *A Teaching Profession: An Address Before the Massachusetts State Teachers Association*, Traper argued: "A teaching profession cannot be established on a basis which only covers the work of the common schools. The knowledge that is to be conveyed to the child is not all that is required on the part of the teacher. A teaching profession will be controlled by the same laws as other professions. In advance of professional training there must be a scholarship foundation."[43] A critical dimension that Traper was concerned about was the need for those who were members of it to excel in their endeavor, such as conducting research for publication. This endeavor began in the graduate college of education where students, under the direction of their professors, conducted research and wrote dissertations as part of meeting requirements for doctoral degrees. They were also encouraged to become members of professional organizations. This is the practice that is followed today.

SUMMARY AND CONCLUSION

This chapter traced the evolution of theory of education from the Latin Grammar school to teacher education. The evolution of this theory was heavily influenced by changing conditions in the country, different stages of its development from the colonial period to the present. This suggests the conclusion that theory must change because conditions keep changing. The evolution of this theory led to specific developments that had a profound impact on both education and society. The change from the Latin Grammar school, through the academy, to the emergence of the modern high school, was a reflection of this evolution. In the same way, the evolution of theory to address change from normal school to professional school was also a result of change in the conditions that affected it. The ability of the nation to adjust to both evolution of theory and change of conditions is the engine that moves the national vehicle forward.

NOTES

1. Robert E. Potter, *The Stream of American Education* (New York: American Book Company, 1967), p. 160.

2. John D. Pulliam , *History of Education in America*, 5th ed. (New York: Merrill, 1991), p. 66.

3. Gerald L. Gutek, *An Historical Introduction to American Education* (Prospect Heights, IL: Waveland Press, 1991), p. 99.

4. This was the origin of one-room and one-teacher schools that continued to operate until the 20th century. The author saw a few of these schools in Iowa and Nebraska in 1961.

5. Gutek, *An Historical Introduction to American Education*, p. 101.

6. Potter, *The Stream of American Education*, p. 161.

7. Quoted in Potter, *The Stream of American Education*, p. 161.

8. John D. Pulliam and James van Patten, *History of Education in America*, 6th ed. (Englewood Cliffs, NJ: Merrill, 1995), p. 66.

9. Ibid., p. 67.

10. Theodore R. Sizer, *The Age of Academies* (New York: Bureau of Publications, Teachers College, 1962). Quoted in Gutek, *An Historical Introduction to American Education*, p. 99.

11. This author recalls that when he went to high school in Zimbabwe in 1956, Latin was one the core subjects his class was required to study. There were two American Methodist missionary teachers who taught it. One of them, Edith Parks, who had studied Latin in college in Michigan, told the student she regretted the decision by U.S. schools to drop Latin in the 1920's, when she went to college, from being a required course.

12. Gutek, *An Historical Introduction to American Education*, p. 99.

13. Edward Krug, *The Shaping of the American High School* (New York: Harper and Row, 1964), p. 5.

14. Potter, *The Stream of American Education*, p. 314.

15. Reports of Cases Determined in the Supreme Court of Michigan, 1784–1875, Vol. 30, p. 69.

16. Gutek, *An Historical Introduction to American Education*, p. 104.

17. Cleveland was elected to his first term as twenty-second president in 1884 and to his second term as twenty-fourth president in 1892.

18. Gutek, *An Historical Introduction to American Education*, p. 105.

19. William van Til, *Education: A Beginning* (Boston: Houghton Mifflin, 1974), p. 43.

20. Ibid., p. 44.

21. National Commission on Excellence in Education, *A Nation at Risk: The Imperative of Educational Reform* (Washington, DC: Government Printer, 1983), p. 5.

22. Gutek, *An Historical Introduction to American Education*, p. 138.

23. Potter, *The Stream of American Education*, p. 148.

24. James L. Kingsley was a recognized as an eminent and outstanding authority on classical languages, mathematics, sciences, and history of New England. That is why Day invited him to co-author the Yale Report.

25. "Original Papers in Relation to a Course of Liberal Education," *The American Journal of Science and Arts*, 1829. Quoted in Richard Hofstadter and Wilson Smith, *American Higher Education: A Documentary History* (Chicago: University of Chicago Press, 1968), p. 275.

26. Among the best known examples of Catholic colleges are Georgetown University (1789) in Washington, D.C., and Notre Dame University (1842) in Southbend, Indiana. The Catholic Church has more colleges and universities than Protestant organizations.

27. "The Trustees of Dartmouth Colleges Woodward," in Reports of Cases argued and Decided in the Supreme Court of the United States, 1882. Quoted in Hofstadter and Smith, *American Higher Education*, p. 202.

28. Named by President John Adams in February 1801, Marshall was a strong believer in a strong federal government. He, therefore, disagreed with James Madison and Thomas Jefferson about states rights. In addition to the *Dartmouth* case, Marshall ruled in *McCulloch v. Maryland*, also in 1819, that the U.S. government had constitutional authority to establish the U.S. Bank. In *Marbury v. Madison* (103) Marshall ruled that the U.S. Supreme Court had the power to rule on the constitutionality of any laws passed by the Congress.

29. Quoted in Hofstadter and Smith, *American Higher Education*, p. 213.

30. Ibid., p. 214.

31. Edward Miner Gallaudet was joined by his brother, Thomas Gallaudet (1822–1902), in carrying out pioneering work in the education of the deaf and blind. Their father, Thomas Hopkins Gallaudet (1787–1851), had pioneered education for deaf-mute students in 1817.

32. Some people have argued that the Freedman's Bureau was the first affirmative action ever initiated in the United States, and that Reconstruction was part of it. Those who oppose affirmative action today only need to remember what happened

when President Rutherford Hayes (1822–1893), who served from 1877 to 1881, ended Reconstruction in 1877.

33. Between 1860 and 1861, when seven of the twelve slave states seceded from the Union due to differences of opinion between those states and the federal government about slavery, Buchanan refused to use force to keep them in the Union citing states rights as reason for his refusal.

34. Benjamin F. Andrews, *The Land Grant of 1862 and the Land Grant Colleges* (Washington, DC: U.S. Government Printing Office, 1918), p. 7.

35. Gutek, *An Historical Introduction to American Education*, p. 145.

36. Ibid., p. 188.

37. Quoted in Hofstadter and Smith, *American Higher Education*, p. 305.

38. Ibid., p. 306.

39. Gutek, *An Historical Introduction to American Education*, p. 191.

40. Potter, *The Stream of American Education*, p. 282.

41. In 1931 Butler, who served as president of Columbia University from 1902 to 1945, shared the Nobel Peace Prize with Jane Addams (1860–1835) for his contribution to the development of teacher education, and for her work in settling immigrants from Europe in Chicago, where she had founded and directed Hull House.

42. Gutek, *An Historical Introduction to American Education*, p. 284.

43. Andrew Traper, *A Teaching Profession: An Address before the Massachusetts State Teachers Association* (Albany, NY: Weed, Parsons, and Company, 1890), p. 5.

6

The Courts and the Theory of Education for African Americans

> Segregation of white and colored children in public schools has a detrimental effect upon colored children.
> —Earl Warren, Chief Justice of the U.S. Supreme Court, 1954

THE SEARCH FOR NEW IDENTITY: 1875–1896

The evolution of education for African Americans is a narrative of their struggle for development in educational opportunity, political, economic and social advancement. Because it was illegal to teach slaves to read, there was no hope that their conditions of life would change any time soon. When the Constitution was adopted slaves were more deeply disappointed by the failure of its framers to take decisive action to end slavery. The only hope African Americans had for development was to take advantage of Reconstruction programs. This chapter is limited to the struggle of African Americans for development. It does not suggest that the struggle of other ethnic groups is not important in the history of the United States. However, no other ethnic group has endured the humiliation of the institution of slavery. Therefore, the purpose of this chapter is to trace the major developments of this struggle and to attempt to see the implications that it has had in the education of black Americans. The reaction of white Americans to social and legal action taken by the courts on issues that deeply affected them in terms of African American development will be explained.

When the Emancipation Proclamation was issued on September 22, 1862, to take effect on January 1, 1863, it was recognized that "none of the Confederate States accepted the implied offer of immunity from abolition if they were to lay down their arms."[1] In 1866 the Fourteenth Amendment was adopted to prevent states from depriving any persons of life, liberty, or property without due process of law. A year before, the Thirteenth Amendment had been adopted to abolish slavery. Then, in 1867 the Reconstruction Act passed. The aim of these actions was to protect the interests of all people and to recreate the spirit of national unity. Southern states ignored the spirit of reconciliation which the country was trying to extend to them by enacting their own state or local laws such as Black Codes. These were designed to restore the essential elements of slavery in various forms.

The southern states also imposed serious disabilities on African Americans with respect to ownership of property, legal and constitutional rights, and education.[2] In 1868 President Andrew Johnson (1808–1875) issued a general amnesty proclamation which, among other things, resulted in the charges of treason dropped against Jefferson Davis (1808–1889), President of the Confederate States. The Civil Rights act of 1875 sought to give the African Americans greater rights as citizens. To this cause President Ulysses Grant (1822–1885), who served from 1869 to 1877, was committed. But his record of action to give effect to the action required by the new spirit of national development left much to be desired. Grant admitted, "Social equality is not a subject to be legislated upon, nor shall I ask that anything be done to advance the social status of the colored man, except to give him a fair chance to develop whatever good there is in him, give him access to the schools."[3] It is quite surprising that when the opportunity made itself available, national leaders, other than President Abraham Lincoln, did not see it as important to move aggressively to resolve a major national problem. Grant's reaction is a typical example. In his own response to the conditions of African Americans, Grant was enunciating his own theory consistent with his own beliefs.

During the presidency of Rutherford Hayes (1822–1893) from 1877 to 1881, the question of African American progress was hanging in the balance. Following the bitterly contested presidential election of 1876, Hayes was picked as compromise candidate over the bitter issue of Reconstruction programs in the South. Knowing how vulnerable he was to coordinated political opposition, Hayes simply let go of the hold on the South when he promised to restore to the South control over its own political process. Hayes stated, "I am sincerely anxious to use every legitimate influence in favor of honest and efficient local self-government as the true resource of those States for the promotion of the contentment and prosperity of their citizens."[4] Hayes, in political exchange for support of the South, was made to believe that African Americans would be better off if the South were left alone to solve its own racial problems. He forgot that Reconstruction was not designed to reflect this line of thinking.

These, and many other similar events, attitudes, and political views of post–Civil War developments had serious implications on the development of education for African Americans during the Reconstruction period and after. The unfortunate pattern of events that shaped future developments appeared to have been set during the administration of Rutherford Hayes. For Hayes to formulate his "let alone" policy was a recognition that the South was increasingly becoming an important factor in national politics. No longer was the North able to dictate the terms of political progress as was the case during, and the period immediately following, the Civil War.

The South, far from being repentant of its sin, became more deeply entrenched in its concept and philosophy of the black man as an inferior being who did not deserve equal treatment as a citizen of the country, as national leaders in the North were trying to express the idea of racial equality. No national leader ever hoped to be elected without appealing for the support of the South, and the South could not give that support as long as the appeal was made on equal rights for African Americans. It was clear that the South intended to use its new form of power and influence to its own advantage.

RECONSTRUCTION AND STRUGGLE FOR DEVELOPMENT

The question may be asked: What did African Americans achieve during the period of Reconstruction from 1865 to 1877? Throughout the South, African Americans were going through a very difficult period of change and re-adjustment from slaves to free citizens. However, they looked to the future rather than to the past. Their participation in a national economy took a new form. A new kind of relationship emerged between black and white. There was "anxious locomotion among Negroes changing homes, moving luggage, hunting places,"[5] and planning for the future. Under the direction of the Freedman's Bureau they made a concerted effort to secure the kind of education that they needed to make progress.

But African Americans of 1865 were confronted with one serious problem; the vast majority of them were illiterate, and so, they were badly exploited by the white businessmen, farmers, and landlords for whom they worked. But African Americans had to endure this humiliation in order to earn a living. This was not easy to get used to since slavery had not provided them with the necessary experience to exercise their proper responsibility for themselves. Therefore, sooner than later, African Americans realized that to secure the bright future promised by their newly found freedom, they had to attend seriously to the business of securing an education. But subsequent events would show that the Southern whites were equally determined to deny them this opportunity and right.

Although education for African Americans had received some attention before the Civil War, it began to take formal shape during the Civil War itself. E. F. Frazier concluded, "As the Union armies advanced into the South, they were faced with the problem of caring for the freed slaves who fled from the plantations and sought refuge in the army camps."[6] The run-away slaves, now freed people, were protected by the Union army, put to work, provided with food, and with education. The American Missionary Association established day schools for them, and among the first teachers was a black woman from the North.

But the South became intensely apprehensive over African Americans getting any form of education because some earlier leaders among them had advocated violence as a means to gain their freedom. These include Gabriel Prasser who, in 1800, planned a revolt and an attack on whites in Virginia; Denmark Vesey, who, in 1822, had recruited about 900 followers to plot against whites in South Carolina; Nat Turner and his followers, in 1831, killed a number of whites, including Turner's master and his family. So, when moves were made to enable former slaves to acquire some formal education, the Southern whites were sadly reminded of these acts of violence by African Americans and came to the conclusion that they must never be given an opportunity for education. It is quite surprising that this was the thinking among colonial officials in Africa after World War II. If African Americans would commit these acts as slaves, what more would they do as freed people with some education? The conventional thinking was that they would take the law into their own hands. So, the South was not too interested in African Americans getting any formal education.

The period of the African American search for a new identity began during slavery. As early as 1857 the Supreme Court found itself faced with an unusual case. In 1834 John Emerson, an army surgeon and resident of Missouri, took his slave, Dred Scott, to Illinois and then to Wisconsin. In 1838 Emerson returned to Missouri. But on his return Scott brought suit against his master for his freedom. He argued that the trip outside the slave state had actually liberated him. In a 7–2 decision rendered by Justice Roger B. Taney (1777–1864) on March 6,1857, the Supreme Court ruled that because Scott was a slave he had no right to bring any suit against his master, that a slave did not become free by merely going outside the slave state, and that Congress and the territorial legislature could not stop slavery in a territory that wished to maintain slavery.[7] However, the clouds of a civil war were gathering rapidly across the national sky and only a few years later was the whole issue of slavery resolved. For a black man and a slave to bring suit against a white man, and for the Supreme Court to find time to hear the case, showed a remarkable degree of progress by the African Americans. The importance of the Dred Scott case underlined, among other things, the urgency of the need for education among African Americans.

Perhaps the post–Civil War effort to help African Americans in their search for a new identity was symbolized by the formation of the Freedmen's Bureau by the federal government under the direction of Oliver Otis Howard. This agency was designed to look after the needs of former slaves in social, health, and educational areas. The Bureau relocated 30,000 former slaves to areas of the country where they were able to acquire land. A number of schools were started. Some hospitals were built. But unfortunately the Bureau's life was short because in 1872 the Congress refused to continue to support it. The American Missionary Association suffered severe limitations in its function of educating freed slaves in the South.

In spite of the many difficulties that confronted them during the postwar period African Americans were able to make substantial progress in social and political life during the Reconstruction. Their participation in the political activity of the country was a revolutionary event. Not a single black person had voted in a southern election since 1835 when only a few states had allowed some free slaves to vote. Suddenly 703,000 blacks out of 1,330,000 persons who qualified to vote under the Reconstruction Act of 1867 could now vote. However, 90 percent of them were illiterate.[8] As a result many were misled by dishonest white politicians who wanted to maintain the status quo. In spite of these difficulties, many recognized their shortcomings and were determined to overcome them.

Beverly Nash, an illiterate former slave in the South Carolina constitutional convention put it more clearly when he said in 1868, "I believe, my friends and fellow citizens, we are not prepared for this suffrage. But we can learn. Give a man tools and in time he will learn a trade. We may not understand it at the start, but in time we shall learn to do our duty."[9] Nash was certainly speaking for many. The tools African Americans wanted were in the form of education. By this time African Americans were convinced that they were American citizens who were entitled to the rights exclusively enjoyed by whites. Nash's view and hope may have been an indication that African Americans had found the means with which to carve a new identify for themselves.

While this was taking place, African American politicians of the Reconstruction era assumed positions of leadership. Many of them were ministers and teachers. A few were better trained than whites for the positions they held during the Reconstruction. A few of these were: J. C. Gibbs, who became Florida's Secretary of State from 1868 to 1872, and later became superintendent of schools in that state. Gibbs established Florida's first public school system. He had been a graduate of the famous Dartmouth College. R. B. Elliot was a prominent South Carolina politician. Born in Massachusetts, he was educated at Eton College, Britain. He read French, German, Italian, Spanish and became a distinguished speaker. J. T. Rapier had his education in Canada and had a powerful following in his native Alabama. Eloquent P. B. Pinchback attained the highest state office of any Reconstruction African American. He served as acting governor of Louisiana, where he led the fight for universal suffrage. J. J. Wright became a distinguished lawyer from Pennsylvania and served as associate justice of the South Carolina Supreme Court. B. K. Bruce served as a U.S. senator from Mississippi from 1875 to 1881. Other African Americans of varying abilities served as lieutenant governors, state treasurers, justices of peace, and sheriffs. Rev. H. R. Revels from Mississippi filled the Senate seat that was formerly held by Jefferson Davis, President of the Confederacy.

These African American individuals exerted themselves and a tremendous influence on the development of education among their own people. Both races came to recognize what education could do to raise people from the dark caves of ignorance to the highest level of national service. African Americans gradually recognized that for them to get anywhere, to make a better contribution to society, they needed education more than anything else. The whites equally recognized that education for African Americans would not be a lethal weapon with which to threaten the privileged positions that they had enjoyed for so long, but a means by which they were trained to make a contribution to society. If they had readily recognized this reality, they would not have been determined to do everything in their power to put a stop to this development.

Among the African American congressmen who won respect for their diligence, intelligence, and common sense, coupled with a high sense of goodwill, was R. Smalls, self-educated former slave who served five terms in Congress as a member from South Carolina. Another is J. R. Lynch, the speaker of the Mississippi house at the age of twenty-four, and who later became a friend of President Grant. J. W. Menard, a congressman from Louisiana, showed no anger when whites refused to seat him. These examples serve as a reminder of the goodwill among Reconstruction African American leaders. They also show a surprisingly "amazing lack of bitterness towards their former masters. They often supported efforts to have the government remove political restrictions on leading former confederates."[10]

This was considerable progress, and one would have hoped that the stream of this progress would continue. But unfortunately, the progress made so far was not to last; the gains acquired were not to continue. The national political events of 1876 set the clock back for African Americans under the administration of Rutherford Hayes. The federal government washed its hands of the enormous problems that African Americans were left to face alone as Jim Crow returned with a vengeance. The South became free to do as it pleased. In 1878 the Congress went on to pass "legislation that forbade the use of troops in matters relating to elections."[11] This took away the protection of voting rights that African Americans had gained during Reconstruction.

In 1894 the federal government ended all funds which were used to pay special federal marshals and supervisors of elections. The process of disfranchisement of African Americans was then set in motion. The educational opportunity that they had utilized to advance themselves, the social and political rate of progress that they had maintained now began to quickly erode. One by one the southern states deprived African Americans of advancement when they realized that the federal government could do nothing to stop the erosion of their rights in American society.

However, the African American search for a new identity brought the realization that they had to secure an education to enable them to secure, in turn, the rights of citizenship granted to them by the Fourteenth and Fifteenth Amendments to the U.S. Constitution. After the failure of Congress to pass legislation to provide equal opportunity for education for all Americans, philanthropic organizations took it upon themselves to provide the desperately needed education for African Americans. Soon after Reconstruction came to an end in 1877 and federal troops were withdrawn, white supremacy was once again restored and the opportunity for African American education was severely restricted, as was the opportunity for political and social activity in general. Most schools for African Americans were taught by white teachers, who, because they had some influence in their community, were able to obtain local sympathy and some support for the African American schools. But as time went on, it became less socially acceptable for whites to teach in black schools.

Therefore, teaching in African American schools fell on the shoulders of poorly trained African American teachers. This, in turn, had a most unfortunate effect as support from the influential people of the community sharply declined. The schools became the prey of unscrupulous politicians and the object of blatant prejudice. They became badly discriminated against in the distribution of school funds; the school buildings received no proper attention, so they simply became shabby and totally unsuitable and unsafe to occupy. Worse still, corruption became the accepted practice in the appointment of African American teachers.[12] In short, in the attitude of the Hayes administration, African American education was dying a slow and painful death. In 1878 fourteen southern states and the District of Columbia passed laws that required separate schools for white and black children. A number of states sugarcoated their segregated school policies by providing for what they called equal facilities in the two systems including the notion of equal fund distribution. It would be unrealistic for anyone to believe that, after fighting to stop equality in education as a prerequisite of denying equality in society, Southern whites were now ready to accept African Americans as their social equals.

Indeed, the South did not live by this criterion. Distinction based on race permeated every level of national life. For African Americans even to hope that some day they would enjoy equal treatment would also be unrealistic and would constitute an offense. This is the reason why, by 1898, the per capita expenditure on an African American child's education was still a very small fraction of the amount spent for a white child.[13] The only criterion that the South considered was the preservation of the social status quo. For members of the white community in the South, maintaining this status quo was believed to be in the best interest of African Americans themselves, and that they would resent and oppose anything that was calculated to change things. Even change in the way of financing education was considered to have a detrimental effect on what was considered to be proper relationships between the races. Table 6.1 shows how these funds were distributed during this period.

During this time some states, like Florida, passed laws that made it an offense for any school to enroll both black and white students in the same school. It was quite clear that with a segregated school system a new set of

Table 6.1
Distribution of Funds for Education by Race per Child, 1898

State	White School	Black School
District of Columbia	$14.82	$10.64
North Carolina	1.17	1.07
Florida	5.92	2.27

Source: R. E. Potter, *The Stream of American Education*, p. 350.

problems was created, especially in the area of African American education. The financial burdens of separate school systems, the plight of African American children, the adversities and the odds under which African Americans had to obtain an education all had to remain a pattern, a way of life, for African Americans for years to come. The philosophy of separate but equal educational facilities, enunciated in the Plessy decision, became solidly established and a permanent order of things.

To alleviate the difficulties imposed on education for African Americans by segregated school systems, some philanthropic organizations, mainly based in the North, tried with some degree of success to give financial support to those schools. One example is the Peabody Education Fund, which was established in 1867 by George Peabody (1795–1869), a wealthy Massachusetts merchant and banker. Peabody gave about $ 3.5 million "to be used in those states which had suffered from the destructive ravages and disastrous consequences of civil war."[14] Mississippi and Florida did not accept these funds because doing so would provide African Americans an opportunity for a better education. This would not be in the best interest of whites in the South, although Peabody made provisions for using the funds in general educational developments, including education for whites.

African Americans were once again aware that their education was vital to their future and that they had to secure it somehow, so they just did not lose heart, though the odds were heavily against them. For them it was better to struggle along the unbeaten path to the future, rather than look back to the dreadful past and its horrors. They recognized the injustices of the philosophy of the separate but equal systems, but they came prepared to make the best of the existing situation. Ten years after the Civil War, schools for African Americans began to get organized once more. African American colleges and universities began to appear all over the country. Although many of these institutions took care of the large part of primary and high school education, their entrance requirements were as high as any college in the nation. These colleges offered a general education program as well as professional, technical, and industrial training, which was badly needed to enable African Americans in Alabama, Arkansas, and Delaware to acquire the skills that American society needed as a result of the great Industrial Revolution of the nineteenth century (see Table 6.2).

Table 6.2
Predominantly Negro Colleges and Universities in Alabama, Arkansas, and Delaware

Institution	Location	Date of Founding	Enrollment in 1967	Type
Alabama				
Alabama A. & M.	Normal	1875	1,222	Coed

Alabama A. & M. offers a liberal arts and general programs, as well as teacher-preparatory and terminal-occupational training leading to a master's and/or second professional degree.

| Alabama State | Montgomery | 1874 | 2,082 | Coed |

Alabama State offers a liberal arts and general program, as well as teacher-preparatory training leading to a master's and/or second professional degree.

| Daniel Payne Jr. College | Birmingham | 1889 | 312 | Coed |

Daniel Payne is a two-year college with a three-year professional school.

| Miles College | Birmingham | 1907 | 816 | Coed |

Miles College offers a liberal arts and general program, as well as teacher-preparatory training leading to the bachelor's and/or first professional degree.

| Oakwood College | Huntsville | 1896 | 410 | Coed |

Oakwood College has a liberal arts program, and offers A.B. and B.S. degrees.

| Selma University | Selma | 1878 | 224 | Coed |

Selma University is a junior college and school of religion owned and operated by the Alabama State Baptist Convention.

| Stillman College | Tuscaloosa | 1876 | 522 | Coed |

Stillman College offers a liberal arts and general program, as well as teacher-preparatory training leading to the bachelor's and/or first professional degree.

| Talladega College | Talladega | 1867 | 413 | Coed |

Talladega College offers a liberal arts and general program, as well as teacher-preparatory training leading to a bachelor's and/or first professional degree.

(continued)

Table 6.2   (*Continued*)

Institution	Location	Date of Founding	Enrollment in 1967	Type
Tuskegee Institute	Tuskegee	1881	2,482	Coed

Tuskegee Institute offers a liberal arts and general program, and has a number of professional schools which grant a master's and/or second professional degree.

Arkansas

| Arkansas Agr., Mech. & Normal College | Pine Bluff | 1873 | 2,490 | Coed |

Arkansas A., M. & N. offers a liberal arts and general program, as well as terminal-occupational training leading to a bachelor's and/or first professional degree.

| Philander Smith College | Little Rock | 1868 | 614 | Coed |

Philander Smith College offers a liberal arts and general program, as well as teacher-preparatory and terminal-occupational training leading to a bachelor's and/or first professional degree.

| Shorter College | Little Rock | 1886 | 216 | Coed |

Shorter College, a two-year college with a three-year professional school, offers a liberal arts and general program leading to a bachelor's and/or first professional degree.

Delaware

| Delaware State | Dover | 1891 | 788 | Coed |

Delaware State offers a liberal arts and general program, as well as teacher-preparatory training leading to a bachelor's and/or first professional degree.

The founding of these colleges was made possible in part by the collective effort of some philanthropic organizations and the federal government. In addition to George Peabody, Andrew Carnegie (1835–1919) gave some $10 million in 1902 toward schools and education for African Americans. General Education Board, enriched by J. D. Rockefeller

(1839–1937), the Rosenwald Fund, and the Anna T. Jeanes Fund, all played a major role in the founding of many schools for African Americans. J. S. Roucek and T. Kierman concluded: "As the last century wore on some groups started to emphasize the need for more adequately trained ministers, teachers, or tradesmen at scores of schools, variously styled as normal, institute, academy, seminary, college or university. Some of the appellations were surely misleading. Many of these schools survived, some changed their names or purpose, some were absorbed by the states. And some lived as landmarks."[15]

J. S. Roucek and T. Kierman also added that the literacy rate was improving quickly as a result of self-determination among the African Americans, as shown by the following figures, and was not due to any significant action by the whites. These two authors cite the following figures to prove their point: In 1860 literacy was 5 percent. By 1890 it had increased to 60 percent. By 1910 it had gone up to 70 percent, and in 1940 it had gone up to 92 percent.[16] H. A. Ploski and R. C. Brown concluded in 1967 that the thirty years between 1860 and 1890 saw a revolutionary change in African American education as a reflection of the importance that they themselves attached to education as a means to securing the full citizenship rights granted to them by the 1866 Fourteenth Amendment and the 1869 Fifteenth Amendment[17]—civil rights. But this remarkable progress was short-lived. The whites were gaining ground in their effort to put an end to African American social and political advancement although the number of black institutions of learning were increasing. The unfortunate events of 1876 national politics played into the hands of white southern strategy.

In 1876 the Democratic candidate for president, Samuel Jones Tilden (1814–1886) of New York, was believed to be the winner in the election until Republicans in some southern states accused the Democrats of intimidating black voters to give Tilden a victory margin. A complicated, confused investigation was then conducted, and in the end the Democrats agreed to let Republican favors, such as subsidies for southern railroads, a southern Postmaster General, removal of the federal troops from the South, and, most important of all, not to interfere in the manner in which the South would handle the Negro question, go unpunished. This political deal has become known as the compromise of 1876. To fulfill his part of the deal, Hayes withdrew federal troops from the South and Reconstruction thus came to a close in 1877.

These tragic developments set a new stage for the South to strip African Americans of their gained and earned advancement. The southern whites, who now had a free hand to do as they pleased, turned to violence as a method to achieve this end. First, a variety of schemes were introduced to make it harder for African Americans to claim or cast their vote in any election. Changes in the polling places, complicated ballots, long and difficult literacy tests, and physical obstruction, were all used to discourage African Americans from voting. As northern and federal support for black education declined, terror of incredible proportions increased. Hayes, during a visit to the South soon after the elections in 1876, told whites the federal government would let them do what the leaders in the South saw fit. The whites cheered Hayes wildly, and yelled to him "let alone" wherever he went. Hayes seemed to enjoy it, as this was how he had come to power. Yet, by the end of his administration in 1881, Hayes regretted that the South, when "let alone," would never seek to give support to general development schemes among the African Americans. It was too late, the damage was done, and his "let alone" policy set a tragic pattern that was to cost the nation heavily. It took many years for meaningful change to come about.

Nearly a hundred years had to pass before the tragic pattern was changed. By the time of his death in 1893, Hayes might not have known the extent of the damage and disservice that his policy had inflicted on the struggle of African Americans for advancement. The harm to the national cause and the mission to bring the two races true freedom and equality, were so greatly cherished that Lincoln chose the passage to national conflict to bring them about to all Americans. The setbacks that African Americans suffered during the Hayes "let alone" policy was a signal that more was to come. In 1868 Tennessee became the birth place of the Ku Klux Klan, the dreadful organization that was to cause so much terror and suffering among African Americans until about 1968. S. W. Webster sums up the activities of KKK and other similar organizations saying that these groups were usually secret societies and had as one of their prime goals the subjection of African Americans and non-Christians. The most commonly used means of oppression included murder, physical violence, intimidation, arson, and ostracism in business or social affairs.[18]

However, these organizations were not restricted to the South. Most states made some effort to control the activities of such organizations as the KKK, but they were not very successful. The inability of the states in the South to deal with these terrorist organizations led to the passage of federal legislation designed to halt such anti-civil rights activity. The main goal of organizations such as the KKK was the preservation of white supremacy. "To do this they realized that they would have to prevent blacks, who were quite a number in most states of the South, from voting."[19] The U.S. Congress, seriously weakened by Hayes' "let alone" policy, appeared powerless to act decisively and promptly, though it tried. In 1890 the Congress considered two seemingly important bills that were designed to restore the vote to African Americans by seeking to improve their education so that more African American voters would qualify for the deliberately difficult literacy tests. The second bill was meant to supervise national elections, so that anti-Negro frauds would be reduced. By this time the public schools had been well established, but African Americans had a long way to go before they enjoyed them as well.

These bills had the support of President Harrison (1833–1901), in office from 1889 to 1893, and appeared to have a good chance of success. However, aware of the power and influence they now exercised, the Southern politicians reacted violently and with great bitterness against such legislation. Senator James Z. George of Mississippi spoke against the bill in very strong terms and a tone that seemed to represent the Southern attitude towards African Americans in general. Said George, "If you will not stop this 'Force Bill' then, remembering the history and traditions of our race, we give you notice of your certain and assured failure, it will never come to pass in Mississippi, in South Carolina, or in any other state in the South, that the neck of the white race shall be under the foot of the Negro, or the Mongolian or any created being."[20]

The threat of possible renewed sectional violence, as well as a number of other political problems, sadly led to the defeat of both bills, and despite campaign pledges, Harrison and the Republicans were forced to abandon the fight for the constitutional rights of African Americans. In 1891 Mississippi had shown disregard and contempt for federal intervention and interference in state affairs by calling a special constitutional convention for the sole purpose of disfranchising the state's remaining black voters. A new amendment to the constitution required that black voters pay a poll tax of $2.00 as a condition and price for voting, and refused the vote to any black accused (not convicted) of some minor criminal offense and those who could not read or interpret a section of the Mississippi constitution. Since the literacy test was always administered by the white judge, it could be used to disqualify educated African Americans without embarrassing or reducing the rolls of the uneducated, ignorant white people. Soon other southern states followed the Mississippi example.

By 1900 Congress was so silent, so weak, so afraid to do anything that the southern congressmen openly boasted on the floor of the Congress about their unlawful, unconstitutional and criminal behavior. Benjamin Pitchfork of South Carolina, stated in the Senate that his state had disfranchised all the Negroes, and went on, to add, "We have done our best. We have scratched our heads to find out how we could eliminate the last one of them. We stuffed ballot boxes. We shot them. We are not ashamed of it."[21] Pitchfork was not joking; he meant what he said. While the congress failed to act, African Americans were being lynched at the rate of three per week during the last two decades of the nineteenth century. Between 1882 and 1900 alone, some 3,011 African Americans were lynched in the South. Behind all this despicable cruelty and senseless violence was the desire of white men to put the African Americans back to their original place as second class citizens. But African Americans were fully aware that, although fate had seemed to turn against them, some day they would overcome these imposed difficulties.

While this was happening, some African Americans began to wonder whether there was room for them in the white American inn. If the U.S. Congress could not give them protection under its laws, where could they turn for help? They were more determined than ever to save themselves from destruction, from returning to a new form of slavery, from second class citizenship. They looked to the future more boldly than ever before. They also recognized that the road to this destination would be slow, costly, and painful, but it seemed the only way to proceed on their long march to the promised land.

The Fourteenth Amendment of 1868 and the Civil Rights Act of 1875 were meant to give African Americans a more secure feeling as citizens, and greater protection than in the past. The Fourteenth Amendment states that no state shall "deprive any person of life, liberty or property, without due process of law, nor deny to any person within its jurisdiction the equal protection of the law."[22]

Then, there was the 1875 Civil Rights Act, which states: "All persons within the jurisdiction of the United States shall be entitled to the full and equal enjoyment of the accommodations advantages, and privileges of inns, public conveyances on land or water, theaters and other places of public amusement, subject only to the conditions and limitations established by law, and applicable alike to citizens of every race and color, regardless of any previous conditions of servitude."[23]

But these laws proved most ineffective as the violence against African Americans increased with the end of Reconstruction in 1877. So, what purpose did their enactment serve? African Americans knew that the federal government was totally unable to enforce its own laws. They also knew that more suffering was to come. Nonetheless, they were prepared to try to change the course of events in the things that deeply affected their lives.

Meanwhile, African Americans were being subjected to other forms of psychological, social, economic, and social humiliation. The Jim Crow movement was now having a great influence on the attitudes of the whites. Every effort was being made to portray the Negro as a creature less than a human being with less intelligence and less ability than the white man. But still African Americans looked forward to the day when they would arrive in the promised land.

THE ROLE OF THE COURTS IN ENUNCIATING
NEW THEORY

In their continuing search for a way to the promised land, and having been let down by and disappointed with the Congress, African Americans now turned to the most important institution in the country—the courts. They looked to the courts as the arbiter and guarantor of their constitutional rights as citizens of the country. They hoped that their rights, so flagrantly violated by politicians, would be restored. They did not have much good luck there either, especially from 1873 to 1927. This section of the study examines some of the court action on cases that have become so important in the history of the African American struggle for advancement, justice, and equality. It also presents some implications of the court decisions on African American life in general and in education in particular. It is not possible to discuss the hundreds of court cases that have been decided by either the state courts or the U.S. Supreme Court. So, this section will take some representative cases to illustrate the argument presented that in each decision the courts reached they were, in effect, enunciating their own theory.

Between 1873 and 1910 the courts and the American public were so racially conservative that many court decisions during this time went against African Americans. Also, African Americans were not legally organized until about 1910, five years after the founding of the Niagara movement in 1905, which became the National Association for the Advancement of the Colored People in 1910, which, in turn, set up a legal and education defense fund. Although there were other civil rights cases, the cases of that year were a result of the suit brought against hotel and other public accommodations for refusing to accept African Americans in defiance of the 1875 Civil Rights Act. In this case the Supreme Court simply ruled that the U.S. Congress, in passing this legislation, did not know what its members were doing. In that case Justice Bradley delivered the majority opinion when he wrote, "The essence of the law is not to declare broadly that all persons shall be entitled to the full equal and enjoyment of the accommodations, advantages, facilities, and privileges of the inns, public conveyances, and theaters, but that such enjoyment shall not be subject to any conditions applicable only to citizens of a particular race or who had been in a previous condition of servitude."[24]

One must note that this strong position held by the Supreme Court against African Americans was taken by a vote of 8–1, and that this attitude of the Court was to prevail well into the 20th century. The one dissenting opinion came from Justice John Marshall Harlan (1833–1911),[25] who served on the Supreme Court from 1877 until his death in 1911. Justice Harlan stated that the Constitution was color blind, it did not recognize its citizens based on race, and that it protected all people on the basis of total equality. In his own way Harlan was enunciating a new theory for the development of African Americans.

Whatever good reasoning Justice Harlan put into his thinking and opinion, which he based on the Fourteenth Amendment and the 1875 Civil Rights Act, he failed to persuade his colleagues on the court to view things the way he did. The era of conservative attitudes during which he served did not allow more positive attitudes toward African Americans. But his views provided a solid foundation upon which to build the powerful strategy that African Americans and their supporters were to utilize later. For now, high emotional feeling expressed by the Court in this fateful decision signaled to

African Americans that they were not to expect much from the Supreme Court. Nevertheless, they were not disheartened, nor did they stop their journey to the promised land. The message coming out of the decision to both the African Americans and the white people was simply that the white society had closed ranks against African Americans, that a new trend was in the making, that the white people meant serious business in their declared intention to deny African Americans their rights.

There were a number of other important civil rights cases that came before the Supreme Court for decision, and, one by one, African Americans lost. In education the pattern was the same. There were schools which would not take black students even though their parents paid taxes to support them. In 1883 the Atlanta school board experienced serious financial problems and decided to close the schools for African Americans and continued to operate schools for white students. The African American taxpayers sought an injunction which they hoped would require the defendant school board either to allow African American students into white schools, or to close the white schools until the board was in a financial position to reopen the schools for both races. After appeals through the state supreme court, the case came before the U.S. Supreme Court in 1886. The Court argued that the education of African American children of the county would not be promoted by compliance with the board in ceasing to give support to high school for white children. We have here no case to be determined. The Court upheld the action of the board. But Harlan warned prophetically that segregation by law would inevitably cause racial hatred and create a feeling of distrust between the groups. However, the warning fell on deaf ears, and in this decision of 1896, the Court seemed to put the stamp of approval on the principle of separate schools.

Let us see what action the Court took in other cases dealing with the education of black Americans. Berea College in Kentucky was started by missionaries from the American Missionary Society, soon after the Civil War, mainly for black students. By 1908 Berea was operating on an integrated basis, disregarding the practices and patterns of segregated schools in the South, and in defiance of a state law which made racial segregation mandatory. The college was ordered to segregate, but, because Berea saw no reason to do that, it brought suit against the state. Its officials argued that the association of the races at the school was purely voluntary and harmonious, and that there was no tension between the students of both races. The college also argued that integrating educational facilities on a voluntary basis was a model that other institutions should follow and state officials must support.

But the state supreme court established the rule, which was upheld by the U.S. Supreme Court, that the section which forbade mixing of the races in schools was not a denial of equal protection or of due process, but that "Teaching in different rooms of the same building or in different building, so near each other as to be practically one, would violate the statute, as it was such intimate personal association of the pupils that was being prohibited."[26] When the case came before the Supreme Court, as was expected, the decision of that court was in agreement with the Kentucky state supreme court ruling against Berea College. Said the Supreme Court opinion, "We need concern ourselves only with . . . the first section of the Kentucky constitution of 1891, which states that 'Every grant of a franchise, privilege, or exemption, shall remain, subject to revocation, alteration, or amendment.'"[27] The Court argued that this was the power the state had over its own people, and that it was of the opinion that the decision of the lower courts came within that power. On this basis the decision of the Court of Appeals of Kentucky was affirmed. Berea College was ordered to segregate its students.

Once again, the lone voice of dissent in the Supreme Court, Justice Harlan, disagreed when he said, "I am of the opinion that in its essential parts the statute is an arbitrary invasion of the rights of liberty and property guaranteed by the 14th Amendment against hostile state actions, and, is, therefore, void."[28] Justice Harlan concluded that if the lower court was right, then a state may make it a crime for white and colored persons to attend the same market places at the same time, or appear in a place of assembly convened to consider questions of a public or political nature. In that case all citizens without regard to race would be equally interested. He concluded that in his opinion the judgment should be reversed for the reason that the statute was in violation of the Constitution of the United States.

Certainly the views held by Justice Harlan were good, more in line with the law, and would provide the basis for future, important developments. But given the attitudes of the court at the time, the conservative thinking of the Supreme Court, and the circumstances that rendered the U.S. Congress ineffective and unable to correct the deteriorating situation that African Americans faced, the opinions of Justice Harlan were simply a far cry in the wilderness. Time was not yet on his side; he would have to wait for a change of attitudes by both the nation and the Supreme Court. The effect of the Berea decision extended far beyond the bounds of the South. The notion of equality, of even the simplest and easily seen aspects of the schools, was rendered farcical to many northern communities where segregation became common, especially in big cities, because residential system by race became a pattern of the American society.

In some communities boundaries of school districts were constructed so as to ensure the greatest possible separation of the two races. Under these conditions the difference between black schools and white schools was so great that it was easy to see that the theory of separate but equal was simply a farce. But some states, like Indiana, New Mexico, Kansas, and Wyoming allowed local school authorities to segregate students by race, and Arizona made segregation at grade school level mandatory until 1951, when a new state law made such segregation optional. In short, the Berea College decision had a tremendous impact on the character of education for African Americans in the country.

Until 1896 the notion of separate but equal had been practiced without any legal basis. A law passed in 1890 in Louisiana required that all railway companies provide separate but equal accommodations for African American and white passengers, either in separate cars or separate compartments. In 1892 Homer Plessy, an African American of light skin, attempted to board a coach reserved for whites, and refused to vacate the seat when ordered to do so. He was forcibly removed from the coach and was imprisoned for violating a state law. Plessy took his case all the way to the U.S. Supreme Court, and, in 1896, the Court reached the momentous decision of endorsing the "separate but equal" principle, and the doctrine. The notion which had been in place since it was suggested by Rutherford Hayes in 1877, now became the law of the land, and was destined to remain a constitutional guide until 1954. Deciding against Plessy in *Plessy v. Ferguson* in 1896, the Supreme Court made particular reference to the school situation saying in the majority opinion rendered by Justice Brown, a Yale Law School graduate and considered legal scholar from Michigan,

The object of the Fourteenth Amendment was undoubtedly to enforce the absolute equality of the two races before the law, but in the nature of things it could not have been intended to abolish distinction based upon color or to enforce social, as distinguished from political, equality or a commingling of the two races upon terms unsatisfactory to either. Laws permitting, and even requiring, their separation in places where they are liable to be brought into contact do not necessarily imply the inferiority of either race to the other, and have been generally, if not universally, recognized as within the competency of the State legislatures in the exercise of their police power.[29]

Once more the vigorous, prophetic dissenting opinion was written by the far-sighted Kentuckian legal prophet, Justice Harlan, who argued that the arbitrary separation of citizens on the basis of race was a badge of servitude wholly inconsistent with the civil freedom and the equality of the law established by the Constitution. He concluded that it could not be justified upon any legal grounds. He suggested that the country boasted of the freedom enjoyed by all Americans above all other peoples, but that it was difficult to reconcile that boast with a state which placed a brand of servitude and degradation upon a large class of Americans. The disguise of "equal" accommodations for passengers in railroad coaches would not mislead anyone.[30] In this opinion Justice Harlan set the tone for future action, but for the time being, this was yet another far cry in the wilderness. The whole nation wildly acclaimed the wisdom of the Supreme Court in its action of legally justifying "separate but equal" laws, and for the segregation of schools. For the next sixty years "separate but equal" became the household word in all aspects of life in the nation. If the "separate but equal" philosophy was applied in daily living conditions and association of people, it was more evident in the schools, where it took a heavy and costly toll in the education of African Americans.

For those next sixty years the schools were established and developed according to the notion of "separate but equal" as a viable philosophy and principle. The school districts were restructured or redefined and population patterns shifted in accordance with this concept. Transport and related economic and social aspects came into line with the notion of "separate but equal." American society was consolidating itself on the basis of the harsh realities of the notion of "separate but equal." From 1896 to 1954 the notion had been universally accepted. African Americans appeared to have resigned themselves to the new order of things. Although so far they had not experienced success, they kept trying in the hope that with the passage of time the nation would begin to see reason in the views expressed by Justice Harlan. When would that possibility come about? Was it remote and distant, or was there a real chance that a change of attitude on the part of the nation and the Supreme Court would come sooner rather than later? African Americans kept hoping, so they kept working toward the realization of their dream searching for the way to the promised land, toward their dream of their constitutional rights as promised by the U.S. Constitution—not as Justice Brown saw it, but as Justice Harlan predicted.

In 1927 the Supreme Court delivered yet another blow to the efforts of African Americans to secure equality in education. Gong Lum, a Chinese resident of Mississippi, resided in the Rosedale Consolidated High School district, which was a white school. Lum was the father of Martha Lum, about twelve years of age. In 1924 Martha, then about nine years old, was sent by her father to attend Rosedale Consolidated High School. At the opening of the school, she appeared as a pupil, and was able to take her seat and place in the school. At noon recess, she was told by the school superintendent that she would not be allowed to return to the school because an order had been issued by the board of trustees to exclude her from the school because she was Chinese, and therefore not white.

Her father took the case to the courts, arguing that there was no school in the district for Chinese children, and that there was none in Bolivar county, where Martha would go. Gong Lum, a mercantile businessman, had been paying tax to support Rosedale, and Martha was not a member of the black race, nor of mixed blood, but pure Chinese. He argued that the 1890 Mississippi state constitution provided for separate school halls to be maintained for children of the white and colored races and that distinction classified Martha as a white child. When the Mississippi state supreme court ruled against Gong Lum, he took the case before the U.S. Supreme Court for determination. The decision was reached in 1927, and Justice William Howard Taft (1857–1930), who served as U.S. President from 1909 to 1913, wrote the majority opinion, saying, "We must assume that there are school districts for colored children in Bolivar County, but that no colored school is within the limits of the Rosedale Consolidated High School District. This is not inconsistent with there being at a place outside of the district and in a different district, a colored school which the plaintiff Martha Lum, may conveniently attend."[31]

It was of little help or comfort to African Americans to realize that other racial groups in the country suffered the same fate under the law as they did. It was, however, surprising to them to know that Chinese people were classified as colored people according to the Mississippi constitution for purposes of education, as confirmed by the U.S. Supreme Court. Gong Lum, however, was shocked by the fact that he was paying tax to support the public schools that now denied an education for his daughter. Well, maybe Gong Lum would be reminded, as Justice Taft stated, that paying tax to support a school did not entitle him to send his child to that school. It was the function of the board of trustees to determine how the funds would be used without taking into consideration the source of such funds. The county board in Georgia, as has already been discussed, did just that earlier when African American taxpayers petitioned that white schools admit African American students, or have them closed until money was found to reopen schools for African American students closed due to financial difficulties. One would think that, judging by the decisions of the Supreme Court in these two cases, there was something basically wrong with the American system of justice at the time. One could ask: What is the difference between taxation to support the schools to which one's children are denied entrance and taxation without representation. This was a hot issue, which was a battle cry during the colonial days, and the main issue that seemed to trigger the American Revolution? Justice Taft and the Court confirmed that the right and power of the state to regulate the method of providing for the education of its youth at public expense is clear. Taft stated, "The education of the people in schools maintained by state taxation is a matter belonging of the Federal authority with the management of schools cannot be justified."[32]

This conclusion seemed to assure the States that they had a free hand in the matter of black education in their own states. They would do as they pleased; the federal constitution did not mean a thing as far as this aspect of American life was concerned. Did federal law mean anything to the states? Did they respect and recognize it as the supreme authority? Could they recognize it when the Supreme Court, which was to give guidance in this area, took a lead in the wrong direction?

Eleven years after Gong Lum, an interesting case came before the U.S. Supreme Court in 1938. In 1935 Lloyd Gaines, an African American student, graduated from Lincoln University, an institution maintained by the state of Missouri for the higher education of African American students. Gaines then submitted an application for admission to the Law School of the University of Missouri because Lincoln University did not have a law school or department. When his admission was refused, Gaines sued the state for denying him equal protection under the Fourteenth Amendment. Finally, after the lower courts had ruled against him, his case came before the U.S. Supreme Court. It was possible that the conservative era was now giving way to the more realistic views of Justice Harlan. In that case, Justice Charles Evans Hughes (1862–1948), who was appointed in 1930 to replace Howard Taft as Chief Justice and served until he retired in 1941, delivered the majority opinion saying: "The equal protection of the laws is a pledge of the protection of equal laws. Manifestly the obligation of the state to give the protection of equal laws can be performed only where its laws operate. It is here that the equality of legal rights must be maintained."[33]

Coming 27 years after Harlan's death, this decision signaled things to come. It seems that, for the first time, the Supreme Court was giving an indication in this decision of a possible change of attitude. Was this a representative trend, or was the decision influenced by the nature of the case—legal education? However, Justice McReynolds dissented when he said, "It appears that never before has a Negro applied for admission to the law school and none has ever asked that Lincoln University provide legal instruction. The problem presented obviously is a difficult and highly practical one. A fair effort to solve it has been made by offering adequate opportunity for study when sought in good faith."[34]

Now, it was time for Justice McReynolds to experience the frustration that Justice Harlan did on the other side of the issue. A few months before the Gaines appeal in 1935, Donald Murray, who was denied admission to the University of Maryland Law School, filled a complaint in the courts arguing that his denial was a violation of equal protection under the law. The Maryland court of appeals ordered the university to enroll Murray on the grounds that the instruction at the branch of the University in Princess Anne reserved for African Americans was "far from equitable and equal, and the out-of-state scholarships for Negroes would not suffice."[35] By the time of the Sipuel case at the University of Oklahoma in 1946 there was indication that the walls of the "separate but equal" philosophy were already beginning to show signs of cracks.

EFFORT TO IMPROVE EDUCATION FOR AFRICAN AMERICANS, 1940–1952

The *Gaines* decision appeared to have shocked many people, as did the *Murray* decision. The American people did not believe that the Supreme Court would suddenly decide to recognize the fact that African Americans had rights guaranteed by the U.S. Constitution, and they would not expect a change in the Court's attitude in the matter. Many began to wonder if Justice Hughes, in the Gaines ruling, reflected a possible change of thinking. Or, was it because the petitions dealt with the topic that it knew best—law school and legal education? Whatever the real reasons of the decisions were, the country could no longer base separation of schools on the basis of "separate but equal." Political leaders could no longer capitalize on "separate but equal" philosophy as they had done over the previous decades. They saw the immediate issue of "separate but equal" as one that needed change in the conditions of schools for African Americans. So, there was a visible effort between 1940 and 1952 to improve the schools for African Americans in order to avoid court orders to admit African American students into the white schools. Both the North and the South gradually began to recognize that the foundation of segregation and other barriers to racial justice and equality were now standing on loose ground.

However, in order to save face, Northern legislatures began to enact anti-segregation laws which would affect schools and other social institutes. Southern legislatures and legislators, fearing that the integration movement would eventually spread to the public schools, began to work towards removing some of the visible inequalities from the segregated school system. They began to spend more money on education and schools for African Americans then they had ever done before. The change in education expenditures between 1940 and 1952 reflected the feeling of "too little, too late," which was beginning to show in the political attitudes of the times. Table 6.3 shows the increase in the amount of money spent on education for African Americans during the twelve-year period from 1940 to 1952, as compared to the amount of money spent on white education per child.

Table 6.3 shows that in 1940 the South spent 43 cents per black child for each $1.00 that it spent on each white child. But by 1952, each African American child received 70 cents for each $1.00 spent on a white child. In Mississippi, in an attempt to improve schools for African Americans so that the state would avoid petitions or suits on the basis of unequal facilities, 34 percent more was spent for African American schools than for white schools. But the difference in the quality of education between the two school systems had become so great over the years that to correct it demanded far more than matching expenditures. Further, the South was not in a financial position to afford the type of crash education programs that were

Table 6.3
Expenditure on Education, 1940–1952

Education Cost (per child)	1940		1952	
	White	Black	White	Black
1. Operating costs	$50.14	$21.54	$164.83	$115.08
2. New buildings	$ 4.37	$ .99	$ 36.25	$ 29.58

Source: Robert E. Potter, *The Stream of American Education*, p. 480.

required and needed in order to produce the quality physical facilities, by which people could judge the effectiveness of the schools.

If the 1938 Supreme Court decision was influential on the Southern effort to improve the schools and to avoid suits, African Americans began to recognize other types to inequalities in their schools. They felt that their teachers, who were graduates of the poor schools and poor colleges, were not as well-educated as white teachers, even if they had the same qualifications as white teachers. They also recognized the negative psychological effect of being segregated. African American leaders now began to speak about the personality factors which were caused by separate school systems. These effects were at first recognized by the leaders of the integration movement. Eventually the overall effects of segregation on the character of African American children became increasingly apparent to African Americans. First, Americans began to question the entire structure of "separate but equal" philosophy. Even if the facilities for African Americans were equal to those of white schools, the mere fact of separate school systems now posed a serious question as to its effects on African American students, who appeared to suffer a general disability as a result.

What must be done? African Americans now recognized that the "separate but equal" philosophy was, in fact, a method of keeping their schools in an inferior position and giving them an inferior education. "Separate but equal" simply did not mean anything; as long as the schools were separate, they could not be equal. African Americans began to work towards convincing the courts that the two systems could not be regarded as equal, and so they would have to go. Integration of schools was the only means to give the black students equality in education. This new theoretical line of thinking began to form during the *Gaines* case when Charles H. Houston (1895–1950), a graduate of the Harvard Law School and dean of the Howard Law School, carried out an investigation of the impact of "separate but equal." Houston came to the conclusion that the notion of "separate but equal" was an instrument of keeping the education of African Americans in an inferior position.

The case which was to put this thinking to test in the courts was the famous *McLaurin v. University of Oklahoma Board of Regents*, which came before the U.S. Supreme Court in 1950. G. McLaurin, an African American citizen of Oklahoma, applied for admission to the University of Oklahoma Graduate School. His application was denied solely because of his race, as specified by Oklahoma law, which made it an offense to operate mixed schools. McLaurin then filed a complaint, alleging that the action of the school to deny him admission and the law upon which that action was based were unconstitutional and deprived him of equal protection under the U.S. law. When a U.S. court reversed the action of the University, and stated that the law upon which the action of denial was based was unconstitutional, the Oklahoma Legislature amended its law to permit the admission of McLaurin and other African American students to institutions of higher learning in the state. However, the amendment provided that the program of instruction on a segregated basis would be maintained. McLaurin was then admitted but required to sit apart at a designated desk or in an anteroom adjoining the classroom, to sit apart at a designated desk on the mezzanine floor of the library, to avoid using the desks in the regular reading room, and to sit at a designated table and to eat at a different time from the other students in the school cafeteria.

McLaurin filled suit with the District Court to have this form of segregation removed, but that court held that such treatment did not violate the provision of the Fourteenth Amendment, and so rejected the suit. McLaurin then appealed to the Supreme Court in 1950. Chief Justice Frederick M. Vinson (1890–1953), who was named to the Supreme Court in 1946 by President Harry S. Truman, delivered the majority opinion. Vinson recognized that in the interval between the decision of the lower court and the hearing by the Supreme Court the treatment afforded McLaurin had been changed. He acknowledged that for some time the section of the classroom in which he sat was surrounded by a rail where there was a sign stating "Reserved for Colored," but that these had been removed and he was now assigned to a seat in the classroom in a row specified for black students. He was also assigned to a table in the library on the main floor and was permitted to eat at the same time in the cafeteria where he could stand and talk with his fellow students. But while he ate he must remain apart. Vinson then concluded: "The result is that appellant is handicapped in his pursuit of effective graduate instruction. Such restrictions impair and inhibit his ability to study, to engage in discussion and exchange views with other students, and in general to learn his profession."[36] For the first time in its history, the Supreme Court had referred to the effects of segregation on African American students. The Vinson Court readily recognized and accepted the truth that the "separate but equal" theory had no validity and the sooner it was eliminated, the better. With each successful court action and decision, African Americans became more determined than ever to secure the rights of citizenship granted to them by the Constitution. African Americans now set their minds to have the Supreme Court rule on the notion of "separate but equal." After Houston died in 1950, Thurgood Marshall (1908–1983), who had studied under Houston at Howard University, accepted the responsibility of leading this crusade. The decisions since the Gaines case, combined with slowly changing attitudes among the members of the Supreme Court and the public, and the determination of African Americans, brought the matter to final showdown. This dramatic event came in *Brown v. the Board of Education of Topeka* in May 1954.

By this time African Americans had some experience in legal issues and procedures involved in their struggle for equality. The NAACP had become well organized and informed about the law in reference to their constitutional rights. In the *Brown* cases of 1954 and 1955, there were about five separate cases from some five states including Kansas, South Carolina, Virginia, Delaware, and the District of Columbia. These cases began as early as 1952 and all challenged the constitutionality of segregated public schools on racial grounds. In short, the Supreme Court went a step further than its 1950 *McLaurin* action by making provision for the implementation of its decision of 1954.

In 1952 a number of African American students in these cases complained that they were denied admission to public schools attended by white children solely because of their race. The students sought the help of the District of Columbia in obtaining admission, and the court dismissed their complaint; but because there was a constitutional question in the petition, the cases were referred to the Supreme Court for determination. Because of the importance of the decision, and because it was a landmark and a new high watermark in the history of social justice in the country, we will attempt to reproduce the main current thinking, attitudes, and views of the Supreme Court on the whole question of racial equality, as written by the Chief Justice himself, who delivered the unanimous opinion. Chief Justice Earl Warren (1892–1974), who had been recently appointed to that position by President Dwight Eisenhower to replace Frederick Vinson who died suddenly, appeared deeply disturbed by the racial injustice that was still present in the country. Now, he was in a position where he could influence an end to it, at least constitutionally. Warren wrote the unanimous decision saying:

Segregation of white and colored children in public schools has a detrimental effect upon the colored children. The impact is greater when it has the sanction of the law, for the policy of separating the races is usually interpreted as denoting the inferiority of the Negro group. Segregation with the sanction of law, therefore, has a tendency to retard the educational and mental development of Negro children and deprive them of some of the benefits they would receive in a racially integrated school system. We conclude that in the field of public education the doctrine of "separate but equal" has no place. Separate educational facilities are inherently unequal.[37]

The decision was certainly a milestone in the progress of education for African Americans. It meant that no state legislature could pass laws permitting segregation in public schools any more. It also meant that "separate but equal" practices in education were over. In short, no form of racial segregation whatsoever could be permitted in the public schools. The nation was tired of this meaningless, empty phrase. Something more positive, more constructive must take place. The decision of the Warren Court made it more clear than the Vinson decision of 1950 in stating the psychological effects of segregation on African American students and that all forms of segregation had to go. African Americans could not have been happier. The momentous decision provided them with a new hope and a bright future. They were going to forget the past and strive toward a new era of racial

Table 6.4
Summary of Supreme Court Decisions Affecting Black Americans, 1857–1954

Year of Case	Title of Case	Issue	For or Against
1. 1857	Dred Scott v. Sangfroid	Slavery	Against
2. 1873	Slaughter House	Privileges	Against
3. 1883	Civil Rights		Against
4, 1884	Ex. Part	Voting	Against
5. 1896	Plessy v. Ferguson	Facilities	Against
6. 1899	Cummings v. Board of Ed.	Education	Against
7. 1908	Berea Col. v. Kentucky	Education	Against
8. 1927	Gong Lum v. Rice	Education	Against
9. 1938	Missouri et rel v. Gaines	Education	For
10. 1948	Sipuel v. Oklahoma	Education	For
11. 1950	Sweatt v. Painter	Education	For
12. 1950	McLaurin v. Oklahoma	Education	For
13. 1954	Brown v. Board of Ed. of Topeka	Education	For

equality. If this hope was misplaced, as the decade of 1955–1965 would show, certainly African Americans were not aware of it as successive court action was generally in their favor since 1938. Table 6.4 shows a summary of some highlights in court action that indicated progress toward granting African Americans their rights. The listing is not exhaustive, it is simply meant to give an idea of the change of attitude the Supreme Court adopted toward African Americans and their education. Table 6.4 shows that the Court's decision followed a definite pattern. In similar cases that came after 1954, the pattern was to continue. Once that change of attitude was made in 1938 it remained the order of things even into the era of the controversial busing issue of the 1970s.

SUMMARY AND CONCLUSION

The discussion in this chapter began with the Emancipation Proclamation issued by President Abraham Lincoln in September 1862. From that point other developments followed with the intent of giving African Americans the rights they had been denied by the institution of slavery. For example, the ratification of the Fourteenth Amendment to the U.S. Constitution in July 1868 giving African Americans the right to citizenship and the Fifteenth Amendment, ratified in March 1870, giving them the right to vote were a natural sequel to the emancipation. The beginning of Reconstruction programs under President Andrew Johnson offered a real opportunity for African Americans to gain some real ground in their struggle for development. But faced with a high illiteracy rate, that struggle was particularly difficult.

The election of Rutherford Hayes in 1876 changed the agenda that had been set and reversed the progress that had been made. But while the Reconstruction was in place, African Americans made some progress. With the help they received from the Freedman's Bureau, African Americans demonstrated that if they were given the opportunity, they would make the best of it. Many served in a variety of roles—congressmen, leaders in education, and successful businessmen. All made a viable contribution to their society. But due to the political deal that Hayes made with southern whites, this progress was short-lived and African Americans were stripped of their rights as citizens and Jim Crow laws took effect. But African Americans looked to the future, not to the past, as they continued their struggle for development.

Having been disappointed by the end of Reconstruction, African Americans now turned to the courts to restore their rights. But from 1873 to 1938 the courts, including the Supreme Court, were functioning in a period of conservative attitudes. The *Dred Scott* case of 1857 set the stage for the courts to disregard the call from African Americans to restore their rights. In decision after decision the courts enunciated theories that intimately affected African Americans in their struggle for educational development. But once change came about, beginning with the *Gaines* case in 1938, the courts became persistent in enunciating theory that affirmed the right of African Americans to education. The evolution of this theory was long in coming. But once it was in place it began to show real results.

NOTES

1. Richard Bardolph, *The Civil Rights Record: Black Americans and the Law, 1949–1970* (New York: Thomas Crowell, 1970), p. 20.

2. Ibid., p. 25.

3. Ibid., p. 30.

4. Ibid., p. 31.

5. R. S. Henry, *The History of Reconstruction* (Glocester, MA: Free Press, 1963), p. 143.

6. E. F. Frazier, *Bourgeoise: The Rise of the New Black Middle Class* (New York: The Free Press, 1965), p. 61.

7. S. W. Webster, *The Education of Black Americans* (Berkeley: University of California Press, 1974), p. 11.

8. R. E. Dennis, *The Black People of America* (New York: McGraw-Hill, 1970), p. 139.

9. Ibid., p. 140.

10. Ibid., p.143. This shows a remarkably similar response among the Africans of South Africa who were subjected to the indignities of apartheid from 1910 to 1994. For details see Dickson A. Mungazi, *Defenders of the Laager: Ian D. Smith and F. W. de Klerk* (Westport, CT: Praeger Publishers, 1998).

11. Webster, *The Education of Black Americans*, p. 17.

12. R. E. Potter, *The Stream of American Education* (New York: American Book Company, 1967), p. 349.

13. Ibid., p. 350.

14. Ibid., p. 341.

15. J. S. Rouceck and T. Kierman, *The Negro Impact on Western Civilization* (New York: Philosophical Library, 1970), p. 207.

16. Ibid., p. 217.

17. H. A. Ploski and R. C. Brown, *The Negro Almanac* (New York: Belleweather Publishing Corporation, 1967), p. 487.

18. Webster, *The Education of Black Americans*, p. 15.

19. Ibid., p. 14.

20. Dennis, *The Black People of America*, p. 168.

21. Ibid., p. 19.

22. Bardolph, *The Civil Rights Record: Black Americans and the Law, 1949–1970*, p. 49.

23. Ibid., p. 55.

24. Ibid., p. 68.

25. Harlan is an enigma in the history of the U.S. Supreme Court. He owned slaves, but fought on the side of the Union to abolish slavery. He persistently disagreed with his colleagues on the question of civil rights believing that all Americans were entitled to equal treatment by the the law.

26. Bardolph, *The Civil Rights Record: Black America and the Law, 1949–1970*, p. 156.

27. J. Tussman, ed., *The Supreme Court on Racial Discrimination* (New York: Oxford University Press, 1963), p. 12.

28. Ibid., p. 14.

29. Potter, *The Stream of American Education*, p. 363.

30. Bardolph, *The Civil Rights Record: Black America and the Law, 1949–1970*, p. 151.

31. Tussman, *The Supreme Court on Racial Discrimination*, p. 20.

32. Ibid., p. 21.

33. Ibid., p. 26.

34. Ibid., p. 30.

35. Potter, *The Stream of American Education*, p. 479.

36. Tussman, *The Supreme Court on Racial Discrimination*, p. 37.

37. David Fellman, *The Supreme Court and Education* (New York: Teachers College Press, 1976), p. 138.

7

Theory to Address National Problems: From Warren G. Harding to Bill Clinton

> The defense of this nation depends upon the mastery of modern techniques developed from complex scientific principles.
> —The National Defense Education Act, 1958

POLITICAL AND ECONOMIC CONDITIONS IN 1928

The naming of the Committee of Ten in 1892 coincided with the beginning of the second term of Grover Cleveland (1837–1908) as president of the United States.[1] The Industrial Revolution was at its height. The high school was steadily taking its modern structure. The evolution of the college of education was almost complete. Higher education was reaching a level of development that had not been reached in the past. Cleveland's dedication of the Statue of Liberty and Henry Ford's first car in the same year suggested the conclusion that the country was about to enter the twentieth century with great expectations. This is why the period from 1893 to 1920 provides a transition from the nineteenth century to the twentieth century. The educational process was getting established. John Dewey (1858–1952) was busy developing his theory of progressive education. Charles Eliot was preoccupied with the activities of the Committee of Ten. Politicians were struggling to introduce amendments in the U.S. Congress to allow women to vote. In 1902 Theodore Roosevelt (1858–1919) successfully mediated a mine workers strike. In 1904 he concluded a peace treaty between Russia and Japan.

These events set the stage for the country to enter a new phase of development. From that time dramatic and unprecedented events began to take place in the United States with the announcement in February 1928 by Herbert Hoover (1874–1964) that he was a Republican candidate for president of the United States. Hoover seemed a natural successor to President Calvin Coolidge (1872–1933), who was elected in 1924 to a full term on his own right after he had succeeded President Warren G. Harding (1865–1923) who died suddenly in San Francisco on August 2, 1923. Harding was elected in 1920 and was the first president to run for office after the ratification of the Nineteenth Amendment[2] giving women the right to vote. Coolidge had announced six months earlier, on August 2, 1927,[3] that he would not seek a second term. That Coolidge succeeded to the presidency when President Harding died added an irony to events that were already rapidly unfolding during that period. In 1921 President Harding had named Hoover as Secretary of Commerce, an office he continued to hold under President Coolidge giving him both the exposure and the experience he needed as president. At the Republican Convention held in Kansas City in 1928, Hoover was nominated on the first ballot giving the impression that he was well groomed and qualified to assume the high office of president of the United States.

The year 1928 is also important in the history of the United States. It was the year during which Amelia Earhart (1897–1937) captured the national spirit by becoming the first female pilot to fly solo from Newfoundland to Burry Port in Wales. On May 20, 1932, when her spirit of adventure led her to fly across the Atlantic, Earhart rekindled a new level of determination to overcome the devastation caused to national morale by the Great Depression. In doing so she put the fear that President Franklin D. Roosevelt (1882–1945)[4] said was the only thing Americans had to fear into proper perspective. In this way she galvanized the national determination that was critically needed to meet the challenges posed by the Depression. If the Depression had created the impression in the minds of Americans that all was lost, Earhart's determination and spirit of adventure proved that human spirit can prevail over adversity of immense proportions. If the years from 1928 to 1932 represented the worst of times for the country in terms of its inability to predict the economic disaster, the four years that followed proved that the best of times was yet to come. In her tragic death on July 13, 1937, the nation lost a true pioneer at a critical time during a period of great national and international crisis caused by the Depression.

The year 1924 also saw J. Edgar Hoover (1895–1972) appointed director of the FBI, a position he held from that year until his death in 1972. During the formative years of his career, Hoover became famous for his relentless campaigns against persons considered public enemies and those who belonged to organized crime, especially the activities of Alphonse Capone (1899–1947). As soon as he took office, Hoover replaced untrained men with lawyers and accountants, people he believed understood his agenda. This enabled him to develop the FBI into one of the most efficient law-enforcement agencies in the world. Hoover had always admired Scotland Yard in Britain for its success in solving crime, and endeavored to build the FBI so that it would enjoy the same reputation as Scotland Yard. In trying to do so Hoover may have crossed the line. Over the years the abuse of power became a hallmark of his reign.

In 1917, after graduating from high school, Hoover worked as a messenger in the Library of Congress. As director of the FBI he also coordinated investigations of suspected subversive persons and groups in the United States. His books, *Masters of Deceit* (1958) and *A Study of Communism* (1962) discuss the dangers of communism and methods for combating it. By the time of Herbert Hoover's nomination for president of the United States, J. Edgar Hoover was well on his way to becoming an American institution.

In their state of euphoria the Republicans celebrated Hoover's nomination as if it were the election itself. They wanted the entire country to know that the best of times were here at last, totally unaware that the worst of times were about to begin under their leadership. Hoover's Democratic opponent, Alfred E. Smith (1873–1944) held impressive credentials. He was first elected to the New York legislature in 1903. From that time to 1919, when he was elected governor of New York, Smith distinguished himself as a powerful politician and leader. His understanding of critical national issues was comprehensive. He used his failure to win the Democratic nomination in 1924 to build a national image for himself as the Democrat who displayed qualities of leadership far better than anyone else within the party and the country.

But with all the political skills he possessed and in spite of the fact that both Harding and Coolidge manifested weaknesses in national leadership[5] at a critical point in the development of the country, American voters decided to place their trust in Herbert Hoover by electing him president. He garnered 21.4 million votes to Smith's 15.0 million. Hoover was not a particularly exciting politician, nor was Coolidge. In the election of 1924, Coolidge managed to win over his Democratic opponent, John W. Davis (1873–1955), a former ambassador to Britain who was hardly known outside the inner circle of the Democratic party. Davis was an authority on constitutional law and had argued more than 140 cases before the Supreme Court giving him the national exposure he needed to launch a political campaign. However, Davis lost his last case, *Brown v. the Board of Education of Topeka* in 1954. The fact that James M. Cox (1870–1957), the Democratic nominee who ran against Harding in 1920, won only 9.1 million votes against Harding's 16.1 million appeared to indicate by the election of 1928 that Democrats were unable to muster strong candidates for president. This perception clearly worked against Smith. But the Republicans did not know that Hoover's victory would be the last Republican president until Dwight D. Eisenhower was elected in 1952.

As the election campaign got underway, Hoover campaigned on his plan to improve the economy and eliminate poverty. Smith warned against overconfidence suggesting that the economy showed signs of weakness and serious decline within a short time. He suggested that everything possible must be done to strengthen the economy. The voters seemed to believe Hoover, who predicted that American families would have two chickens in the pot and a car in every garage, more than they did Smith, who was seen as not being positive enough to plan the future development of the country. This took away the excitement of the campaign as Smith was unable to generate enthusiasm in his candidacy and in himself as a viable alternative to Hoover. The brilliant lawyer that he was, Smith failed to develop a strategy for both his campaign and a plan to revive the economy. Although some people doubted Hoover's ability to deliver what he was promising, they thought the future of the country would be better under his presidency than under that of Smith.

Among those who believed that Hoover was promising more than he could deliver was John Dewey, the well-known educator whose philosophy of progressive education had attracted the attention of leading thinkers and educators throughout the world. As voters were about to go the polls, Dewey, then sixty-nine years old, not only supported Smith's candidacy, but he also criticized Hoover for failing to develop and fully explain his plan to revive the economy. He also faulted him for not presenting other domestic and international policies that would ensure the development of the country and the security of the world. Dewey went on to add, "If he has any human insight, dedicated by consciousness of social needs, into the policies called for by the day-to-day life of his fellow human beings, either in domestic or international affairs, I have never seen the signs of it."[6] Dewey particularly criticized Hoover for failing to articulate an educational policy that, when implemented, would address the critical issues both at home and abroad. The decline of morale and the threat of communism were problems Dewey believed would be addressed by the implementation of an effective national educational policy based on theory, and Hoover had none.

Dewey's concern was based on his argument that "Lying just below the optimism, apparent prosperity is a binding image of the roaring twenties, there seems to be an influence of a strong undercurrent of dissatisfaction ready to surface as the whole creed of complaisant capitalistic individualism and the right and duty of economic success is the greatest force that exists at present is maintaining unrealities of the social tone."[7] Dewey then predicted that Hoover's economic policies would lead, not to two chickens in the pot and a car in every garage of every family, but to an unprecedented economic disaster. However, the Republicans believed that Hoover had what it took to lead the country into the era of great economic prosperity and so refused to consider the ominous signs of impending doom.

THE DEPRESSION AND THE CHALLENGE OF RECOVERY

With Hoover's election, events began to unfold in dramatic fashion. The country had been on a course toward a major economic collapse. Farmers had not shared in the relatively reasonable prosperity that followed the end of the First World War. In the coal mining and textile industries, working conditions had not improved since President Theodore Roosevelt intervened in 1902.[8] By 1929 the economy was also weakened by widespread buying on credit so that there was little investment in its development and stability. Thousands of Americans borrowed large sums of money to pay for stocks giving Hoover and his administration an erroneous impression that the country was enjoying a new era of social and economic prosperity as stock prices soared to new heights. Then in October 1929 the stock market collapsed and the Great Depression was underway. There was nothing that Hoover could do to stop the collapse. His political fate was sealed.

Unable to comprehend the magnitude and the seriousness of the problem, Hoover tried to assure Americans that the economic problems amounted to nothing more than a temporary setback. But when, by the end of 1929, the collapse had caused losses estimated at $40 billion, everyone knew that the country was in a very serious economic situation. The value of stock listed on the New York Stock Exchange had dropped by 40 percent. Individuals lost their personal savings and employment opportunities. Within a few months the two chickens in the pot and a car in every garage for the American families that Hoover had promised became a delusion that existed only in their minds. Although the Republicans nominated Hoover for the second term as President in 1932, they and he knew that he had little chance of being reelected. To deny him the nomination would send signals to the country and the voters that the party was in disarray.

By the end of the year Franklin D. Roosevelt, then governor of New York, was a force to be reckoned with in the Democratic party. Roosevelt nominated Alfred Smith in 1928, and Smith nominated Roosevelt in 1932. Many people believed that Roosevelt could become a viable candidate in the near future. But for Smith this was his last hurrah. Many people within the Democratic party were hardly aware that the future was only four years away. It was only natural for the Democratic party to turn to Roosevelt as its candidate for president to salvage the party and save the country.

In a nationwide radio address, Roosevelt outlined a program to find solutions to the economic problems the nation was facing. He was nominated on the fourth ballot and went on to defeat Hoover by popular vote of 20.8 to 15.7 million. Roosevelt's victory was largely the result of James A. Farley (1888–1976), chairman of the Democratic party in New York and his campaign manager. There was a new sense of hope, not only within the Democratic party for a new direction, but also within the country in general. Americans began to blame Hoover for the depression because he failed to acknowledge the extent of the problems and so was unable to design a program to combat them.

In 1932, as the country was entering a period of political transformation, tragedy struck an all-American family in a way that devastated the nation.

Charles A. Lindbergh Jr., infant son of an American hero, Charles A. Lindbergh (1902–1974), who had flown[9] nonstop from Roosevelt Field near New York City on May 20, 1927, to Paris, France in 33.5 hours, was kidnapped and murdered. The enthusiasm the citizens of St. Louis had embraced for the future by sponsoring Lindbergh's plane, christened the *Spirit of St. Louis*, quickly gave way to the reality that the Great Depression was having other devastating effects on people's behavior that were hard to measure, let alone accept.

That kidnapping became a very common crime in the United States during the Depression suggests the negative side of human experience and thinking when under stress. Although the Congress responded by enacting the Lindburgh law, which made kidnapping a federal crime if the victim was carried out of state, it did little to curb this crime. The arrest, trial, conviction, and death sentence imposed on Bruno Richard Hauptmann, a German immigrant, added a sad twist to a national tragedy. It reminded Americans that the country was vulnerable to a combination of forces that were working against it. Although Hauptmann protested his innocence, he was executed in 1936 raising questions as to whether he was tried and convicted properly.

By the time Roosevelt took office on March 4, 1933,[10] the Depression had grown steadily worse. The economy had been destroyed. Thousands of unemployed workers were standing in bread lines to receive food aid for their families. Many farmers and workers were rapidly losing their homes, and many more were about to lose them because they could not pay the mortgages. Roosevelt applied a wide range of programs that he had used in New York at the beginning of the Depression to restore the confidence of the people in the future. The New Deal was the first major response to a national challenge and initiated reform in the structure of national institutions. This was the introduction of programs that were designed to enable Americans to have a fresh new vision of the future to restore their confidence and belief that all was not lost.[11] But in initiating these programs Roosevelt was under no illusion. He knew that the task was great and the challenge was compelling. He also knew that it was a challenge that had to be accepted, and a task that had to be undertaken because the survival of the nation was at stake.

The New Deal included successful programs that Roosevelt had applied as governor of New York at the beginning of the depression. He initiated relief programs to farmers in an effort to control the devastation of that segment of the economy which was so vital to the survival of the United States. On March 6, 1933, Roosevelt declared a "bank holiday" to allow his administration to formulate a new monetary policy. Three days later, on March 9, Roosevelt called a special session of Congress to begin dealing with urgent economic matters. Although this special session of Congress lasted ninety-nine days,[12] it is known as the "Hundred Days Session of Congress." On March 12 Roosevelt began the first of his famous fireside chats in which he addressed the many issues that his administration was proposing in order to fight the effects of the depression.

While the main focus of the New Deal was to combat the effects of the depression, it was also designed to initiate long-term solutions to other problems. It included programs designed to bring visible benefits to education as a preparation for the future. One of these programs was the introduction of the school lunch. When it was initiated in 1935 as a method of providing an expanding market for the farmers it was believed that it would be a temporary measure. But by 1946 it had been so successful that it was made a permanent part of educational programs. The national lunch program is still in operation today.[13] The legislation creating this program also authorized the secretary of agriculture to purchase and distribute agricultural surplus among individuals devastated by the depression. The school lunch program became the second largest single program of aid to education totaling nearly $400 million by 1964.[14]

Because agricultural production and development became an important part of the economic recovery, Roosevelt depended upon agronomists to develop technology that would enhance agricultural production. Among these agricultural scientists was George Washington Carver (1864–1943), an African American who won international fame for his research in agriculture. Carver developed products from such crops as peanuts, sweet potatoes, and peas. In all, Carver made 300 products from the peanut and 118 products from the sweet potato, including flour.[15] Although Carver made his discoveries prior to the Depression, they received special application to the challenges of economic recovery. Carver designed a theory of agricultural production: He urged farmers, especially in the South, to reduce their production of cotton in favor of food production. He began his scientific experiments as soon as he joined the faculty of Tuskegee Institute in 1896, a school that Booker T. Washington (1856–1915) founded for Negroes in 1881. A former slave, Carver spent the rest of his life at Tuskegee giving his life savings of $33,000 to the George Washington Carver Institute of Agricultural Research there in 1940.[16] Roosevelt then formulated his theory that the country must depend on human resources not only to recover from the depression, but also to make progress. He then stressed the importance of students to remain in school instead of rushing to secure employment. By the time of his death in 1943 Carver had become a household name in the country.

In spite of his efforts to sustain education as an investment for the future, Roosevelt knew that the depression had a devastating effect on education itself. By 1932 teachers' salaries had been reduced to poverty levels all across the country. Throughout the country, teachers went without pay for months bringing untold misery and financial ruin. To add insult to injury, the leadership of the National Association of Manufacturers attributed the economic disaster to the laziness of the workers and the failure of schools to educate students well.[17] This is why in his study, *Dare the School Build a New Social Order*, published in 1932, George Counts (1889–1972), a prominent educator, argued that the failure of the country to support education created a national disgrace that led to the crisis in which it now found itself. Counts suggested the expansion of the curriculum to assure that students were adequately prepared to play their role in society.[18]

This reaction to conditions of education as one of the chief effects of the depression suggests the conclusion that just as the New Deal initiative was intended to plant a new hope in the minds of the people about the general conditions of the economy, George Counts's initiative in education was generating a new level of confidence in educators as they were collectively trying to restructure the elements of leadership that was needed for the future. By the time he assumed the presidency of the American Federation of Teachers (AFT) in 1939, Counts had become a major national figure in the efforts that were being made to restore the country to its feet economically. By 1934, seeing the persistence of their president, Americans were steadily gaining confidence in themselves to recreate social and economic conditions that would eventually make the country better in the future than it had been in the past.

When a new journal, *Social Frontier*, appeared in 1934, it provided a forum for debate on critical national issues, especially the position of teachers and the direction education was taking.[19] What this indicates is that Roosevelt had planted in the minds of the people that distinct combative determination to rise up to the occasion and meet the challenges posed by the depression, to fight to regain their sense of vision and purpose, to struggle against odds to overcome the problems it created, and to respond to the challenge that came from a variety of sources during a period of great social and economic crisis. He demonstrated to the people that committing national suicide and surrender in the face of seemingly insurmountable problems was an assault on the human spirit and that this option should not be allowed to become part of human existence and enterprise.

UNITED STATES AND THE WORLD SITUATION

In 1931 the situation in the world created problems that placed the United States on the horns of a dilemma. Should it become involved in the effort to create stable conditions beneficial to the international community at the expense of possibly failing to pay adequate attention to problems at home, or to remain isolated and create conditions that could have an adverse effect on recovery programs? It was a crisis that had no easy solutions. In that year Japanese military forces had invaded Manchuria to re-establish its influence after Chinese revolutionary forces invaded it in 1911 and ousted the Manchu dynasty.

Since that time Japan had opposed Chinese action and waited until 1931 when it thought conditions were appropriate to reassert its dominance. The

League of Nations, weakened by the U.S. Senate's refusal[20] to ratify its creation under President Woodrow Wilson's (1856–1924) plan as outlined in his Fourteen Points presented at the Versailles Peace Conference in 1919, was impotent in its calling for the imposition of economic sanctions. The sanctions, however, proved to be ineffective, which served as a green light to Japan and other nations with similar ambitions to expand their boundaries through territorial gains. In 1937, Japan, feeling no ill-effects from the UN sanctions, invaded China itself. This set the stage for the progression of events that culminated in the outbreak of the war in 1939. When the war ended in 1945 the character of international relationships was altered forever.

In 1935, encouraged by the failure of the League to do anything to stop the Japanese occupation of Manchuria, Benito Mussolini (1883–1945) ordered his forces to invade Ethiopia. Its leader, Emperor Haile Selasse (1892–1975), fled and appealed to the international community to do something to force Italy to remove its forces from his land. But, as in the case of the Japanese invasion of Manchuria, the League of Nations was totally unable to do anything to stop this aggression. In both situations, Roosevelt was equally unable to do anything that might have helped find solutions to the escalating international problems. The following year, 1936, the time for presidential elections in the United States, Francisco Franco (1892–1975) led a revolution that established himself as dictator of Spain, a position of absolute power he maintained for nearly fifty years. For much of Franco's dictatorial rule, the standard of living for the Spanish populace remained one of the lowest in Europe.

During this time many locals of the two national organizations, the AFT and the National Education Association (NEA), united in order to do something to resolve the declining economic position of teachers. They formulated various strategies for improvement. This is why the Baltimore Teachers Union passed a resolution in August 1935 stating:

Whereas the teachers in the United States have suffered repeated pay cuts in the past five years of the depression, and whereas the rising cost of living has still further depressed teachers' salaries. Therefore, be it resolved that the American Federation of Teachers begin a national campaign of meetings, public petitions, media speeches, etc. in order to arouse public opinion in favor of restitution of teachers to restore salaries to their previous level and to ensure a further increase to meet the rising cost of living. Be it further resolved that all teachers' unions in the AFT and other organizations sympathetic to labor be enlisted in this campaign.[21]

Although there were no immediate results in the position of teachers as a result of this resolution, the country could not remain ignorant of the plight of teachers any longer.

Members of the AFT were seriously concerned about the critical nature of the world situation and how it could have a profound impact on conditions at home. The Baltimore Teachers Union recognized this fact and passed a resolution in 1935 condemning the preparation for war that was underway in Europe. The resolution stated:

Whereas the danger of an impending war threatens more and more ominously aggravated by a suicidal race in preparing arms and other war materials, and whereas such organizations as the ROTC, CMTC, CCC, etc., are indoctrinating our youth in the military and nationalist spirit, therefore be it resolved that teachers counteract such preparation by the doctrine of peace and internationalism for the settlement of national disputes and international conflict. Be it further resolved that armament expenditures be diverted to educational channels for the benefit of children and under-educated adults. Be it further resolved that this convention urge the AFT to reorganize a nation-wide opposition to imperialist war bringing together all organizations opposed to war.[22]

It is not surprising that those who saw the peril of Nazi and Fascist imperialism regarded the resolution as supporting Hitler and Mussolini. However, the failure of the Munich conference between Hitler and the British leader Neville Chamberlain (1869–1940) cannot be attributed to beliefs of this nature, but to Chamberlain's appeasement of Hitler.

To make sure that the Baltimore Teachers Union was not misunderstood, it passed another resolution the same day stating:

Whereas fascism is a reactionary force in society interested in the destruction of all liberal and progressive thinking about trade unions, fraternal organizations, and political parties, and whereas fascism incites the population against minority races and groups, and whereas fascism is spreading an international network of reaction and race hatred awakening in this country, be it resolved therefore that this convention reiterate its unalterable opposition to fascism. Be it further resolved that the teachers, as directors of the union, use their influence in combating fascist thought and activity. Be it further resolved that the extension of credits or loans to the Nazi government by the United States be condemned and that the AFT request the U.S. government to prevent such credits or loans.[23]

It is clear that the Baltimore Teachers Union saw events in Europe in the context of events that were rapidly unfolding in the United States, especially the deterioration of the economic position of teachers. On that same day the Baltimore Teachers Union passed yet two other resolutions, one addressing the need to recognize human rights for teachers, and the other calling for a system of tenure.

The outbreak of the war in September 1939 transformed the way people thought about themselves and their world. The Japanese sudden and surprise attack of Pearl Harbor on December 7, 1941, a day that President Roosevelt said would live in infamy, forced the United States to end its neutrality. In January the President underscored the importance of four freedoms he believed must be preserved for all people saying, "In the future day, which we seek to make secure, we look forward to a world founded upon four essential human freedoms. The first is freedom of speech and expression everywhere in the world. The second is freedom of every person to worship God in his own way. The third is freedom from want. The fourth is freedom from fear."[24]

When France surrendered to Nazi forces on June 22, 1940, Germany launched its blitz against Britain believing that it would not be able to withstand the power and destruction that its Air Force and missile attack unleashed. For several months Winston Churchill (1874–1965) pleaded with Roosevelt to come to Britain's aid, arguing that united German and Italian forces would force Britain to surrender posing serious implications for the United States. After meeting secretly the two leaders issued what became known as the Atlantic Charter on August 11, 1941, consisting of eight principles. The third principle stated, "We respect the right of all peoples to choose the form of government under which they will live, and wish to see sovereign rights and self-government restored to those who have been forcibly deprived of them."[25]

This statement shows two things. The first is that the United States was now willing to consider its involvement in world events that held implications for its own future. The second thing is that it implied that colonial systems in Africa had forcibly deprived the Africans of their right to self-determination. Both implications would have serious consequences for the future as both Africans and African Americans began to demand better treatment soon after the war. In the United States it meant the beginning of the civil rights movement. In Africa it meant the rise of African nationalism. Both movements had a profound impact on social conditions on both continents.

The passage of the Lanham Act in 1941 made it possible for the federal government to provide funds for school districts to build and operate schools where federal war-related activity created problems that local governments could not resolve. Three years later, in 1944, two events occurred that would have a profound impact on the country. The first was the passage of the Servicemen Readjustment Act, better known as the GI Bill. This legislation provided education and training for returning war veterans. Later the benefits it provided were expanded to include veterans of the Korean and Vietnam wars. The ability of the country to initiate educational plans for the future in an environment of war suggests a critical feature of human struggle for existence. The GI Bill made it possible for Americans returning from war to receive the education that they needed to prepare themselves for the future.

The second event took place in 1944. It was the publication of a report entitled *An American Dilemma: The Negro Problem and Modern Democracy* by Gunnar Myrdal (1898–1987), a Swedish sociologist and researcher. In his well documented study Myrdal predicted that unless racial discrimination soon ended, the United States was likely to encounter serious racial and social problems in the not so distant future. Mrydal suggested the causes of this social conflict saying, "The crowdedness in the Negro ghettos, the poverty and the economic insecurity, the lack of wholesome recreation are factors which all work in the direction of fostering anti-social tendencies leading to conflict. Racial discrimination in the opportunity for school facilities is as spectacular as it is well known. The current expenditure per pupil in daily attendance per year in elementary and secondary schools in ten southern states in 1935 and 1936 was $17.04 for Negroes and $49.50 for white children."[26] This difference meant that black Americans were receiving less educational opportunity than white Americans, a fact that contributed to both the Brown decision in 1954 and the beginning of the civil rights movement in 1955.

The violent deaths of Adolf Hitler and Benito Mussolini, both in 1945, meant that only Japan remained determined to continue the war against the Allied forces. After nearly six years of fighting, the world was getting tired of it. On July 16, 1945, the United States tested an atom bomb in New Mexico. On August 6 of that year the United States dropped one such bomb over Hiroshima killing more than 70,000 persons. Three days later a second atomic bomb was dropped on Nagasaki killing nearly 40,000 people. This brought the war to an end, but the use of the bomb created increasing conditions of global insecurity and danger. The atom bomb had ushered in the era of nuclear weapons that posed the possibility of destroying the world. In spite of the end of World War II, the wars in Korea and Vietnam brought the United States into the arena of international relationships more intimately than it had done in the past.[27] Since that time the world has not been the same. The United States has since been involved in seeking solutions to a plethora of global problems.

PROBLEMS ON THE HOME FRONT

One year following the end of the war in 1945, dramatic events began to take place in rapid succession on the home front. In 1946 a thirty-eight-year-old conservative Republican politician from Wisconsin, Joseph McCarthy (1908–1957), was elected to the U.S. Senate. Four years later, in 1950, McCarthy attracted public attention when he accused some members of the U.S. State Department of harboring Communists. McCarthy used this publicity to write two books, America's Retreat from Victory (1951) and McCarthyism: The Fight for America (1952). Although both books were less than successful, McCarthy used them to stage a massive investigation of individuals he suspected of communist activity. In the process of carrying out his self-assigned inquisition, McCarthy initiated a witch hunt that violated the basic constitutional principles he claimed he was trying to protect.

When Dwight Eisenhower (1890–1969) was elected president of the United States in 1952, McCarthy was already at the height of his investigations. He singled out teachers and college professors because of their activities during the depression. During what has become known as the McCarthy Era, careers were destroyed. Eisenhower, fearing to divide the Republican party, tried to ignore McCarthy and his activities. But, by 1953, Eisenhower and his administration realized that McCarthy was an embarrassment to both the Republican party and the country.[28] The president tried an approach of quiet diplomacy to have McCarthy cease his activities. In 1954 McCarthy was censured by the U.S. Senate, bringing his infamous activities to a halt. Education scholar Diane Ravitch concluded, "With Eisenhower as President, McCarthy could no longer fall upon and sustain an atmosphere of suspicion. The efforts to oust teachers suspected of being communists continued for a time in some school districts."[29]

Among the dramatic events that had a profound impact on the United States during this time was the Supreme Court decision in *Brown v. Board of Education of Topeka* in 1954. Since the end of Reconstruction and the beginning of Jim Crow laws, there developed a thinking that differences in skin color represented differences in intellectual potential and that the black race was inferior to the white race. A conclusion was then reached that, because of this difference, separate facilities must be established for whites and blacks. This thinking was seen as an official approval by the U.S. Supreme Court in its 1896 *Plessy v. Furgeson* decision. From this the doctrine of "separate but equal" became the modus operandi until the *Brown* decision.

From 1952–1953 the Supreme Court heard arguments against this policy and the specific application of "separate but equal" relative to segregation in education. These arguments were directed at schools in South Carolina, Virginia, Delaware, District of Columbia, and Kansas. These collectively constituted the *Brown v. Board of Education of Topeka* case. Lawyers arguing in favor of maintaining segregation cited the *Plessy* decision to conclude that the issue of race had been settled once and for all, the constitutionality of racial segregation had been substantiated by that decision, and that nothing must be done to change it. The lawyers in favor of integration argued that segregation did great damage to black students because separate was not equal. Robert L. Carter, arguing for the plaintiffs advanced a compelling argument saying, "No state has any authority under the equal protection clause of the Fourteenth Amendment to use race as a factor in affording educational opportunity among its citizens."[30] Thurgood Marshall (1908–1982), the chief counsel for the plaintiff, who had attended the Howard Law School directed by Charles H. Houston, added, "that there were no recognizable differences from a racial standpoint between children."[31]

On May 17, 1954, after hearing the arguments, the Supreme Court reached a unanimous decision that the doctrine of "separate but equal" as enunciated by the *Plessy* decision was no longer applicable to conditions of the day. Chief Justice Earl Warren (1891–1974)[32] wrote the decision saying, "Does separation of children in public schools on the basis of race, even though the physical facilities and other tangible factors may be equal, deprive the children of the minority groups of equal educational opportunity? We believe that it does. Such segregation is a denial of equal protection of the law."[33] The reaction to the historic decision can be understood in the context of the events that began to immediately unfold. The formation of the infamous White Citizens Council in close cooperation with the KKK to coordinate efforts to disobey the ruling was the beginning of a decade of unprecedented social turmoil. Some U.S. senators from the South, especially South Carolina and Mississippi, were actively involved in efforts to disregard the decision and to maintain racial segregation. James Eastland and John Stannis, U.S. senators from Mississippi, both took the center stage in their resistance to the *Brown* decision.

When Albert Einstein (1879–1955) died on April 18, 1955, the theory of relativity that he first enunciated in 1915 had become a touchstone that physicists tried to apply to a variety of situations to find solutions to problems of human existence. In that year some individuals, one being Albert E. Shanker (1928–1997), then an aspiring mathematics teacher, saw the applicability of the theory of relativity to conditions of education by recognizing its central tenet that all laws of physics have the same mathematical form regardless of the system of reference to which they are applied. This is why Shanker tried to adopt "a strong stand and not allow the school district to renege on its contract in order to satisfy an experiment in education and allow a superintendent to use the community against the union."[34] In this approach these individuals were now trying to apply the scientific and mathematical method that society required to solve problems.

On August 20, 1955, Emmett Till, a black youth of fourteen years, almost missed his train from Chicago to the Mississippi delta, where he was going to spend part of the summer with his relatives. Till caught his train but never made it back to Chicago. He was murdered for being black and those responsible for his death were acquitted of the crime. A decade after the end of the war, southern states, especially Mississippi, felt that the *Brown* decision had plunged the United States into "another war to protect its way of life."[35] Those responsible for Till's death did not know that they were helping arouse a new level of consciousness among black Americans about the need to initiate a protest movement to gain their civil rights.

In the same year that Till was murdered in Mississippi, a crisis was rapidly developing in Alabama. Racial segregation on Montgomery transit bus lines had been entrenched by tradition. When black passengers bordered the bus, they paid the fares at the front and then were expected to leave the bus to reboard at the rear door because the front seats were reserved for white passengers. Black passengers were also expected to give up their seats to allow white passengers to have them if there were more white passengers. On December 1, 1955, Rosa Parks, secretary to the Montgomery branch of the NAACP and a tailor's assistant in the Montgomery Fair department store, was on her way home after a long and tiring day. There was one vacant seat on the Cleveland Avenue bus that she took to go home. She took the seat in front across the aisle from one white man and two black women. By the time the bus got to the third stop, all seats in the front were taken and a white man stood next to Parks. The driver, in accordance with the practice, asked Parks and the other two black women to give up their seats to the white passengers. The two black women gave up their seats, but Parks refused to give up hers. The driver called the police and Parks was immediately arrested. E. D. Nixon, chairman of the local NAACP, posted bail and got her out of jail. The next morning Nixon called a number of people, including Martin Luther King Jr. (1929–1968), a young minister at the Dexter Street Baptist Church, to discuss a strategy for action. Coretta Scott King, Martin's wife, explained what they planned to do, "They decided that they wanted to call together the ministerial group and some leaders. They had the meeting at Dexter Street Baptist Church to formulate a plan of action. The plan called for a one-day boycott of the buses for one day in December. They sent out leaflets all over town."[36] When the boycott extended beyond the one day the committee had recommended, Montgomery city authorities were compelled to change the policy in 1956 because the boycott had imposed severe economic strains. Thus, the civil rights movement was underway and the United States would never be the same.

On September 4, 1957, the world awoke to a major crisis that was emerging in Little Rock, Arkansas. There, national guardsmen with fixed bayonets stopped a fifteen-year-old girl from entering the Central High School as a mob of white protesters threatened to lynch her. In a scene reminiscent of the Reconstruction Period, a major crisis was rapidly developing between the Governor of Arkansas, Orval Faubus (1910–1995), and President Eisenhower. To enforce the *Brown* decision, the president federalized the Arkansas national guard depriving Faubus of the means to resist integration. But the anger and outrage with which the white community responded in being forced to give up its exclusive power and position of privilege manifested itself in violence meted out against black Americans. By 1955 there were still efforts in the South to avoid implementing the *Brown* decision. There was a new thinking that the Supreme Court had not demanded that the schools be integrated, but only that "separate but equal" was no longer constitutional because, while it required the end of discrimination, it did not order integration, and "The Constitution does not require integration as a result of voluntary action, it merely forbids the use of governmental power to enforce segregation."[37] Regardless of this action the United States was forging ahead with plans for the future. There was no going back to conditions of the past. This was the course of action the AFT had advocated since 1937.

The crisis in Little Rock occupied the back pages of national newspapers when the Soviet Union launched the first satellite Sputnik ("voyager") on October 4, 1957. The satellite circled the earth once every ninety-five minutes at a speed of 18,000 miles her hour until it returned to the earth on January 4, 1958. The entire world was caught by surprise. Few people believed that the Soviet Union, coming out of World War II weakened to the point where its recovery would take years, was capable of rising above its third rate development to the status of a major nuclear power the way that it did.[38] By 1959 the Soviet leader, Nikita Khrushchev (1894–1972), exploited the Sputnik's success for his own political advantage and threatened to bury the West in the intense ideological competition that was rapidly developing as part of the cold war.

The impact of Sputnik was felt more profoundly in the United States than in any other country in the world. The United States saw the success of the Sputnik as a challenge and decided to respond in two specific ways. The first had to do with a change of attitude about the involvement of the federal government in education. Out of this new thinking emerged a national call to arms for the federal government to think of new ways of encouraging development in key areas of research and technology. This required making a thrust towards funding certain academic areas, especially mathematics and the hard sciences. President Eisenhower had vigorously opposed any federal role other than that of offering encouragement in education.

Eisenhower's reason for this position was that federal involvement would lead to federal control of education, a position the Constitution of the United States cautioned against by delegating education to the states. However, knowing that the era of the baby boom was placing considerable financial strains and demands on formulating strategies for action, conditions of the times compelled President Eisenhower to seek congressional action in initiating construction projects to improve education.[39] But many Americans saw the country's response to an educational call to arms in terms of a number of political factors that included religion, gender, and race. That the southern states saw this effort as a way of seeking to impose the *Brown* decision accentuated the controversy surrounding the federal involvement in education. It now seemed that Eisenhower was seeking to ensure educational development as a response to Sputnik.

The second specific way in which the United States reacted to Sputnik was that as soon as it returned to the earth, President Eisenhower pushed the National Defense Education Bill through Congress. Due to congressional procedures the bill did not become law until September 1, 1958, which was still a relatively short period in the history of legislative action in the U.S. Congress. The first paragraph of the act stated clearly what its purpose was saying, "The Congress hereby finds and declares that the severity of the nation requiring the fullest development of the mental resources and technical skills of its men and women. The present emergency demands that additional and more adequate educational opportunities be made available. The defense of this nation depends upon the mastery of modern techniques developed from complex scientific principles."[40] "Among the major provisions of this legislation designed to respond to Sputnik was the need to include in the curriculum at all levels more comprehensive studies in science, mathematics, foreign languages, and research. University professors saw in these provisions opportunities to initiate research in various areas related to the U.S. efforts to promote its efforts to sustain its interests during the cold war. It was the beginning of new graduation requirements in both high school and college."[41]

In 1959, while attempting to gain technological ground lost to Sputnik, Eisenhower invited Khrushchev to visit the United States. In June of that year, Soviet First Deputy Premier F. R. Kozlov, visited the United States to prepare for Khrushchev's visit.

Khrushchev seemed to understand the impact that Sputnik was having on the thinking of people in the United States. On his return to the Soviet Union, Kozlov carried an official letter of invitation from Eisenhower to Khrushchev. Khrushchev reacted:

Our relations had been extremely strained. Yet here was Eisenhower, President of the United States, inviting us to head a government delegation on a friendly visit. America had been boycotting us completely, even to the point of issuing a special ban on the purchase of crab meat from the Soviet Union. They said our goods were manufactured by slave labor. They also refused to buy our caviar and vodka. How does one explain this sudden invitation? What did it mean? It was hard to believe. Recognizing Sputnik's success Eisenhower was being forced to listen to voices within the democratic circles and in the business community which advocated concrete measures to reduce tensions between the two countries.[42]

Conscious of the impact of the invitation, Khrushchev submitted the letter of invitation to the Soviet Presidium for discussion and decision. It was decided to accept the invitation in principle, but urged the United States to do more to reduce the tension that was building up between the two countries. M. A. Menshikov, the Soviet ambassador in Washington from 1958 to 1961, was instructed to relay the acceptance of the invitation to Eisenhower and to make appropriate arrangements for the visit. The trip lasted thirteen days in September 1959 shortly after the first anniversary of the passage of the National Defense Education Act. Khrushchev and his entourage would visit seven cities and the United Nations. His entire family—including his wife; his son, Sergei; his two daughters, Yalia Gentor and Rada Adzhubei, and her husband, A. J. Adzhubei—and the editor of *Izvestia* were among the party. This raised the question in Moscow about the wisdom of taking the entire family to the United States in one plane during the height of tensions between the two countries.

Khrushchev's tour of the United States would have been completed without incident were it not for the remarks made by Norris Poulson, the mayor of Los Angeles, during a reception hosted by the World Affairs Council. Poulson chided Khrushchev for his "We will bury you" remark. Khrushchev recalled his reaction in an interview with his biographer, Strom Talbert:

Everything was going fine until the mayor got up to make a speech. His remarks were brief but very offensive to us. He stuck all kinds of pins in the Soviet Union and our system, most in the form of comparisons with the United States. I was furious. I could not pretend that I did not know what he was really saying. So I decided to deal a counterblow as I said, 'Mr. Mayor, I am here as a guest of the President of the United States. I did not come to your city to be insulted or to listen to you denigrate our great country and our great people. If my presence is unwelcome, then my plane is always ready to take me straight back to the Soviet Union. In my indignation I might have been a bit rude.[43]

Instead of returning to the Soviet Union with a favorable impression of the United States, Khrushchev returned with a strong suspicion that the United States was about to increase its anti-Soviet activity, including espionage. Indeed, Khrushchev did not have to wait too long to substantiate his suspicion. Early on May 1, 1960, Marshall Malinovsky, head of the national security system, called Khrushchev to report that an American U-2 reconnaissance airplane had crossed the border of Afghanistan into Soviet airspace and was flying towards Sverdlovsk, a strategic defense center. Khrushchev ordered the Soviet defense forces to shoot the plane down and not to allow it to get away as had been done in April when another U-2 plane had flown into Soviet airspace.

As soon as the plane was shot, the pilot, Francis Gary Powers (1929–1977), a lieutenant in the U.S. Air Force who was also in the service of the CIA, parachuted and was immediately placed under arrest. When Eisenhower refused to acknowledge the espionage purpose of the flight, Khrushchev angrily denounced the United States and canceled the summit conference that was scheduled for mid-May between him, Charles De Gaulle (1890–1970), and Eisenhower to discuss postwar German issues and disarmament in general. This incident represented the lowest point in Eisenhower's presidency. He even purportedly considered resigning because he felt that he had let his country down. This incident saw the cold war take a dramatic turn for the worse. Neither leader could trust the intentions of the other. Khrushchev's recent visit to the United States was no more than a minor episode in the relationships between the two countries.

These developments had placed the United States in what a film documentary called the dangerous years.[44] By the time the Cuban missile crisis presented itself in 1962, the United States was increasingly coming to the realization that the diplomacy initiated in order to improve relationships and reduce tension between it and the Soviet Union must take a backseat to the need to strengthen its military forces. The arms race represented a bold approach that included space exploration to counteract the prediction that Khrushchev had made during his tour of the United States. His expressed opinion was that the United States must abandon its capitalist policies in favor of adopting a socialist agenda, otherwise the country would fall further and further behind the Soviet Union. On February 20, 1962, John

Glenn became the first American astronaut to orbit the earth. The arms race soon acquired expanding and perilous dimensions.

The Association of Federated Teachers, like the rest of the world, became helpless participants in the doctrine known as MAD (mutually assured destruction) that these two superpowers obsessively embraced. School children all around the world soon took part in two kinds of emergency classroom drills—fire and atom bomb.

KENNEDY'S VISION OF THE NEW FRONTIER

The tragic death of President Kennedy on November 22, 1963, did not slow down the intensity of the competition in the arms race and the cold war in general. Kennedy's successor, President Lyndon B. Johnson (1908–1973), continued the programs he had started. The installment of the Kennedy administration gave Americans an opportunity to reevaluate the relationship that their country was having with other countries. This could only be realistically done in the context of posing fundamental questions about the United States's own national character and domestic programs. This is why, on taking office on January 20, 1961, Kennedy recognized the need to develop a national program that would improve relationships with other nations.

Kennedy's concept of the new frontier was born out of this endeavor. It had the significance of acknowledging a basic tenet in human relationships, manifested in the principle that the freedom of all people was essential to stability and peace among all nations. For Kennedy the exploration of space was only meaningful within the context of seeking to recognize the exploration of the aspirations of all people both in fulfilling their personal ambitions and to scale new challenges leading to national enrichment. This is why in 1961 Kennedy enunciated new policies regarding the rise of African nationalism. The appointment of Dean Rusk as U.S. secretary of state brought a fresh new approach that saw a departure from past policies pursued by the State Department under John Foster Dulles. Up until the Kennedy years, prior administrations believed that the consequences of the rise of African nationalism was the sole responsibility of the colonial governments.[45]

Kennedy also fully recognized the momentum that the civil rights movement was gathering in the United States. In it he saw a struggle that gave the country an emerging national character that was necessary to enable the country to recognize its proper role in critical issues of international relationships. His basic conviction was that unless the United States found solutions to problems at home, it would not be able to play an effective role in international developments. The new frontier demanded taking all pertinent factors into account in designing a domestic policy and agenda that were closely related to events abroad. This is the reason behind his submitting to the Congress the most comprehensive bill on civil rights, which became law in 1964.

The inauguration of the Peace Corps in 1961, under the direction of Sergeant Shriver, Kennedy's brother-in-law, proved to be the ultimate new frontier. A cultural bridge that helped build international relationships by providing the U.S. government and its people an opportunity to understand the nature of the culture and the problems that other countries faced in their struggle for advancement.

Under the Peace Corps, Americans from all walks of life were called upon to participate in a national program to give Kennedy's transformation vision a practical application to human understanding and cooperation. They were asked to live and work with people in foreign countries, studying and advising them on various aspects of national development. They would immerse themselves in foreign cultures and avoid trying to persuade the people in those lands to adopt the American culture. They symbolized mankind's ability to show the appreciation of cultural diversity as a means towards global enrichment. Kennedy envisioned this as constituting an understanding which was a prerequisite in creating an atmosphere of peace and cooperation. Nurses, teachers, agricultural specialists, engineers, and industrial workers all came forward in the spirit of Kennedy's call to offer their service in a national program designed to improve understanding between the United States and other countries.

In this rare new venture Americans came to understand themselves within the context of a global community. It also enabled their country to rediscover itself in an effort to refine its proper role in international relationships. In this context Peace Corps volunteers were found all over the world. The quest for human understanding came alive when agricultural specialists worked alongside people in Chile to raise food, when educators went to the Philippines to be both student and teacher, when health workers helped establish health care facilities in Tunisia, and when geologists went to Tanzania and assisted in extracting minerals needed to reap the benefits of natural resources without doing damage to the ecosystem. That there was no age limit to be a Peace Corps volunteer indicates the awareness that all Americans had the potentiality for accepting an appointment in a foreign country in the service of their nation. The AFT fully supported the Peace Corps mission. It allowed Peace Corps teachers to return to American classrooms with a wealth of experience and knowledge to share.

This approach to national policy created an environment that helped define a new paradigm which held new meaning for the United States. This new frontier manifested itself in a variety of program initiatives at home. The Higher Education Act of 1963 authorized $935 million in matching funds and $360 million in loans extended over a period of five years to institutions of higher education, both public and private, for building new educational establishments that included athletic and recreational facilities, and buildings for all purposes, even sectarian.[46] At the same time the Vocational Education Act, also passed in 1963, "extended and expanded all previous vocational programs including the Smith-Hughes Act of 1917."[47]

In 1965, having won the 1964 presidential election on his own merit against his Republican opponent, Barry Goldwater (1909–1998) of Arizona, Lyndon B. Johnson set out to define in his own way the "New Frontier." On April 11, 1965 President Johnson initiated what he regarded as a new definition of the New Frontier by signing the Elementary and Secondary Education Act. This legislation represented the most comprehensive provisions for education since the National Defense Education Act of 1958. The law provided for annual appropriations for education that enabled students from low income families to avail themselves of educational opportunities. The implementation of the law began with $100 million for the 1965 academic year. It allowed for the purchase of textbooks, library resources, and other published materials needed in the promotion of education among the children of economically deprived families. States were required to assure that fiscal control of the funds was exercised to ensure fair and equitable distribution of resources.

On November 8 President Johnson expanded the concept of the "New Frontier" in the area of higher education by signing the Higher Education Act. Coming one year after the passage of the Civil Rights Act of 1964, this legislation prompted Johnson to acknowledge its importance by saying, "This is only one of more than two dozen educational measures enacted by the first session of the 89th Congress. History will forever record that this session did more for the cause of education in America than all the previous 176 regular sessions of Congress did put together."[48]

While this was happening African Americans were trying to define the new frontier in their own way. Since the *Brown* decision they were increasingly demanding their fair share of the educational pie. The constitutional conclusion of the Supreme Court in that decision—that separation of children on the basis of color gave them the stamp of inferiority—became the basis of a fresh approach to their quest for educational opportunities. Those who continued to argue that the black race was intellectually inferior, such as Arthur R. Jensen,[49] saw the earlier *Plessy* decision as supporting their line of thinking.

Those who argued that race was not a factor in human intelligence also used the *Plessy* decision to support their view. This brought the question of research into play. The *Brown* decision, however, validated a new line of thinking that environment plays a major and crucial role in academic achievement. This belief led African Americans to argue that society had a duty to provide an environment that was conducive to their learning. The reality of this aspect of the new frontier is that success or failure in both education and society in general must be measured by the guarantee of equality in all aspects of national life.

This line of thinking was why, from provisions of the Civil Rights Act and of the Economic Opportunity Act of 1964, efforts were made to assist students from economically disadvantaged family backgrounds. They received special attention to help them overcome the effects of the denial of equal opportunity. Known as the anti-poverty law, this legislation was intended to help students recognize their potential and to encourage them to use it in their educational efforts. In this connection Johnson's understanding of the new frontier was evident in his desire to initiate Head Start, a program for preschool children. The rationale behind Head Start was that students from culturally disadvantaged backgrounds were being placed in socially disadvantageous situations that made it hard for them to learn. This was due to the lack of racially integrated social interaction. This also deprived them of access to quality teachers and appropriate educational resources. As it did with the Peace Corps venture, the AFT and Albert Shanker lauded the implementation of Head Start.

This paradigm shift in education held meaning and renewed hope for those responsible for education. They understood that educational materials and an adequate environment were critical variables for educational success. Shanker had persistently addressed the critical nature of the relationships that existed between these educational building blocks. The U.S. Office of Economic Opportunity had also argued that this disadvantage could be corrected by appropriate remedial strategies designed early in the life of students.[50] This is precisely the position that African Americans took in their understanding of Kennedy's original concept of the New Frontier. With the passage of this legislation, they felt that the concept was within their grasp and that they and the country stood on the verge of a new era, an era of social cooperation and acceptance.

RICHARD NIXON, WATERGATE, AND PROBLEMS OF POLITICAL SCANDAL

That Johnson translated the spirit of the new frontier into a vision of the 'Great Society' suggests the critical nature of the national programs he began, especially in education. This gave Americans a clearer sense of what it meant to live in a world of conflict. From preschool through postsecondary education, from rural to urban settings, he regarded education as the chief instrument to give Americans what he believed to be the necessary tool to fulfill their aspirations. In relying on education to accomplish this objective, individuals would also make it possible to become involved in proactively seeking an end to world problems.

Johnson might have gone down in history as one of the great presidents were it not for the war in Vietnam. Realizing that his domestic priorities were misunderstood because of the conflict in Vietnam, Johnson announced in 1967 that he would not seek the nomination of the Democratic Party for a second term as president. The tragic death of Martin Luther King Jr. in April 1968 and of Robert Kennedy (1925–1968) in June of the same year appears to have closed the era of the New Frontier. But was the country ready to enter the period of Richard Milhous Nixon (1913–1994)? Did he understand the importance of the office he was seeking? Although he had served as vice-president to Eisenhower, Nixon appeared to lack the sharpness of ideas that were needed at a period of great national crisis. The war in Vietnam would claim many victims.

The presidential election of 1968 was marked by considerable violent demonstrations throughout the nation. Protesters clashed with police at the Democratic national convention held in Chicago. Mayor Richard Daley (1902–1976) wielded a heavy hand in dealing with the demonstrators. Although Hubert Humphrey (1911–1978), Johnson's vice-president and heir-in-waiting, received the Democratic nomination, he would lose the election to Nixon, the Republican candidate who had lost to Kennedy eight years prior. Nixon exploited the violence in Chicago by portraying Humphrey and the Democratic party as being unable to provide effective national leadership at a critical point in the history of the country. The deterioration of the war in Vietnam had deleterious results for the Johnson administration and the Democratic party as the death of American soldiers was viewed every day on television news.

President Nixon recognized that the Vietnam War must soon come to an end if the United States was to reach a newly defined role as the world's greatest superpower. Nixon dispatched his secretary of state, Henry Kissinger, on what would be coined shuttle diplomacy. This led to a premature announcement in 1973 that peace was at hand. The Supreme Court's decision in *Roe v. Wade* in the same year had further far-reaching social and educational implications for the United States. The issue addressed the question of choice—a concept associated with democracy and freedom. This decision represented a period of time when the Supreme Court stepped boldly forward to address certain social issues that could not be addressed in any other way, knowing full well that it was the final arbiter in the land.[51] Indeed, the *Roe* decision placed the country in a situation that compelled it to reexamine its value system. This reevaluation still continues to plague and disunite large segments of the United States. Whereas protesters in the 1960s and 1970s addressed the moral issue of war in faraway lands, the 1980s and 1990s have witnessed protests about the right to terminate human life while it is yet still gestating in the womb.

The decision in *Roe* was not merely about the right of women to terminate unwanted pregnancies, but about the exercise of their rights in a variety of settings. It has extended to other questions: Should school districts retain an unmarried pregnant teacher? Could the school district employ a couple living together outside marriage? If so, what kind of influence would they have on students and society? These were just some issues the United

States had not yet encountered. During these troubled times, teachers' organizations, especially the AFT, began to formulate their own theoretical positions on the controversies that these issues raised in order to remain effective in discharging their proper responsibility to both education and society.

In 1972 Nixon accentuated the drama of moral decline ascribed to the so-called era of the hippie and the yuppie movements by putting together a highly controversial reelection committee. This group consisted of individuals of questionable integrity. Nixon authorized the burglary of the headquarters of the National Democratic Party, located in the Watergate Hotel, to search for materials he thought might embarrass the Democratic Party and his opponent George McGovern. Nixon hoped to use the information against both McGovern and the Democrats to win the election. Although Nixon won reelection, the action proved to be his political demise.

Two years later, when the full extent of his involvement in this unprecedented scandal was made known, Nixon had no choice but to resign from the presidency on August 9, 1974. In doing so he became the only president in the history of the United States to resign. Gerald Ford, who had become vice-president some months earlier when Spiro T. Agnew resigned because of his questionable financial dealings, assumed the office of president at a period of turbulence in the history of the United States. The last chapter of the Nixon presidency has yet to be written. But at this point it is clear that his political behavior represented a low point in the development of a nation struggling to find an effective place in the world.

Although Nixon helped to bring about formal relations with China through what has become known as the "ping-pong diplomacy," his legacy is rooted in the Watergate scandal. The moment Nixon's name is mentioned, one immediately associates him with political corruption. The introduction of court-ordered busing to achieve racial balance in schools reached a crisis during the Nixon presidency. Both white parents and black parents began to reject the court-ordered busing as a means to achieve equality of educational opportunity. While Nixon expressed his opposition to forced busing he did not offer any viable alternative plan to achieve the objectives the federal courts had outlined. In this regard Nixon failed to exercise proper national leadership when the country needed it.

In 1969 the Vietnam War brought the U.S. Supreme Court into the controversy in a way Nixon never anticipated. In the famous *Tinker v. Des Moines Independent School District* case, the Supreme Court ruled that students had a constitutional right to protest the war. The court stated that students were free to express their opinion, even on controversial subjects like the conflict that was going on in Vietnam. The Court concluded that under the U.S. Constitution, free speech was not a right given only to be so circumscribed; it existed in principle as well as in fact.[52] In May 1993 Albert E. Shanker, president of the AFT from 1974 to 1997, reflected upon the impact that, by 1974, these developments were having on the United States. He told the author,

As you know the country was going through a national crisis caused by the Watergate scandal. Although the scandal affected the political process more than it affected education, it had a tremendous impact on national morale. Inflation was rising rapidly, giving teachers less buying capacity. The war in Vietnam was reaching a critical stage. The curriculum in general was not developing as much as it should have developed. Teachers were in a state of confusion. Students were in doubt about the future. The traditional American family was experiencing unprecedented problems. Social and moral values were in a state of decline. These were among the conditions that prevailed in the country. We felt we had to reflect upon them in the activities of the AFT.[53]

When Ford assumed the presidency he was preoccupied with minimizing the impact of his pardon of Nixon. Because of his presidential pardon, Ford immediately alienated himself from the American people, causing serious political problems for himself.[54] During the primary election campaign beginning in 1975, Ford faced a considerable challenge from former California Governor Ronald Reagan, an actor-turned-politician. Although Ford won the Republican nomination in 1976, he lost the election to Jimmy Carter, a one-term governor from Georgia. In 1993 Shanker looked back upon the Ford presidency, saying, "President Ford was so preoccupied with the damage control of his pardon of President Nixon that he was unable to do anything else. He also vetoed education legislation to the extent that he was known as the veto president. His term of office from 1974 to 1976 was not distinguished in terms of defining an education needed for the future."[55]

When Jimmy Carter assumed office in January 1977 he was keenly aware of the promise he had made to the country during an address to the NEA in 1976. He proclaimed that if elected he would create a separate department of education, replete with cabinet ranking, to make it more effective in responding to the increasing educational needs of the populace. As a result Carter received an enthusiastic endorsement from both the NEA and the AFT. One of his major accomplishments as president was the creation of the U.S. Department of Education, a move Shanker opposed because, as he told the author, "I felt that education should not be isolated from other national issues."[56] But Carter believed he had to help those that had helped elect him. For this reason Shanker changed his position because he saw Carter's commitment to education as a distinct feature of his administration, one that was genuine.

THEORY UNDER REAGAN, BUSH, AND CLINTON: A NEW NATIONAL AGENDA

During the election campaign in 1980, the Republicans formed an educational alliance with special interest groups, such as the Moral Majority led by Jerry Falwell and the Eagle Forum led by Phyllis Schlafly, that attempted to draw votes away from Carter. These groups formed a coalition that functioned under an umbrella organization known as the Committee for the Survival of Free Congress. The organization chose Ronald Reagan as its candidate for president. Throughout his term of office Reagan responded to the wishes of the organization that raised serious questions in some people's minds about the purpose of government in a democracy. Should it dictate a national education policy?

Although Carter was supported by teacher organizations in his bid for re-election, the financial wealth and publicity generated by the special interest groups for Reagan proved too much for Carter as he lost the election. During his two terms of office, from 1981 to 1989, Reagan tried to dismantle the U.S. Department of Education that Carter had created. He appointed Terrel H. Bell to preside over its dissolution; William Bennett presided when Bell could not. Critics of the Reagan administration argued that he failed to accomplish any significant progress in national education programs because he was operating under the influence of special interest groups and was preoccupied with defending himself in the Iran-Contra scandal.

An embarrassing moment for the Reagan presidency came in 1983 with the publication of *A Nation at Risk*. On April 26, 1981, Bell had named the National Commission on Excellence in Education to examine the quality of education in the country and to submit a report making recommendations on how it could be improved. In 1983, after traveling across the country to gather the evidence it needed to reach its conclusions and ancillary recommendations, the commission submitted a report that was a disturbing indictment of education in general and specifically the Reagan administration, saying that if an unfriendly power had tried to impose on the country the mediocre educational performance that existed then on the United States, the country might have regarded it as an act of war. However, the United States had allowed this to happen to itself; the educational gains that had been made in the post-Sputnik era had disappeared, and the essential support systems had fallen away.[57] Bell had no choice but to resign. His successor, William Bennett, did little to confront the educational problems that plagued the administration he served. It appeared to many that he lacked any real understanding of the need to fully stress the ongoing and proactive development of education as the principal component in national development.

When George Bush, Reagan's vice-president, was elected president in 1988, he seemed to recognize the serious nature of the problems that the country faced. He lost the support of the people, however, when he announced that he wanted to be known as the education president, but then added, "People who want Washington to solve our educational problems are missing the point. We can lend appropriate help through such programs as Head Start. But what happens here in Washington will not matter half as much as what may happen in schools. Each local community and, yes, in each home. Still the federal government will serve as a catalyst for change in several important ways."[58]

This suggests that under Bush the federal government had chosen a small role for itself to play in the enhancement of education. Bush also seems to have ignored the perilous concerns that the National Commission on Excellence in Education had raised in 1983. How could he possibly initiate a new policy before solutions to these entrenched problems were found? Bush was not in touch with reality as far as education was concerned. By 1991 the war with Iraq and the declining economy combined to create serious political problems that he wouldn't overcome. These were some of the reasons behind his loss of the presidential election to Bill Clinton, the governor of Arkansas.

During the presidential election campaign in 1992 Clinton outlined his proposals for the recovery of the American economy through education in a clear and articulate manner saying, "Education today is more than the key to climbing the ladder of opportunity. In today's global economy, it is an imperative for our nation. Our economic life is on the line. Washington shows little concern[59] as people pay more and get less for what matters most to them: educating their children."[60] As he took office in January 1993 Clinton faced many national problems that were not solved during the Reagan-Bush and the Bush-Quayle administrations. But the improvement of the economy at the beginning of 1994 gave Clinton and Americans a period of great expectations, a fact he took into account in his State of the Union address delivered to the joint session of Congress on January 25.

The presidential election of 1996 presented the country with both opportunity and challenges. The economy was doing reasonably well. The world was at peace, and Americans were quite contented with their lives. President Clinton was given credit for turning things around for the better. But the election campaign was marked by negative campaigning by both the Democrats and Republicans in a manner that raised a national concern about this disturbing trend. Senator Bob Dole, the Republican candidate for president, and his wife, Elizabeth, focused on the negative, rather than the positive. This worried many people, including this author. On December 16 the author wrote a memo to the Republican head office in Washington, D.C., to express some concerns about the way the campaign was conducted saying:

When Senator Dole announced his candidacy he had been in politics about 35 years. He had served in the Senate reasonably well. When the campaign began he never made an effort to highlight some of his accomplishments of these 35 years. Americans were left to ask the question of who Bob Dole was. Senator Dole's failure to take a definitive position on two critical issues hurt him. One was social security, and the other was education. By opposing both Senator Dole failed to show leadership in two critical national issues. Meanwhile President Clinton restricted himself to addressing those issues. The publication of his *Between Hope and History* is an impressive accomplishment and a contribution to the literature about this nation. This comes from a national leader who sees his country in a positive light, rather than the negative perspective adopted by the Republicans.[61]

When Bill Clinton was reelected in November 1996 he became the first Democratic president elected to a second term since Franklin Roosevelt was reelected in 1944.[62] That in itself was a very important event. On February 25, 1997, President Clinton announced a new federal effort to combat drug abuse among American youth. But the election of 1996 demonstrated the need to reform the campaign process, including the manner in which finances are raised to run them. Soon after the elections there was talk of reform in methods of financing election campaigns. In March 1997 President Clinton addressed the National Governors Association conference held in New York during which he outlined his theory designed to address national problems, especially education, saying:

Our country still has an attitude problem about education that I think we should resolve. Too many people in the United States think that the primary determinant of success and learning is either IQ or family circumstances instead of effort. We can only do better with tougher standards and better assessment. I believe that the most you can do is to have high expectations of students, to make them believe they can learn, to tell them they have to learn really difficult, challenging things, to assess whether they are learning or not, to hold them accountable as well as to reward them.[63]

There is no question that Clinton had recognized the imperative of formulating new theory to address national problems. This is why he went before the nation's governors to explain his agenda for action.

SUMMARY AND CONCLUSION

The discussion in this chapter focused on some events that began to take place in 1892—the year that the NEA named the Committee of Ten and the assumption of office by President Grover Cleveland to begin his second term in 1893. One arrives at two conclusions from the discussion. The first conclusion is that from the beginning of the twentieth century, through the Depression and the administration of Herbert Hoover to the era of economic and educational reconstruction under Bill Clinton, the United States has faced serious social and economic problems that leaders have strived to resolve by applying theoretical considerations they believed would yield tangible results. The national spirit has always surged higher to assert itself in a struggle to sustain a national character consistent with the demands of the time. The challenges presented by such events as the passage of the National Defense Education Act of 1958 demanded action in response to a national call.

The second conclusion is that the era of the civil rights movement that began in December 1955 with Rosa Parks and Martin Luther King Jr. quickly led to a national campaign to recognize the need to extend civil rights for all people. The *Brown* decision in 1954, the passage of the Civil

Rights Act in 1964, the *Tinker* decision of 1969, and the *Roe* decision of 1973 all testify to the degree to which the United States was struggling to put the civil rights movement into proper perspective and to further create conditions that were conducive to the improvement of the lives of all people. Kennedy's concept of the New Frontier held wider significance and implications far beyond the extent of his thinking and vision.

NOTES

1. Cleveland served two unconnected terms, from 1885 to 1889, as twenty-second president, and from 1893 to 1897, as twenty-fourth president. He was defeated for reelection by Benjamin Harrison (1833–1901), whom he had defeated in 1892.

2. The Nineteenth Amendment was first proposed on June 4, 1919, and was ratified on August 26, 1920. Amendments to give women the right to vote were introduced in the U.S. Congress more than 40 years before this one was finally ratified.

3. President Harding died on August 2, 1923. It is not clear why Coolidge chose this date to make his announcement. This author thinks that he chose the anniversary of Harding's death to show his respect for the memory of a man he admired and to give his successor publicity in launching a successful election campaign. Indeed, his successor, Herbert Hoover, won the election in 1928.

4. Roosevelt served from 1933 to 1945, the longest of any president. On March 24, 1947, the Twenty-second Amendment was proposed and was adopted on March 1, 1951, stating, "No person shall be elected to the office of President more than twice."

5. As vice-president in the Harding administration, Coolidge could not escape the Teapot Dome and other such scandals. Although in 1924 he forced the resignation of Attorney General Harry M. Dougherty and replaced him with Harlan F. Stone, Coolidge remained tarnished by the scandals. That as president he pursued Harding's policies added doubt to the problems of confidence he was having with the public. This is partly the reason he decided against running for a second term in 1928.

6. Herbert Kliebard, *The Struggle for the American Curriculum, 1893–1958* (New York: Routledge and Kegan Paul, 1987), p. 180.

7. Ibid., p. 181.

8. Roosevelt assumed the office of president on September 14, 1901, when President William McKinley (1843–1901), who was elected in 1897, died from an assassin's bullet. Roosevelt served until 1909.

9. The record shows that Lindburgh took off at 5:21 P.M. from Roosevelt Field near New York on May 20 and landed at Le Bouget Field near Paris at 10:21 P.M. Paris time on May 21 covering a distance of 3,600 miles.

10. The inauguration was the last to be held in March. Under Amendment 20 to the Constitution proposed on March 3, 1932, and ratified on February 3, 1933, all future inaugurations would be held in January.

11. Robert E. Potter, *The Stream of American Education* (New York: The American Book Company, 1974), p. 371.

12. The special session of Congress lasted from March 9 to June 16, 1933.

13. Potter, *The Stream of American Education*, p. 391.

14. Ibid., p. 340.

182   Evolution of Educational Theory in the United States

15. Anne T. White, *George Washington Carver: Boy Scientist* (New York: Random House, 1954), p. 57.

16. Ibid., p. 59.

17. Kliebard, *The Struggle for the American Curriculum,1893–1958*, p. 187.

18. Ibid., p. 195.

19. Ibid., p. 196.

20. The campaign to keep the United States out of the League of Nations was led by Republican Senator from Connecticut, Henry Cabot Lodge (1850–1924), who had been elected to the U.S. Senate in 1893. When Wilson died on February 3, 1924, his wife asked Lodge to stay away from the funeral. The two men had become bitter political ememies.

21. Baltimore Teachers Union, "Resolution on the Position of Teachers," August 10, 1935. The AFT Files, Walter Reuther Archives of Labor and Urban Affairs, Wayne State University, Detroit, Michigan.

22. The Baltimore Teachers Union, Resolution on the Danger of War, August 10, 1935. The AFT Files, Walter Reuther Archives of Labor, Wayne State University, Detroit, Michigan.

23. Ibid.

24. Franklin D. Roosevelt, The State of the Union Message, January 6, 1941.

25. President Franklin Roosevelt and Prime Minister Winston Churchill, The Atlantic Charter, August 11, 1941.

26. Gunnar Myrdal, *An American Dilemma: The Negro Problem and Modern Democracy* (London: Harper and Brothers Publishers, 1944), p. 332.

27. For example, since the United States recognized the formation of the government of Israel in 1948, it has tried to mediate between Israel and its Arab neighbors. Its efforts remained unsuccessful until September 14, 1993, when the government of Israel and representatives of the Palestinian Liberation Organization (PLO) met in Washington, D.C., to sign an agreement that they had reached.

28. Diane Ravitch, *The Troubled Crusade: American Education, 1945–1980* (New York: Basic Books, 1983), p. 110.

29. Ibid., p. 111.

30. Leon Friedman, ed., *Argument: The Oral Argument before the Supreme Court in Brown v. Board of Education of Topeka, 1952–1955* (New York: Chelsea House, 1969), p. 14.

31. Ibid., p. 15.

32. Warren had been named Chief Justice by President Dwight D. Eisenhower in 1953 to replace Frederick Vinson (1890–1953), who died suddenly.

33. Brown v. Board of Education of Topeka, 347 U.S. 483, May 17, 1954.

34. Marjorie Murphy, *Blackboard Unions: The AFT and the NEA, 1900–1980* (Ithaca, NY: Cornell University Press, 1990), p. 246.

35. Henry Hampton and Steve Fayer, *Voices of Freedom: An Oral History of the Civil Rights Movement from the 1950s through the 1980s* (New York: Bantam Books, 1990), p. 2.

36. Ibid., p. 22.

37. Ravitch, *The Troubled Crusade: American Education, 1945–1980*, p. 165.

38. Ibid., p. 228.

39. Ibid., p. 229.

40. The U.S. Public Law 85-864, National Defense Education Act, 1958, 85th Congress, September 2, 1958.

41. The author recalls that when he arrived in the United States to attend college in 1961, the liberal studies requirements were already in place and he took courses under provisions of the legislation.

42. Strobe Talbott, Edward Crankshaw, and Jerrald Schector, *Khrushchev Remembers: The Last Testament* (Boston: Little, Brown and Co., 1974), p. 369.

43. Twice in 1993 the author requested a copy of Poulson's remarks from the office of the mayor in Los Angeles, but he received no response.

44. A&E, "Eisenhower: The Dangerous Years," a documentary film, July 1988.

45. Dickson A. Mungazi, *The Struggle for Social Change in Southern Africa: Visions of Liberty* (New York: Taylor and Francis, 1989), p. 100.

46. Potter, *The Stream of American Education*, p. 406.

47. Ibid., p. 402.

48. U.S. Senate Committee on Labor and Public Welfare, *Enactments by the 89th Congress Concerning Education and Training* (Washington, DC: Government Printer, 1966), p. 18.

49. William van Til, *Education: A Beginning* (Boston: Houghton Mifflin Company, 1974), p. 346.

50. *Economic Opportunity Act*, U.S. Public Law 88-482 (Washington, DC: U.S. Government Printing Office, 1964).

51. In 1975, during an official visit to Washington arranged by the U.S. State Department, this author had an occasion to visit with then Justice Potter Stewart who said to him and to other guests, "We are final not because we are infallible, but we are infallible only because we are final."

52. U.S. Supreme Court, *Tinker v. Des Moines Independent School District*, 393 U.S. 503, 1969.

53. Albert Shanker, during an interview with the author, in Washington, D.C., May 17, 1993. The interview was part of gathering materials for the author's book, *Where He Stands: Albert Shanker of the American Federation of Teachers* (Westport, CT: Praeger, 1995).

54. During a graduate course in political science at the University of Nebraska, the author conducted a survey that asked 500 people what they thought about the pardon. Eighty percent had a negative response to it.

55. Albert Shanker, during an interview with the author, in Washington, D.C., May 17, 1993.

56. Ibid.

57. National Commission on Excellence in Education, *A Nation at Risk* (Washington, DC: Department of Education, 1983), p. 5.

58. George Bush, *America 2000: An Education Strategy* (Washington, DC: Department of Education, 1991), p. 5.

59. Clear reference to the lack of interest by both the Reagan and Bush administrations.

60. Bill Clinton, *Putting People First: A National Economic Strategy for America* (Little Rock, AR: Bill Clinton for President Committee, 1992), p. 6.

61. Dickson A. Mungazi, "Some Reflections on the Presidential Election Campaign of 1996," memo to the Republican Headquarters, December 16, 1996.

62. Harry S. Truman (1884–1972) was elected only once, in 1948. John F. Kennedy (1917–1963) was also elected once in 1960, so was Lyndon Johnson (1908–1973) in 1964, and Jimmy Carter in 1976.

63. "President Clinton Delivers Message of High Standard and High Account-ability," address to National Governors' Association (Washington, DC: U.S. Department of Education, March 1997).

8

The Evolution of Educational Theory: Summary, Conclusion, and Implications

> In our new complex economic environment, 89 percent of the jobs that are now being created require much higher levels of literacy and knowledge of mathematics. Improving America's literacy rate is just as important to this nation's future economic growth as balancing the budget.
> —Richard Riley, U.S. Secretary of Education, 1996

> The task before American educators today is to take what we know works in schools and spread it more widely among America's public school classrooms.
> —Sandra Feldman, President, AFT, 1997

THE IMPORTANCE OF HISTORY

This study began with a discussion of the origins of theory of Western education and traced some major developments that were part of the philosophy of ancient Greek thinkers through the founding of universities in Europe during the Middle Ages to the Renaissance, the Reformation, and the Age of Reason to the present. It has presented the formulation of theory at the founding of the colonial society, beginning with the establishment of Jamestown in Virginia in 1608 to the present. In doing so, the study first discussed the evolution of theory as it was related to the three major regions of the colonial society: New England, the Middle Atlantic colonies, and the South. The study of the evolution of theory is important to all human endeavors. The old saying, "Study the past to understand the present in order to plan the future," forms an important component in any effort to resolve problems of social or human development.

The reality that any society faces social, economic, and political problems combines with the fact that, throughout history, nations have to make concerted efforts to find a functional basis of educational theory with which to build a new agenda for national development. This is the line of thinking that John D. Pulliam took into consideration to conclude: "In a world marked by war, inflation, population explosion, pollution, social strife, and anxiety about the future, education and schooling cannot be taken for granted."[1] The Soviet educational thinker, Yuri Azarov, took this same line of thinking a step further to argue in favor of developing a theory of education that was designed to serve the needs of individual students in order to serve those of the nation. Azarov concluded, "Education can be effective only when it is intended to help solve problems of the learner and is not divorced from social conditions that have implications for national development and international understanding and cooperation."[2]

Major human developments are a result of lessons learned from the past. It is not easy for man to understand the present and plan the future without an effective knowledge of the past. This is why the astronomer who explains how the universe operates does so from an historical perspective. The biologist who studies how a species can become extinct also does so from a knowledge of the past. The economist who warns nations of the consequences of inflation or makes economic projections also does so from an understanding of similar situations that existed in the past.

Another factor to consider in any human enterprise is that humankind is a product of history. The anthropologist tells us that the study of man's past yields important information about the present and the future. The paleontologist informs us that the study of fossils reveals important information about species in general to tell us about the present and possible future development. The archaeologist advises us that the study of material remains of the past showing how people used to live to indicate how they might live in the future. The fact of the matter is that whether it is in economic issues, political action, religious thought, or educational theory, human action is constantly influencing the character of institutions as a product of history.

The legacy of the Jacksonian era, for example, is that it created a national consciousness that suggested some glaring weaknesses in the existing social and educational American systems. Political and economic power was still the privilege of a few. This undercut the thinking that democracy was at its best when the largest possible number of people participated in the political and economic systems. The exclusivity of the political process generated new fears that the United States was becoming an aristocratic society like that in Europe. With the increase in the U.S. population from 5,308,000 in 1800 to 12,866,000 in 1830, poverty and other social dysfunctions were on the rise, putting the value of social institutions into doubt.[3]

These were the conditions that brought individuals like Henry Barnard, Horace Mann, and William Torey Harris into the arena of educational reform. Mann so believed in educational reform that he gave up his law practice to become secretary of the Massachusetts Board of Education. For eleven years, from 1837 to 1848, Mann championed the cause of educational reform in a way that reflected the ideas of Andrew Jackson for the improvement of American society through educational development. The success of Mann's efforts must be seen in the context of the strategy he utilized to accomplish the objectives he had identified. First, he persuaded the business community to be involved in seeking reforms in education because he convinced them that better educated workers were more productive. Edmund Dwight, a leading industrialist who had nominated Mann for the po-

sition of secretary of the Massachusetts Board of Education, played a leading role in creating a new consciousness among members of the business
community about the need to support the reform movement.

By the time Grover Cleveland began his second term as president in
1893,[4] American society had been transformed by technological and industrial development measured in terms of educational development. Cleveland's dedication of the Statue of Liberty in October 1896 and Henry Ford's
first car in the same year marked the end of the nineteenth century with the
hope that the twentieth century would be even better. This study examines
other aspects of education in the United States. The *Brown* decision of 1954,
enactment of the National Defense Education Act of 1958, and the Civil
Rights Act of 1964 are only three examples that show that American education was conditioned to go through the enunciation of theory and reform.

THE IMPORTANCE OF THEORY

With delegates from all over the world, the San Francisco conference that
was convened at the end of the war in 1945 was an appropriate setting. The
world needed to examine broader theoretical components relative to the education of a new era. This is why what came out of the conference was a
broad perception of the theoretical considerations of education needed to
meet the demands of the changing world situation. However, there were
some critical theoretical elements that the conference did not consider carefully. One such element is what Peter McLaren identified as evincing the idea
that "Men and women are essentially unfree and so inhabit a world rife with
contradictions."[5] The world since 1945 has witnessed unfree people because
man himself, in the universal sense, has taken action, though seemingly intended to serve society, carefully calculated to serve his own interests. For
example, the number of millionaires has rapidly increased among those who
are in positions of political power. At the same time, the number of the poor
has dramatically increased. One might have to argue that this has not happened by chance but by design.

The "asymmetries of power and privileges"[6] that McLaren concluded to
be the major cause of conflict in the world have accentuated differences in
which educational opportunity is extended to the people of a nation at the
expense of the others, and has created a situation that translates into a dire
need for a new theory of education. Failure to recognize the imperative dialectical theory of education has created problems for the global society in a
much broader context than limiting individuals to an environment that ren-
ders them inefficient to function in a larger global social order. The reality of
the resulting situation is that neither the individual, nor the society in which
he or she lives, can have a determining influence on the character of the
other. Dialectical theory in the existing social order provides those in a position to do something positive, to initiate a process with specific objectives,

to serve the educational interests of all students as the only viable means of serving the interests of their nation. This is a critical element of global peace and security.

Peter McLaren also concluded that utilizing a dialectical theory of education makes it possible for society to see the school not only as a place where instruction and socialization take place but also as a basis of the revitalization of broader cultural materials needed to understand the essence of the universal human being. This line of thinking suggests that the theory of education that emanates from this sociocultural perspective becomes a viable channel to embrace the essential elements of what it means to be human in the age of the search for global understanding. McLaren also suggested that without taking these critical elements of education into consideration, the education that emerges loses the real purpose for which it exists.[7] The thinking that national interests must come above those of the world is a result of an educational system that is not based on a theory of the need to embrace broader human values from an inclusive perspective. This is the evolution of theory that must become a deliberate and careful exercise conceived in the intricate components of human survival in a larger social order.

The failure of nations to take this perspective into account means that it is difficult, even impossible, to restructure human relationships on a level different from the past because the process of formulating an education to sustain national interests, rather than global peace, results in projecting a new norm of culture "intimately connected with the structure of social relationships within class, gender and age formations that produce forms of oppression and dependency."[8] One has to look at the results of the war between Iraq and Allied forces in 1991 to understand the importance of embracing a theory of education on a broader scale than is the current practice. The concept of cultural diversity, though recent as an area of study, demands not only tolerance of differences but also acceptance of divergent viewpoints that emanate from cultural differences. This is how theory brings into focus the shared international values that only education can offer to all people as a form of change in the conditions that control the universal person. This is the perspective that Robert Manners took into account when he argued in favor of a theory of education that must be designed to initiate social innovation: "If you introduce change in any part of society, contingent changes of varying intensity will make themselves felt throughout the venture. The very change that may be welcomed by the group in power as a desirable innovation may be resented by those who feel oppressed by society because they feel that such change has been introduced to strengthen the status quo."[9]

Immanuel Kant (1724–1804) added in his *Critique of Pure Reason* (1781) that one major function of the state is to make people happy and secure. The best way to do this is to allow them free will so that they can exercise their options in order to make a viable contribution to the development of their society. This approach demands an education based on a theory that entails dialectical elements. The absence of free will and a theory of education consistent with this objective creates a social climate that generates conflict. The consequences of the failure of the participants of the San Francisco conference to recognize the importance of these elements led to the educational crisis that nations have endured since 1945. What has been emerging as a trend of thinking among nations of the world is the notion that to be happy the people have to identify with the objectives, policies, and programs of their government. In their turn national leaders have built their own popularity among citizens by formulating an aggressive foreign policy as the only viable way to ensure their security. In this approach, national leaders forget the lessons of the war that began in 1939. Let us now attempt to discuss the importance of theory as it is related to the four nations selected for this study.

THE SEARCH FOR NEW THEORETICAL APPROACHES

From the time that slavery was introduced into the United States in 1609, Americans have been seriously handicapped by a preoccupation with race. It is not surprising, therefore, that by 1991 the United States and South Africa were the only countries in the world where race was still a major factor of individual development. That American scholars readily disagree about the impact of race on education suggests its strong influence on the thinking process itself. When it comes to the practice of social precepts, Americans do not seem to share Thomas Jefferson's view that: "All men are created equal." Even then, it is generally accepted that Jefferson was actually referring only to white men. How could he include African Americans in that statement when he was a slave owner? How could he include women when they did not have the vote until 1920? However, what is important to remember is that in making this statement Jefferson was stating a clear theory of education.

Writing in 1988, Peter McLaren argued that formulating a functional theory of education in the United States has been made harder by the consideration of race and that racism has overshadowed the efforts of those who are trying to seek an improvement in the education of all Americans. McLaren stated, "As I write on the anniversary of the slaying of Martin Luther King Jr. (1929–1968), a state holiday rescinded by Governor Evan Mecham of Arizona[10] reports of growing racial unrest rattle the airwaves. Images of violence in Howard Beach, New York, and the shrouded specters of Ku Klux Klan leading a demonstration in Forsythe County, Georgia, appear ominously across the television screens of America."[11] Logic suggests that race and racism in any society become a major problem in finding a theoretical base with which to seek solutions to problems of national development.

As the United States moved into the nineteenth century the emphasis in education began to shift from the development of character to the development of skills needed to function in an industrial society. The search for education as a measure of an enlightened individual gave way to the search for education to enable the individual to be self-sufficient and so make a viable contribution to the development of society. John Dewey took this line of thinking in 1938 when he wrote *Experience and Education* in which he argued that a theory of educational development of the individual was a critical factor of the development of the country. Dewey went on to explain the changing nature of society and how the individual must be educated to play his role effectively: "The political and economic issues which the present generation will be compelled to face demands education. The nature of the issues cannot be understood save as we know how they come about."[12]

Mortimer Adler sees theory of the individual's educational development in relationship to its role in promoting and maintaining democratic values and the consequences that he said may ensue from the failure to formulate an educational program in response to such a theory. He adds, "We are all sufferers from our continued failure to fulfill the educational obligations of democracy. We are all victims of a school system that has only gone halfway along the road to realize the promise of democracy."[13] What Adler seems to suggest is that formulating a theory of education must entail two critical considerations. The first consideration is that education must ensure the development of the individual. This development has a single purpose: to make it possible for a person to function in a larger social order. The second consideration is that the educational process that ensues from this theory must make it possible for all to endeavor to preserve the principles of democracy.

In discussing theory of education as it is understood to apply to education in the United States one must remember that there are two related components. These are learning and teaching. With respect to learning, a relatively recent theory has been developing, known as cognitive psychology. This theory suggests that a student is capable of learning in a variety of ways and at different rates and that capability to learn varies from student to student. In the recent history of education in the United States, teachers have endeavored to apply this theory resulting in a change from individualized instruction to what has become known as cooperative learning. Although the theory of cognitive psychology has some appeal to a variety of educational settings, Edward Ignas argued that it "has had little positive effect on the schools."[14] This does not suggest that the theory does not work. Rather, it indicates that the conditions of its application are not quite right. For this reason, the search for a theory of education must be related to other critical factors, such as the school and home environment, social conditions, and the level of training of teachers.

With respect to the theory of teaching, there is a variety of elements that one sees in American educational settings. These range from the inductive approach to the deductive method. What has been developing in recent years is the thinking that what a good teacher can do is to provide an environment in which students develop confidence in themselves and their ability to discover answers to educational questions. Contemporary American educationists seem to hold the view that education is far more meaningful when students are allowed to discover for themselves those critical aspects of knowledge associated with the educational process. Once this process is applied, it accrues benefits to students that they would not secure in any other way. It generates a concept of individuality so critical to American social settings. It helps develop elements of critical thinking. It helps offer students new perspectives in interpreting old concepts and makes them relevant to contemporary conditions.

A theory of teaching that brings out these features of the educational process does not have to have loud pronouncements from thinkers to be applicable, even though educational thinkers believe that such theories must stand the scrutiny of critics and intellectuals to have universal application. The reality of it all is that teaching, like learning, is essentially a product of individuality. A Marva Collins can be a successful teacher without accepting, or resorting to, the theory of John Dewey or Charles Eliot. American theoreticians seem to ignore the fact that what determines success in teaching is not so much the kind of theory teachers put into practice, but a combination of the goals and objectives they establish to ensure that learning takes place. This demands commitment and clear knowledge of what teaching is all about. If teachers understand these basic requirements of their responsibility, then one would have to conclude that they have demonstrated understanding of the essential elements of a theory of education.

An interesting phenomenon in the theory of education in the United States is that the legal system has been intimately involved in developing it. The historic ruling of the U.S. Supreme Court in *Brown v. Board of Education of Topeka* in 1954 gave new meaning to the quest for a new theory of education. In stating that separate and racially segregated schools were inherently unequal, and so unconstitutional, the Supreme Court was reversing a theory that it had put in place in 1896 in *Plessy v. Ferguson*, which affirmed the notion of "separate but equal." It is ironic that the Supreme Court was less concerned about genuine equality than it was with maintaining the status quo. Gerald Gutek observed that segregated schools were always unequal. He argued that educational expenditures per pupil were greater for white students than for black students, and that salaries paid to teachers were generally higher for white teachers, the white school year was longer, and physical facilities were much better than those for African American schools.[15] What is important here is not that the Supreme Court knew in 1896 that racially segregated facilities were unequal, but that it had enunciated a theory consistent with the thinking of the time. The thinking of the Court that facilities were not inferior as long as the notion of equality was applied was what gave relevance to its theoretical enunciation. It was this same consideration operating in reverse that the Court took into account in reversing the *Plessy* decision in 1954.

It is quite clear that in both 1896 and 1954 the Supreme Court was articulating a theoretical position in relation to the Fourteenth Amendment to the U.S. Constitution. Ratified in 1868 soon after the conclusion of the Civil War, this amendment was intended to ensure that the Bill of Rights extended equal protection of the law to all Americans. "No state shall make or enforce any law which shall abridge the privileges or immunities of citizens"[16] was a constitutional condition that the Supreme Court took into consideration in giving the Fourteenth Amendment its appropriate meaning in the life of the people. The Supreme Court of 1986 and that of 1954 espoused different theories on how that objective could be accomplished.

In the course of trying to implement this theory in 1958, President Dwight Eisenhower found himself in serious conflict with Governor Orvile Faubus (1910–1994) of Arkansas. His successor, John Kennedy, had a similar crisis with Governor George Wallace of Alabama in 1962. In the same way, the U.S. Congress itself has been intimately involved in formulating a theory of education in the form of legislation. The Civil Rights Act of 1964, for example, makes a provision for action against those educational institutions that indirectly or directly attempt to inhibit the concept of equality. Therefore, the responsibility for formulating the theory of education in the United States manifests itself in a collective effort. The function of theory is to address specific issues in education, especially educational objectives, the curriculum, educational administration, and problems. We now turn our attention to this exercise.

THEORY OF EDUCATIONAL OBJECTIVES

Writing on the universality of educational objectives, Mortimer Adler, the American educational thinker, outlined three broad objectives of education in any society. The first objective is to ensure personal and individual growth and development.[17] Adler sees this objective as suggesting that students must utilize the school environment to gain experiences that broaden the horizon of their understanding of themselves, values, and the character of their society. Adler adds that the educational process must prepare students "to take advantage of every opportunity for personal development that society offers."[18] The second objective is to prepare every citizen to play an appropriate role in shaping the character of his society—politically, economically, socially, and in any other constructive manner. The third objective is to prepare individuals to learn a vocation or an occupation that will enable them to earn a living. It is in the process of earning a living that individuals find their appropriate place in society. This is also how they make viable contributions to its development. Without belonging, a person's sense of self is lost and values become confused. This is true of any society, whether it is "civilized" or "primitive." It is important to remember that, from the inception of the formal education during the colonial period, theory was designed to address these objectives.

While these three objectives are important to every educational system and society, they are not the only ones that must become the focus of theory. One universal objective that Adler does not discuss is to help students function within the environment of their culture. Any education that negates the culture in which it is cast loses the purpose for which it is designed. Gennadi Yogodin, the Soviet educator, takes this line of thinking to argue, "To develop education in isolation from national culture means to regard students as people without kith and kin."[19] Yogodin continues to outline a set of educational objectives within the premises of culture to make it possible for the school to teach students to perceive the importance of mature social and cultural values.

Peter McLaren argues that formulating theory to address the process of establishing educational objectives must reflect the cultural values in which the educational process is cast. This action constitutes a search for national meaning made possible by the acquisition of knowledge and national endeavor.[20] Because of the imperatives of the twentieth century, national leaders need to understand that educational objectives that do not reflect the cultural values and national identity derail the educational process itself. It may also suggest that education has no relevance to building a national character. Racial tension in the United States—especially after the Rodney King incident in April 1992—may persuade us to accept McLaren's conclusion that education must seek to refine the cultural framework in which it is cast if national conflict is to be avoided.

In addition to relating education to national culture the United States needs to recognize other complex national problems that must be resolved and for which formulating appropriate educational objectives constitutes an essential step toward finding solutions. In this nuclear age, human problems have become far more complex than in the past, and the only viable means of finding solutions to them is through knowledge both of the conditions that influence human behavior and of human relationships. Since objectives determine the content of education, it is important to remember that formulating educational objectives is a fundamental step toward putting in place educational programs that help minimize the possibility of national conflict. These considerations are essential to the development of any nation.

In discussing theory relative to educational objectives in the United States one must keep two essential theoretical considerations in mind. The first is that schools exist for the purpose of preparing citizens to function within a social, economic, and political environment. These are the elements that sustain American democratic traditions. The second theoretical consideration is that each student must be given an opportunity to learn the essentials needed "to carry out the basic life tasks."[21] Edward Ignas concludes that practices in the American educational system are so varied that it is hard to come up with universal objectives. One must remember that the development of objectives takes a historical perspective. In this section we discuss only a few examples to show that formulating objectives of education is a critical part of responding to theory to make the educational process viable.

During the formative years of the colonial American society, schools were created to impart to students the religious and moral values they needed to function in a larger social order.[22] But as colonial America came to an end in 1776, the purpose of schools changed to suit new situations. This major political change required a corresponding change in theory. What came out of this change is that the authoritarian principles had to give way to the principle that education had a fundamental objective of preparing the individual to function in a new social, economic, and political environment. There was by the beginning of the nineteenth century a move to substitute the Bible as the cornerstone of the curriculum. This move was quite consistent with new theoretical considerations that were pertinent to secular literature, which was considered more important than the Bible.

When John Dewey argued in 1938 that, "The main objective of education is to prepare the young for future responsibility and for success in life,"[23] he was stressing the importance of the secular character of the American society as an outcome of implementing educational objectives consistent with the changing character of society. The advent of modern industrial technology during the latter part of the nineteenth century ushered in a different perspective in recognizing the need to redirect the task of formulating educational objectives based on new theory in accordance with the expectations brought about by change of social and economic conditions. Mortimer Adler seems to sum it all up when he argues, "To achieve the desired quality of democratic education,"[24] students must be trained "to earn a living in an intelligent and responsible fashion, to function as intelligent and responsible citizens and to enjoy as fully as possible all the goods that make human life as good as it can be."[25] These theoretical elements were in place to shape the direction that educational development was taking as a result of seeking to fulfill objectives.

Edward Ignas argues that the problem of articulating educational objectives in an effort to bring the country to a new level of equality of opportunity is often complicated by "attempts to balance the needs of the individual and those of society."[26] He suggests that those charged with this responsibility of formulating educational objectives must function from an operational base of articulating theory so that they eliminate the specter of failure both in their undertaking and in the educational process. Beyond this imperative, Americans must recognize that extending equality of educational opportunity to all students as an objective of education sustains the backbone of its national life. Efforts to define objectives of education for this century appear to have taken a new form. When the Committee on the Reorganization of Secondary Education enunciated seven basic objectives in 1918, it was actually enunciating its theory of education. The thinking that objectives were important to the success of education took on a powerful theoretical dimension. The chairman, Charles Eliot, approached his task with religious fervor worthy of its importance. The commission utilized theoretical elements to outline the famous objectives as: to ensure good health; to enable all students to gain a functional knowledge of the fundamental processes; to enable students to demonstrate their worth as members of the family; to train students to gain the essentials of a vocation; to demonstrate good citizenship; to teach students to understand the values of leisure time and to use it for recreative and creative purposes; and to gain an essential understanding of ethical character.[27]

Twenty years later, in 1938, to underscore the importance of these objectives, the Education Policies Commission of the National Education Association (NEA) stressed the importance of establishing educational objectives in four critical areas of education: self-realization, human understanding, socioeconomic competence, and civic or community responsibility. In 1961 NEA added a new theoretical dimension in considering these objectives when it concluded, "The purpose which runs through and strengthens all other educational purposes is the development of the ability to think."[28] Recognition of the teacher's ability to inspire students to think is a fundamental objective of education and is accentuated by the knowledge that social issues are becoming far more complex than they were in the past. Answers to critical questions are no longer sought in the context of "yes/no" settings, but within a social environment that demands a critical appraisal of all pertinent factors.

For the United States in 1973, applying moral values or principles in the context of applying the principle of choice could only be done in the context of new theoretical considerations. The U.S. Supreme Court did this in that year in *Roe v. Wade*. Changing conditions have always compounded the conditions of the environment to the extent that issues, even those pertaining to personal choice, have added enormous theoretical dimensions. This is the context that a pregnant high school girl faces as she ponders the consequences of exercising her choice—to have an abortion or not. Her decision is solely based upon theoretical considerations. In the era of freedom of choice recent developments in the country advise her that she does not need to consult her parents to carry out her choices. Therefore, the ability to think as an objective of education carries enormous practical theoretical dimensions that were not part of the educational process in the past.

The mere fact that each year an increasing number of American girls get pregnant suggests two things. The first thing is that the definition of morality has been radically changing: pregnancy outside of marriage no longer carries the social and moral stigma that it did in the past. The second thing is that American schools need a new set of objectives based on new theory, not only directed at teaching students to function in a new moral and social order, but also to impart a sense of who they are as individual human beings sufficiently trained to delineate elements of what is right and what is wrong for themselves as being synonymous with what is right and what is wrong for society. A girl who has more than one abortion has obvious problems of understanding who she is. The first thing she needs to learn is to go back to the basics of moral values for herself. This demands an understanding of clear elements of theory even in her personal life.

In a similar manner, the United States, like other countries, is facing some critical problems in the fabric of its national life. The disintegration of the traditional family has eroded many traditional values that were the basis of institutional structures. The phenomenon of the single parent family has exerted tremendous pressures on women and children. The uncontrollable surge of subcultures invariably threatens the very survival of a struggling nation. While her efforts were a gallant demonstration of her commitment to rid the country of the scourge of the drug culture, Nancy Reagan's strategy of "Just say no" was a simplistic approach to a major national problem. The problems that the United States is now facing can effectively be addressed by redefining new objectives that seek to implant in students an ability to exercise critical thinking and judgment. This is where theory becomes paramount.

The last example of the importance of formulating objectives of education based on theoretical considerations in the United Sates is that education must address the question of social justice. Although Ignas concludes that "disagreement and controversy are so common that there is little chance of any new consensus,"[29] it seems that Americans understand that social justice is a sustaining theme of their society. Since the end of the war in 1945, various national organizations have tried to apply pressure on those who have political power to do something to seek solutions to social problems. By recognizing that eliminating poverty and promoting racial integration, they believe that national issues can best be addressed by formulating a set of educational objectives based on theory and designing an educational system that may give the country a renewed sense of purpose. The plight of the homeless, a bulging and disturbing new social phenomenon, is a national problem whose solution can be found by articulating new theory. The imperative of redefining theory to address educational objectives is itself an effort to resuscitate the throb of the falling pulse of a nation that finds itself in doubt about its values and the future. The decade of prosperity in material comfort from 1980 to 1990 was not matched by corresponding values of national institutions. The demise of the American family in 1996 is a long shot from the Puritan family of 1642.

THEORY OF THE CURRICULUM

A theory has been stated that, while objectives determine the curriculum, the curriculum determines the outcome of fulfilling those objectives. In this context, the curriculum also becomes an instrument of fulfilling a larger national purpose—shaping the character of society itself. In all societies, developed or underdeveloped, Western or non-Western, the character of education largely depends on the extent to which the curriculum seeks to fulfill objectives. This reality suggests a relationship between objectives and the curriculum as an operational principle of the educational process. Writing about the imperative of theory to address the functions of the curriculum, John Dewey observed, "Finding the material for learning is only the first step. The next step is the progressive development of what is already experienced into a fuller, richer, and more organized form."[30]

But Dewey cautioned against the danger of designing a curriculum that attempts to sustain its own interests—that is, those who design it must be influenced by the balance in the interests of the nation and those of the students. Dewey offer an impressive theoretical explanation for this position saying, "Because the studies of the traditional school consisted of subject matter that was selected and arranged on the basis of the judgment of adults as to what would be useful to the young sometime in the future, the material to be learned was settled upon outside the present life experience of the learner."[31] Dewey suggests that one way of helping students sustain their interest in the educational process is assuring them that the curriculum and the related activities are designed with their best educational interests in mind.

Therefore, in designing the curriculum a nation must remain conscious of the importance of a theoretical question: How best can the curriculum serve the needs of students? The curricular structure that emerges as a result of an effort to provide an answer to this question brings to the educational process benefits that would otherwise be lost. It generates a new level of interest among students in the educational process because they begin to see themselves as its primary beneficiaries. It makes it possible to have an education that extends to all students a new sense of their individuality so essential to building diversity as an environment of building a new national character. It provides for broadly based educational programs that offer a unique opportunity for students to engage in various areas of study. It offers students an opportunity to meet the labor and manpower needs of their country. Only the curriculum that is developed from this theoretical perspective embraces the essential elements of national development.

Peter McLaren takes this line of thinking to discuss the importance of theory relative to the development of the curriculum saying, "To view the curriculum as a form of cultural politics assumes that the social, cultural, political and economic dimensions are the primary categories of understanding contemporary schooling."[32] This way of looking at education suggests that the curriculum creates a national climate in which students see themselves as active and indispensable political, social, and economic entities that the nation needs to build a foundation for the future. Once this reality becomes part of the school system, both students and the community in which they live begin to understand the curriculum not as an institutional structure created to serve the super interests of the nation, but as a sociocultural establishment with varying shades of accommodating interests that are in harmony with each other, and not on a collision course.

The question of the curriculum in the United States has always been an important one since the inception of formal education during the colonial period. An important characteristic feature of the curriculum has been the involvement of the school board in its development. In all systems of education teachers must be in the forefront of developing curriculum because they are the ones who come into direct contact with students. The basic theoretical consideration behind this thinking is that teachers know best what the learning needs of their students are, and that they can best prepare students for effective roles in society. William van Til observes that, whereas some school systems attempt to have curricular uniformity, the concept of local development is still practiced[33] because the idea of control of the curriculum by any agent other than local authorities is against American traditions.

Because education during the colonial period had two primary purposes—to enable students to function and survive in the wilderness, and to impart religious and moral values—the development of the curriculum was a result of cooperation between the church and the state. By 1690 the *New England Primer* had become one of the most widely used textbooks in elementary school.[34] That the primer combined basic rudiments of literature and religious instruction suggests the elements of the curriculum considered essential to successful education at that time. The practice that emerged during the colonial period (that the state can support education of a religious nature) was not considered a conflict between church and state because it was believed that the state could benefit from individuals educated from the standpoint of religious values.

During and after the Revolution individuals began to articulate new theory to address the curriculum. Among these was Thomas Jefferson, who tried to assess the conditions of education and attempted reforms that were needed to assure the development of the country as a sovereign and progressive nation.[35] This is why in 1779 Jefferson introduced into the Virginia legislature a "Bill for the More General Diffusion of Knowledge," and based it on three theoretical considerations. The first was that America could develop more rapidly as a democracy if education was available to as many people as possible. To make this a reality, the curriculum must be broad enough to allow for diverse interests among students. The second theoretical consideration was that state control of education was the only viable method of ensuring a broad curriculum because the federal government was likely to exercise red tape that might handicap progress. The third theoretical consideration was that the curriculum must include more courses on social and political studies than religious courses because the country was slowly becoming a secular society.[36] Today these three theoretical considerations are still in operation in American schools, but they need reform.

Benjamin Franklin shared Jefferson's articulation of theory of the curriculum and suggested a broad range of courses to give effect to it. These included mathematics, English grammar, trade courses, history, geography, literature, agriculture, Latin, and Greek. Franklin felt that because the country was going through a period of transition, it was necessary to make the curriculum as broad as possible to ensure that students were properly trained to play an effective role in society. In the same way, Noah Webster advanced his theoretical perception that schools must play a major role in shaping the building of a developing society. He argued that the only way to accomplish this objective was to make the curriculum more inclusive than it had been in the past. Webster also felt that teaching American English, not British English, was important in giving the nation a new direction. This is why in 1783 he published *A Grammatical Institute of the English Language.*

One can see that the development of the curriculum from theoretical considerations envisaged by Jefferson, Franklin, and Webster began to take on social, economic, and political dimensions that were important to the reshaping the country. Today these dimensions seem to take two forms that exert important influence on the curriculum: international events and national developments. The surprise attack of Pearl Harbor in December 1941 by Japan demanded a change in theoretical perception of the way schools thought of the curriculum in adopting to conditions imposed by the war.[37] This meant that the curriculum had to be changed because theory had to change. In the same way the launching of the Sputnik on October 4, 1957, and the shooting down the U-2 plane in 1960 created an international environment that demanded a new articulation of theory of the curriculum in the United States to address new situations. In a similar manner, the beginning of the civil rights movement in December 1955 led to the Civil Rights Act in 1957 and 1964. The curriculum has always been expected to provide the kind of education that would prepare Americans to address social problems. William van Til concluded that, confronted by angry youths and dissenting African Americans, a general dismay at crime, and a tendency to revolutionary action, the country turned to the school for much needed help.[38]

Seeking to understand the articulation of theory of the curriculum in the United States is best done from a historical perspective. The curriculum has developed on the theoretical belief that it is designed to serve the needs of students and of society in response to changes in social conditions at various stages of the history of the country. The classical curriculum that came into being as a result of the Yale Report of 1828 was considered important because education was intended to prepare an elite class who would run the country. The election of Andrew Jackson to the presidency in the same year introduced a new way of thinking that, because the country would require participation of all people to make progress, the curriculum must be designed so that it would afford all students an opportunity for education. This line of thinking was the beginning of questioning the idea of the classical curriculum and the role of the elite. New powerful theoretical dimensions were in place. As immigration got underway in the mid–nineteenth century, there was a need to articulate a new theory to address the nature of the curriculum because the education that was being envisaged for the future was going to be different from that of the past.

The declaration by President George Bush at the beginning of his administration in 1989 that he wanted to be known as an education president yielded little to substantiate his claim because he failed to articulate a clear theory that could be applied with success. His idea of a thousand points of light was good but he failed to follow it up with substance. Bush's inability to live by his own expectations to realize the aspirations of the people contributed to his defeat by Bill Clinton. As Clinton prepared to assume office in January 1993, he was acutely aware of the serious nature of the problem the country faced.

State and local education authorities, faced with enormous budgetary problems, have given up the struggle because the task is too heavy. In June 1991 the controversy between President Bush and Congress over the Civil Rights Bill, combined with the trauma that many servicemen and women were facing on their return from the Persian Gulf and with the recession, created formidable socioeconomic problems. If President Bush was not able to solve these problems, how, then, was he going to create the new global order that he said was going to result from the defeat of Iraq?

During a graduate class on December 3, 1992, J. Otto Berg, professor of adult education at Northern Arizona University, put the problems of education in the United States within the context of a search for a new theoretical approach, saying, "America faces a dilemma of choice: Either to have low levels of education and low wages and unemployment, or to have high skills and high wages brought by America being competitive in the global economic marketplace. Only then will the standard of living rise once again for a high percentage of the American population."[39]

Participating in the Clinton economic conference held in Little Rock in December 1992, John Scully, education advisor to Bush, discussed the same dilemma when he rhetorically asked, "Do we want high skills or do we want low wages? High skills and high paying jobs will come from a better school system."[40] Scully, like Berg, was advancing a new theoretical perspective that has had an impact on the development of educaion in the United States. In 1992 Scully, a Republican, was disappointed to see that President Bush ignored his suggestions to improve education. This is why he endorsed Bill Clinton for president. What both Berg and Scully were suggesting is that a strong national character can only come from an effective educational policy based on sound theoretical perspectives.

One is led to the conclusion that, while American education has served the needs of the people at various stages of its development, it is going through a major crisis that has to be resolved if the future is to be more meaningful than the past. With the recession having a serious impact on the U.S. economy in 1992, confidence in President Bush rapidly deteriorated to the extent that he lost the election to Bill Clinton. The crisis in Los Angeles in May 1992, caused by the trial and acquittal of four white police officers accused of using excessive force against Rodney King, a black motorist, accentuated the extent of the problems the United States was facing.

President Bush's pardon on December 24, 1992, of Caspar Weinberger and five other top officials in the Reagan administration involved in the Iran-Contra scandal raised new questions about his understanding of the need to restructure an emerging national character based upon an effective educational policy. In discussing its reasons for selecting Bill Clinton as its choice for man of the year for 1992, *Time* of January 4, 1993, portrayed Bush as a national leader who did not seem to understand the elements of character of the nation he was leading.[41]

The wish that Bush expressed at the beginning of his administration to be regarded as the education president became a victim of his elusive grand plan to build a new global order sustained by the military might of the United States. This is what gave *Time* reason to paint a picture of Bush leading an administration in disarray.[42] Bush's limited success in defining an educational policy to sustain the national character of the United States at a critical period in its development compounded the problems that the Reagan administration had not been able to resolve from 1981 to 1988. This is why, in 1992, as part of his election campaign, Bill Clinton put forward an impressive package recognizing the inadequacy of the educational system, saying, "The 1980s witnessed the emergence of immense education gaps between America and the world, and among our own people. Test scores went down while in general enrollment in schools went up."[43]

During an address on February 28, 1996, Richard Riley, U.S. secretary for education, put three new theoretical elements in place to suggest new approaches to education, saying:

American education must reach for a new level of excellence. Our challenges are many. Here are three of them. The first challenge is to get America reading again. Our national mathematics and science scores are up because we have invested more than ten years of hard work in that effort. Improving America's literacy rate is just as important to the nation's future economic growth as balancing the budget. I urge every family to follow the first rule of education and read to their children. Our second challenge is to give parents the power to help their children learn. Strong families make strong schools. When parents get involved in their children's education, good things start to happen. Our third challenge is to keep our schools safe, orderly, and disciplined.[44]

Riley supported these theoretical elements by saying that, in the complex economic environment, 89 percent of the jobs that are currently being created required much higher levels of literacy and knowledge of mathematics to function. He concluded that success in education, especially in the kind of the curriculum offered, was an imperative for national success.

In a similar line of thinking, Sandra Feldman, who was elected May 6, 1997, to replace the late Albert E. Shanker as president of the American Federation of Teachers, concluded, "I believe that every child can learn, and I believe that there are proven ways to ensure that every child does learn. The task before American educators today is to take what we know works in schools and spread it more widely among America's public school classrooms. What works? The answer is: orderly classrooms that are a serious environment for learning, teachers trained to teach high standards, and appropriate assistance to students who are unable to meet high standards. Our children are capable of the best, but it is up to adults around them to challenge and help them to do their best."[45] This kind of faith in the ability of students to learn should serve as a guide for those teachers like Sandra Feldman who are interested in the evolution of new theory of education to ensure the success of the educational process for all students.

THEORY OF EDUCATIONAL ADMINISTRATION

The relationship between educational objectives and the curriculum is that their operation depends on the administrative structure. In essence, the administrative structure is the vehicle that carries the educational system to its destination—national development. A good and effective educational system will need a sound theoretical base, a good set of objectives, and a carefully structured curriculum.[46] But without a properly designed administrative structure, the educational process that emanates from these educational components may still fail to help in accomplishing their intended purpose. This suggests that the success of any educational system depends on an effective system of administration.

An important theoretical question must now be asked: What does it take to have an effective system of educational administration? There are three important considerations that those charged with the responsibility for the administration of education must keep in mind. The first consideration is that they must have a clearly demonstrated understanding of three essential elements of educational theory: objectives, curriculum, and problems.[47] Without a clear knowledge of these three basic components of education, the administrative structure has little purpose because it may not be based on substantiated theory. Conversely, without an effective administrative system, seeking to give effect to these three components may be elusive, and, as a result the educational process loses its direction. Other aspects of education, such as the relationship between the school and the community, are also important, but these three seem to demand articulation of theory more than others.

The second consideration is that the educational administrative structure must be such that implementation of the curriculum must begin to show ex-

pected results by a specified time. There must be a timeline in which to expect outcomes. This will enable planners of educational programs to assess
their impact on national life and the nature of the contribution students
make after their education is completed.[48] If no tangible results are demonstrated, the failure may suggest two things. The first is that the objectives
and the curriculum are incompatible. This failure demands a fresh start in
evaluating both to see where a dysfunction lies. The second thing is that
there are substantial shortcomings in the administrative structure itself. If
this is the case, then the entire administrative structure must be reexamined
in accordance with specific guidelines.

The third consideration is that working out an implementation instrument
or plan is an essential part of an effective administrative structure. This exercise cannot be taken lightly. It demands thorough knowledge of all pertinent issues and skills in the dynamics of human interactions and the
responsibility that each segment of the educational process must assume,
such as the role of teachers and members of the community. It demands
opening effective means of communications and negates dictatorial behavior
so typical of bureaucratic machinery. Education is no place to play political
power games. In the process of developing an instrument of implementation,
it is important to keep some theoretical questions in mind, such as: Who
must be involved in the implementation process? What level of the administrative system must take part in the implementation process? Should the responsibility for educational administration be shared between the national
level and the local level?

There are three dimensions of educational administration at the federal
level—the executive branch, represented by the president; the legislative
branch or Congress; and the judiciary branch, or the courts. Although the
president can involve himself in the administrative system through executive
action, the federal courts and the Congress play the decisive role even
though the U.S. Constitution does not delegate education a federal responsibility. The Congress takes action in the form of legislation. The enactment of
the Morrill Land Grant Act in 1862, for example, made it possible to establish the U.S. Office of Education in 1867. One of this office's major functions was to administer the dissemination of information and oversee the
opening of colleges in accordance with the provisions of the Morrill Land
Grant Act.[49]

Once the legislative role was established, it became an important part of
the administrative structure. But political considerations were to play a critical role in its operations. For example, in 1945 the National Education Association (NEA) and the American Federation of Teachers (AFT) sponsored
two bills providing federal financial aid to education. After three years of debate and amendments the bills were defeated because members of Congress
felt strongly that the law would violate the principle of state's rights and responsibilities to conduct education in their own way. Moreover, they be-

lieved the federal courts might rule it unconstitutional if the bill came to them for arbitration. No one will ever know what the federal courts might have done if the bill had actually become law.

Believing that it had achieved a reasonable degree of success in responding to the critical international issues of the day, the U.S. Congress now turned its attention to seeking answers to critical national problems. The beginning of the civil rights movement in December 1955 convinced the Congress that it must do something to find an answer to the problems of educational inequality as a result of practicing racial segregation. By 1964 it had become evident that legislative action was needed to direct the course of education to meet the needs of an emerging society. That action was in the form of the Civil Rights Act of 1964. That Title IV of this law authorized federal authorities to withhold federal funds to any educational institution that practiced discrimination against any students on the basis of race shows the importance of two issues. The first issue is that federal funds were becoming increasingly important as an instrument for shaping the development of education. It was no longer possible for school districts to ignore this reality without falling out of place on the line of thinking about the role of the Congress on the administrative character of the educational process. The second issue is that the Congress wanted the country to understand that educational opportunity must be open to all students on the basis of equality and without regard to race.

The theoretical perception that equality of educational opportunity would result in equality of opportunity for economic and political development of all people was an outcome of the belief that ending poverty, especially among minority groups, was essential to national development. This was why the Congress enacted the Elementary and Secondary Education Act in 1965. Under this law the famous Head Start programs were initiated across the country to help children of deprived socioeconomic backgrounds to begin their education early to reduce the likelihood of failure in the future.[50] This legislation became a major weapon in fighting the war on poverty, the hallmark of Lyndon Johnson's presidency. The educational benefits of this legislation were felt in school districts across the country in profound ways.

Still wishing to ensure the concept of equality for all students as an operative principle of American education, Congress now turned its attention to seeking ways of ending inequality based on gender. In 1972 it passed the Higher Education Act to make sure through Title IX that, "No person in the United States shall, on the basis of sex, be excluded from participating in, be denied the benefits of, or be subjected to discrimination under any education program or activity receiving federal assistance."[51] Enactment of this legislation represented an effective response to the century-old struggle that women in the United States had launched in 1848 to achieve social equality with men. The political victory that they won in 1920 by gaining the right to vote provided a new imperative to continue their struggle.

In 1974 the federal role in promoting and protecting the concept of equal opportunity was expanded by the Buckley Amendment.[52] The amendment, part of the Education Amendment Act of 1974, required that educational institutions allow parents access to the school records of their children or they would lose the funds that came from the federal government. The reason for the Buckley Amendment was that educational institutions routinely placed materials in student's files that might later prove damaging, without either the parents or the students themselves knowing about their existence. That the Buckley Amendment gave students and their parents the right to examine these files and eliminate any inaccuracies demanded a substantial change in the manner in which educational institutions kept records on students. This revealing administrative procedure initiated by Congress at a changing stage in the administrative process had acquired a meaning that had not been understood in the past about the nature of educational administration.

The question of how to achieve equality of educational opportunity inevitably led to an examination of how schools could best achieve integration. In 1971 the Supreme Court ruled in *Swann v. Charlotte-Mecklenburg Board of Education* that busing students was a proper constitutional means of achieving equality. In reaching this decision the Supreme Court warned school districts that schools of one race in racially mixed neighborhoods must not hide under the state statute that permitted segregation.[53] Three years later, in 1974, the Supreme Court went further in ruling in *Oliver v. Michigan State Board of Education* that any school district found guilty of practicing racial discrimination must submit its plan for integration developed with the assistance of independent experts. From this decision one is led to the conclusion that the federal courts were assuming a major role in enunciation theory of the administrative system of education in the country.

In the structure of educational administration local school boards have important educational functions to fulfill. They establish a hiring policy. They determine conditions of service for teachers and administrators such as superintendents, principals, and other school officials. They set conditions of leave for teachers, including female teachers in their child-bearing years. They maintain school equipment such as school buses, buildings, equipment, school grounds, and educational facilities. They set guidelines for teachers in dealing with various aspects of student life. They establish an annual budget and a general policy. This practice dates back to colonial days. The formulation of theory relative to the local school board began to take its present form during the reform movement. As the number of women seeking employment as teachers rose, there developed a new set of theoretical considerations to control both their professional conduct and personal life.

By 1872 school boards across the country had formulated theory to develop sets of regulations to control the conduct of teachers. The following is a set of regulations developed by the Cashion School Board in the territory of Arizona:

1. Each day teachers will fill lamps and clean chimneys.

2. Each teacher will bring a bucket of water and a scuttle of coal for the day's session.

3. Make your pens carefully. You may whittle nibs to the individual taste of your pupils.

4. Male teachers may take one evening each week for courting purposes, or two evenings a week if they go to church regularly.

5. After ten hours in school the teachers may spend the remaining time reading the Bible or other good books.

6. Female teachers who marry or engage in unseemly conduct will be dismissed.

7. Every teacher should lay aside from each pay a goodly sum of his earnings for his benefit during his declining years so that he will not become a burden to society.

8. Any teacher who smokes, uses liquor in any form, frequents pool or public halls, or gets shaved in a barber shop will give good reason to suspect his worth, intention, integrity and honesty.

9. The teacher who performs his labor faithfully and without fault for five years will be given an increase of twenty-five cents per week in his pay, providing the Board of Education approves.[54]

Young women were very careful to observe these regulations because failure to do so would result in severe consequences. In February 1997 Carolyn Hardison of Arlington, Arizona, whose great-grandmother, Janie Kerr, was a teacher in Missouri in 1885, was kind enough to share with the author some of the correspondence she had with her boyfriend, Charles Wallis. One such correspondence addressed the need to respect the board of education regulations. Miss Kerr wrote:

It is a violation of the rules of school for the girls to accept the company of young gentlemen except on Sunday. I did not think of the rules when I promised you my company on Saturday evening, and as I do not want to be demerited I feel it my duty to ask you to excuse me. I would have enjoyed your company and I hope you will not think that I asked to be excused for any other reason only that I have given. Unless something happens more than I know of now, I will go to Mr. Pauliss Saturday night anyway and I would prefer your company at church on Sunday morning and at home in the afternoon. Let me know if this will be agreeable to you, for if it is not I will have to make some other arrangements as I would not like to come home alone on Sunday evening.[55]

To conclude that both Janie Kerr and Charles Wallis understood the expectations placed on them by their society is to recognize the importance of the values that they were determined to operate under in order to be effective in their endeavor. These were the values that have enabled teachers to become members of a unique professional organization.

By the beginning of the twentieth century, when it was an accepted practice for women to become teachers, articulation of theory of educational administration emphasis shifted from developing academic, intellectual, and professional skills to developing moral character and deportment as the desirable qualities that female teachers must acquire. By 1915 it was quite common for school boards to prescribe rules of conduct for female teachers different from those prescribed for male teachers. For example, the board of education in Virginia outlined the following rules for female teachers:

1. You will not marry during the term of your contract.
2. You must be home between the hours of 8:00 p.m and 6:00 a.m. unless you are attending a school function.
3. You may not loiter downtown in ice cream stores.
4. You may not travel beyond the city limits unless you have the permission of the chairman of the school board.
5. You may not ride in a carriage or automobile with any man unless he is your father or brother.
6. You may not smoke.
7. You may not dress in bright colors.
8. You may, under no circumstance, dye your hair.
9. You must wear at least two petticoats.
10. Your dress must not be any more than two inches above the ankle.
11. You must:
    (a) keep the school room clean
    (b) scrub the floor at least once a week with soap and water
    (c) clean the blackboard at least once a day
    (d) start the fire at 7:00 a.m. so that the room will be warm at 8:00 a.m.[56]

However, the female teacher of today has important responsibilities to exercise in the educational interests of her students. The absence of a national system of public examinations gives teachers both an opportunity to respond to the real educational needs of their students and the responsibility to develop skills that are essential in the exercise of her duties to the students. This practice exists in the American system of education because there is a basic theoretical assumption that the teacher knows about the needs and progress of the student more than any other person. What this shows is that the teacher plays an important role in the administrative system of education. The evolution of theory to govern this component of education suggests that the entire system of administration of education is a shared responsibility by the federal, state, and local levels. The question now is: Does this shared responsibility improve the effectiveness of the system, or does it create problems? The reader is at liberty to express some opinions.

THEORY TO ADDRESS PROBLEMS OF EDUCATION

Finally, the evolution of theory has always sought to address problems of education. To understand the problems of education in the United Sates one needs to understand their origin. When the educational reform movement initiated by Horace Mann became a reality, the central theoretical question that everyone asked was how education in the common schools would be financed. The consensus that taxation was the best form of support created a new level of controversy because, at the time, the argument that not every member of the community had children in school was a powerful argument against general taxation. Although the practice that has evolved over the years to use a property tax to support public education has been accepted, it has left a trail of controversy that has not been fully resolved to this day. Across the United Sates today communities have wrestled with this problem without finding an adequate solution.[57]

Since the proclamation of the Fourteenth Amendment to the U.S. Constitution on July 28, 1868, granting equal rights to former slaves, the United Sates has not been able to solve its racial problems. The *Plessy* decision seemed to underscore the thinking that, even though the Fourteenth Amendment explicitly stated that equal protection of the law for all people must be an operative principle of national life, the Supreme Court's interpretation of it in *Plessy* left no doubt that it was still operating under the thinking of distributive justice. When the Court tried to function by the intent of the Fourteenth Amendment in its ruling in *Brown*, it created an entirely new racial situation that had not existed before—an intensity of white opposition to the idea of racial equality. Formation of the White Citizens Council accelerated the deterioration of a situation that was taking a heavy toll on national purpose. The crisis in Little Rock in 1957 and at the University of Alabama in 1963 showed that the United Sates was entering a new phase of racial conflict. The increase in racial violence among young people, an age group that is traditionally intolerant of racism, troubles many people. An educator told the author in Florida in November 1990: "Racial unrest in the United Sates has taken a more serious twist than in the past. Young people are known for their liberal political views. It is painful to see that in the United Sates young people are in the front line of promoting racial intolerance. What are our schools doing? Any nation that fails to teach its young to understand their social responsibility spells it own demise. I am afraid that this seems to be the direction we are moving as a nation. Why can't our young people take lessons from the social movements of the 1960s?"[58]

Two problems emanated from this federal aid to education. The first problem is that the Elementary and Secondary Education Act provided for aid in special areas such as improving educational programs. Many state departments wanted financial assistance for their total budget. By limiting financial aid to specific programs, this legislation was restrictive and so limited educational expansion. By limiting the ability of local school boards to decide how federal funds should be used, this legislation also made it possible for Congress to determine educational programs. In this context, the concept of local control of education had little application beyond basic administrative systems. The second problem is that because the federal government and the state departments had conflicting priorities, a new form of conflict emerged in the educational process, a conflict that often takes political dimensions.

The inflexibility of federal financial aid to schools is a situation that has "forced school districts to cheat and deny the existence of large numbers of poor students in order to get federal money to support their general educational programs."[59] By 1972 the misuse of federal funds designated to specified educational programs had become a serious problem. In that year Eliot Richardson, who was Secretary of Health, Education, and Welfare, went before a congressional committee to testify that the provisions made by the Elementary and Secondary Education Act forced school districts to use the designated funds to meet other financial costs. Richardson then indicated that his office had recently requested eight states to return $6.3 million which they had misused and was soon to ask another fifteen states to return an additional $23 million.[60] These must have been the realities that President George Bush took into consideration in announcing his educational reform package in April 1991.

When the National Commission on Excellence in Education released its report, *A Nation at Risk: The Imperative for Educational Reform* in 1983, it sounded an alarm of crisis:

If an unfriendly foreign power had attempted to impose on America the mediocre educational performance that exists today, we might have viewed it as an act of war. As it stands, we have allowed this to happen to ourselves. We have even squandered the gains in student achievement made in the wake of the Sputnik challenge. Moreover, we have dismantled essential support systems which helped make those gains possible. We have, in effect, been committing an act of unthinking, unilateral educational disarmament. Our society and its educational institutions seem to have lost sight of the basic purpose of schooling, and of the high expectations and disciplined effort needed to attain them.[61]

There is no question that the commission was articulating its own theory to address a major national problem. Out of this alarm the full extent of the problems that American education was facing was now known. But this knowledge did not translate into a set of actions designed to find solutions. In many respects solutions to the problems that education in the United Sates is facing have not been found. The elusive nature of these problems has compounded the problems of society. Illiteracy has been increasing. Laura Cavazos, secretary of education in the Reagan administration, concluded in 1988 that there were 27 million illiterate adults in the United Sates and that the dropout rate from high school would cost the nation $240 billion over their lifetime in lost income and productivity.

Although Cavazos suggested that the $22 billion proposed in federal spending for education for fiscal year 1989 be directed toward disadvantaged students, she was not optimistic that this action constituted a workable solution. Cavazos did not address the question of the rapidly rising numbers of disadvantaged students caused by the combination of factors that included increasing poverty, unemployment, disintegration of the nuclear family, continuing racial disparity, the widespread use of illegal drugs, and, in 1991, the crisis in the Persian Gulf, which was partly responsible for the recession. Indeed, a nation at risk that the National Commission on Excellence in Education saw in 1983 had, by 1991, become a nation in crisis.

The election of Bill Clinton as president in 1992 and his reelection in 1996 generated a new enthusiasm towards the development of education. At his inauguration for the second term, Clinton indicated that education would be the main focus of his administration. His theory was very simple, saying that the United States needed to provide the young people with skills so that they could develop confidence in both themselves and in the future of the country. As part of his strategy to improve education Clinton also directed the efforts of his administration towards eliminating drugs and smoking among students. He also offered a phased-in $10,000 tax deduction for college tuition or job training.[62] This plan of action was part of Clinton's theory of building the bridge to the twenty-first century.

CONCLUSION

This book has attempted to discuss the evolution of theory of education in the United States in terms of its effect on major developments, both historical and contemporary, that have impacted education and society since 1608. It has concluded that there are four critical areas of education that the formulation of theory must address. These are objectives, curriculum, administration, and problems. What one learns from the effect of these critical components of education is that an effective education cannot develop if it does not utilize theory in addressing them. These four components are at the center of the educational process and finding solutions to them will help find solutions to other problems.The study has also identified four other critical areas of national life that the evolution of theory of education must address if it is intended to serve the purpose for which it is initiated. These are social values, the national political character, finance, and reform. Let us briefly discuss the implications that each has, not only on the educational process, but also on society itself.

IMPLICATIONS

In many respects education is the process of adjusting to social values in the same way education defines social values. It is highly sensitive to the operative social norms. Any change in society and the values of society itself must be reflected in the educational process. The education that students receive has little or no meaning if it is not related to their needs and those of society. Students who are educated to play a role in a society that operates by a different set of values are miseducated and may find it hard to adjust to its institutional functions. This study has furnished evidence to show that all the functions of education must come into play to enable students to prepare themselves fully for that role. It has also discussed evidence to suggest that the rapid pace of social change in the United States has not been fully reflected in the educational system. This is why students have found it hard to bear the social pressures that society imposes on them. It is the function of both society and the school that must ensure that students are properly educated so that they adjust to society without experiencing any difficulties.

The study has also presented evidence to show that the United States has at its disposal technological skills and financial resources to initiate continuing reform in education from the federal level to the local level. All levels of authority, as well as individuals, such as scholars, must share in the process of formulating theory. But each level encounters serious problems that inhibit its ability to contribute its best. For example, the manner in which funds are distributed, the difference in educational practices, the curriculum, the manner of promotion of students, the setting of regulations, all are carried out in a fashion that is detrimental to the coordination of efforts to serve the educational interests of students. The involvement by the courts and Congress leaves local authorities confused as to what they must do to secure adequate financial resources to operate their schools. Here the formulation of theory is desperately needed. When things go wrong, as they often do, both the federal authorities and the local authorities blame each other when they should appreciate each other. In the era of great technological development communication should facilitate the process for the benefit of the country. America, be well advised and be wise!

NOTES

1. John D. Pulliam, *History of Education in America*, 5th ed. (New York: Merrill, 1991), p. 1.

2. Yuri Azarov, *Teaching: Calling and Skills* (Moscow: Progress Press 1988), p. 30.

3. David Nasaw, *Schooled to Order: A Social History of Public Schooling in the United States* (New York: Oxford University Press, 1979), p. 29.

4. Cleveland had been defeated in 1888 by Benjamin Harrison, whom he defeated in 1892.

5. Peter McLaren, *Life in Schools: An Introduction to Critical Pedagogy* in *The Foundations of Education* (New York: Longman, 1989), p. 166.

6. Ibid.

7. Ibid., p. 167.

8. Ibid., p. 171.

9. Robert Manners, "Functionalism, Reliability, and Anthropology in Underdeveloped Areas," in *To See Ourselves: Anthropology and Modern Social Issues*, ed. Thomas Weaver (Glenview, IL: Scott, Foresman Company, 1973), p. 117.

10. Evan Mecham rescinded the holiday in 1988, the year he was impeached and removed from office. In 1990 Mecham again led a strong opposition to the King holiday. When voters in the state rejected the holiday, the National Football League rescinded its decision to have the Super Bowl game played in Arizona in 1993, costing the state millions of dollars in revenues.

11. McLaren, *Life in Schools*, p. 2.

12. John Dewey, *Experience and Education* (New York: Macmillan, 1938), p. 77.

13. Mortimer J. Adler, ed., *The Paideia Proposal: An Educational Manifesto* (New York: Collier-Macmillan Books, 1982), p. 4.

14. Edward Ignas, "The Traditions of American Education," in *Comparative Educational Systems*, ed. Edward Ignas and Raymond Corsini (Itasca, IL: F. E. Peacock, 1981), p. 12.

15. Gerald Gutek, *An Historical Introduction to American Education* (Prospect Heights, IL: Waveland Press, 1991), p. 284.

16. Pathfinder Publications, *The Constitution of the United States with the Declaration of Independence* (Boston: Pathfinder Publications, 1973), p. 34.

17. Adler, *The Paideia Proposal*, p. 15.

18. Ibid., p. 16.

19. Gennadi Yogodin, *Towards Higher Standards in Education Through Its Humanization and Democratization* (Moscow: Novosti Press, 1989), p. 17.

20. McLaren, *Life in Schools*, p. 168.

21. Ignas, "The Traditions of American Education," p. 2.

22. Ibid., p. 3.

23. Dewey, *Experience and Education*, p. 18.

24. Adler, *The Paideia Proposal*, p. 18.

25. Ibid., p. 19.

26. Ignas, "The Traditions of American Education," p. 3.

27. Ibid.

28. Ibid., p. 4.

29. Ibid., p. 3.

30. Dewey, *Experience and Education*, p. 73.

31. Ibid., p. 76.

32. McLaren, *Life in Schools*, p. 185.

33. William van Til, *Education: A Beginning* (Boston: Houghton Mifflin Company, 1974), p. 462.

34. Gutek, *An Historical Introduction to American Education*, p. 17.

35. Ibid., p. 23.

36. Ibid., p. 33.

37. Van Til, *Education: A Beginning*, p. 463.

38. Ibid., p. 464.

39. J. Otto Berg, "America Faces a Choice," lecture given to a graduate class at Northern Arizona University, December 3, 1992.

40. John Scully, "America's Choice," in *USA Today* (December 15, 1992).

41. "Bill Clinton, Man of the Year: The Torch Is Passed," *Time* (January 4, 1993), p. 21.

42. Ibid.

43. Bill Clinton, *Putting People First: A National Economic Strategy for America* (Little Rock, AR: Bill Clinton for President Committee, 1992), p. 14.

44. "Secretary Riley Defines Education Challenges," in *Community Update* (Washington, D.C.: U.S. Department of Education, No. 33, March 1996), p. 1.

45. Sandra Feldman, President, the American Federation of Teachers, response to the author, August 12, 1997.

46. George Psacharopoulos and Maureen Woodhall, *Education for Development* (New York: Oxford University Press, 1985), p. 43.

47. For a discussion of these problems see chapter 7 of Dickson A. Mungazi, *Educational Policy and National Character: Africa, Japan, the United States, and the Soviet Union* (Westport, CT: Praeger, 1993).

48. Psacharopoulos and Woodhall, *Education for Development*, p. 44.

49. Joel Spring, *American Education: An Introduction to Social and Political Aspects* (New York: Longman, 1978), p. 40.

50. Ibid., p. 140.

51. U.S. Title IX, Amendment to Higher Education Act, 1972.

52. Named after its author, Senator James Buckley, a Republican from New York.

53. Spring, *American Education*, p. 63.

54. Cashion School Board, "Rules for Teachers, 1872." The author obtained these rules on February 13, 1997, from Carolyn Hardison of Arlington, Arizona, whose great-grandmother was a teacher in the late nineteenth century.

55. Janie Kerr, a letter dated March 4, 1885, addressed to Charles Wallis. Carolyn Hardison, Arlington, Arizona, February 13, 1997.

56. Virginia Board of Education, Rules of Conduct for Female Teachers, 1915.

57. A case in point, in April 1991, local school districts in Arizona attempted to organize a discussion forum involving members of the legislature to find a formula for equitable distribution of funds to support the schools.

58. An American professor during a conversation with the author while attending the National Social Science Conference, Fort Lauderdale, Florida, November 1–3, 1990.

59. Spring, *American Education*, p. 155.

60. Ibid., p. 156.

61. National Commission on Excellence in Education, *A Nation at Risk: The Imperative for Educational Reform* (Washington, D.C.: Government Printing Office, 1941), p. 5.

62. *The Christian Science Monitor* (February 24, 1997), p. 20.

Selected Bibliography

BOOKS

Addams, Jane. *Twenty Years at Hull House.* New York: Macmillan, 1910.

Adler, Mortimer J., ed. *The Paideia Proposal: An Educational Manifesto.* New York: Collier Macmillan, 1982.

Alberty, Harold B., and Boyd H. Bode, eds. *Educational Freedom and Democracy.* New York: Appleton-Century, 1938.

Alexander, Carter. *Some Present Aspects of the Work of Teachers' Voluntary Associations in the United States.* New York: AMS Press, 1972.

Anderson, Ronald. "Japanese Education." In *Comparative Educational Systems,* edited by Edward Ignas and Raymond Corsini. Itasca, IL: F. E. Peacock, 1981.

Andrea, Robert G. *Collective Negotiations: A Guide to School Board–Teacher Relations.* Lexington, MA: D. C. Heath, Heath Lexington Books, 1970.

Arrowood, Charles F. *Thomas Jefferson and Education in a Republic.* New York: McGraw-Hill Book Company, 1930.

Axtelle, George E., and William W. Wattenberg. *Teachers for Democracy.* New York: Appleton-Century, 1940.

Azarov, Yuri. *Teaching: Calling and Skills.* Moscow: Progress Press, 1991.

Babbridge, Homes D. *Noah Webster: On Education, Selected Writings, 1783–1828.* New York: Praeger Publishers, 1967.

Bailyn, Bernard. *Education in the Forming of American Society: Needs and Opportunities for Study.* New York: Norton, 1972.

Banks, James A., and Cherry A. McGee Banks. *Multicultural Education: Issues and Perspectives.* Boston: Allyn and Bacon, 1989.

Bardolph, Richard. *The Civil Rights Record: Black Americans and the Law, 1949–1970.* New York: Thomas Crowell, 1970.

Barnard, Henry. *Normal Schools and Other Institutions, Agencies, and Means Designed for Professional Education of Teachers*. Hartford: Case, Tiffany and Company, 1851.

Barnes's Historical Series. *A Brief History of the United States*. New York: American Book Company, 1885.

Beale, Howard K. *Are American Teachers Free?* New York: Charles Scribner's Sons, 1936.

Bendiner, Robert. *The Politics of Schools: A Crisis of Self-Government*. New York: Harper and Row, 1969.

Berube, Maurice R. *Teacher Politics: The Influence of Unions*. Westport, CT: Greenwood Press, 1988.

Berube, Maurice R., and Marilyn Gittell, eds. *Confrontation at Ocean Hill–Brownsville: The New York School Strikes of 1968*. New York: Praeger, 1969.

Best, John H., ed. *Benjamin Franklin on Education*. New York: Bureau of Publications, Teachers College, Columbia University, 1962.

Bestor, Arthur E., Jr. *Educational Wastelands: Retreat from Learning in Our Public Schools*. Urbana: University of Illinois Press, 1953.

———. *Restoration of Learning: A Program for Redeeming the Unfulfilled Promise of American Education*. New York: E. P. Dutton and Company, 1959.

Binder, Frederick M. *The Age of the Common School, 1831–1865*. New York: John Wiley and Sons, 1974.

Blinderman, Abraham. *Three Early Champions of Education: Benjamin Franklin, Benjamin Rush, and Noah Webster*. Bloomington, IN: Phi Delta Kappa Educational Foundations, 1976.

Bloom, B. *Human Characteristics and Learning in School*. New York: McGraw-Hill, 1976.

Boyd, William, ed. *The Emile of Jean Jacques Rousseau: Selections*. New York: Teachers College Press, Columbia University, 1966.

Boyer, Ernest L. *High School: A Report of Secondary Education in America*. New York: Harper and Row Publishers, 1983.

Brameld, Theodore, ed. *Workers' Education in the United States*. New York: Harper and Brothers, 1941.

Braun, Robert J. *Teachers and Power: The Story of the American Federation of Teachers*. New York: Simon and Schuster, 1972.

Brickman, William F., and Stanley Leher, eds. *A Century of Higher Education: Classical Citadel to Collegiate Colossus*. New York: Society for the Advancement of Education, 1962.

Brinkmeir, Oria A. *Inside the Organization Teacher: The Relationship Between Selected Characteristics of Teachers and Their Membership in Professional Organizations*. Danville, IL: Interstate Printers and Publishers, 1967.

Brooks, Thomas R. *Toil and Trouble: A History of American Labor*. New York: Delacorte Press, 1971.

Brubacker, *John S. Henry Barnard on Education*. New York: McGraw-Hill Book Company, 1931.

Bruner, Jerome S. *The Process of Education*. Cambridge, MA: Harvard University Press, 1960.

Bunzel, John H. *Challenge to American Schools. The Case for Standards and Values*. New York: Oxford University Press, 1985.

Callahan, Raymond E. *Education and the Cult of Efficiency*. Chicago: University of Chicago Press, 1962.

Campbell, Ronald F. *The Organization and Control of American Schools*. Columbus, OH: Charles E. Merrill, 1965.

Campbell, Ronald F., and Donald Layton. *Policy Making for American Education*. Chicago: University of Chicago Press, 1969.

Carlton, Patrick W., and Harold I. Goodwin. *The Collective Dilemma: Negotiations in Education*. Worthington, OH: Charles A. Jones, 1969.

Carter, Barbara. *Pickets, Parents and Power: The Story Behind the New York City Teachers' Strike*. New York: Citation Press, 1971.

Carter, James G. *Essays upon Popular Education*. Boston: Bowles and Dearborn, 1828.

Cash, Wilbur Joseph. *The Mind of the South*. New York: Alfred A. Knopf, 1941.

Chamberlain, Leo M., and Leslie W. Kindred. *The Teacher and School Organization*. Englewood Cliffs, NJ: Prentice-Hall, 1958.

Childs, John L., and George S. Counts. *America, Russia and Communist Party in the Post–war World*. New York: John Day, 1943.

Clinton, Bill. *Putting People First: A National Economic Strategy for America*. Little Rock, AR: Bill Clinton for President Committee, 1992.

Cohen, Sheldon S. *History of Colonial Education: 1607–1776*. New York: John Wiley and Sons, 1974.

Cole, Stephen. *The Unionization of Teachers: A Case Study of the UFT*. New York: Praeger, 1969.

Coleman, J. S. *Equality of Educational Opportunity*. Washington, DC: U.S. Office of Education, 1966.

Conant, James B. *The Education of American Teachers*. New York: McGraw-Hill Book Company, 1963.

———. *The Revolutionary Transformation of the American High School*. Cambridge, MA: Harvard University Press, 1959.

———. *Slums and Schools*. New York: McGraw-Hill Book Company, 1961.

Counts, George. *Dare Build a New School Order*. New York: John Day Company, 1932.

———. *School and Society in Chicago*. New York: Harcourt Brace, 1928.

———. *Secondary Education and Industrialism*. Cambridge, MA: Harvard University Press, 1929.

———. *The Selective Character of American Secondary Education*. Chicago: University of Chicago Press, 1922.

———. *Social Foundations of Education*. New York: Charles Scribner's Sons, 1934.

Cremin, Lawrence. *The American Common School*. New York: Teachers College Press, Columbia University, 1951.

———. *American Education: The Colonial Experience, 1607–1783*. New York: Harper and Row, 1970

———. *The Republic and the School: Horace Mann on the Education of Free Man*. New York: Bureau of Publications, Teachers College Press, Columbia University, 1957.

———. *The Transformation of the School: Progressivism in American Education, 1876–1957*. New York: Alfred A. Knopf, 1961.

Cruse, Harold. *Plural but Equal: A Critical Study of Blacks and Minorities and America's Plural Society*. New York: William Morrow, 1987.

———. *The Struggle for Social Change in Southern Africa: Visions of Liberty.* New York: Taylor and Francis, 1989.

———. *Where He Stands: Albert Shanker of the American Federation of Teachers.* Westport, CT: Praeger, 1995.

Murphy, Marjorie. *Blackboard Unions: The AFT and the NEA, 1900–1980.* Ithaca, NY: Cornell University Press, 1990.

Myrdal, Gunnar. *An American Dilemma: The Negro Problem and Modern Democracy.* London: Harper and Brothers Publishers, 1944.

Nasaw, David. *Schooled to Order: A Social History of Public Schooling in the United States.* New York: Oxford University Press, 1979.

Nelson, Jack L., Kenneth Carlson, and Stuart B. Palonsky. *Critical Issues in Education: A Dialectic Approach.* New York: McGraw-Hill, 1990.

Newell, Barbara W. *Chicago and the Labor Movement: Metropolitan Unionism in the 1930s.* Urbana: University of Illinois Press, 1961.

Noll, James W. *Taking Sides: Clashing Views on Controversial Educational Issues.* Guilford, CT: Dashkin Publishing Group, 1983.

Ozman, Howard A., and Samuel M. Craver. *Philosophical Foundations of Education.* Toronto: Merrill, 1986.

Page, David P. *Theory and Practice of Teaching or the Motives and Methods of Good School-Keeping.* New York: A. S. Barnes and Company, 1885.

Perkinson, Henry. *The Imperfect Panacea: American Faith in Education.* New York: Random House, 1979.

Perry, Charles R., and Wesley A. Widman. *The Impact of Negotiations in Public Education: The Evidence from the Schools.* Worthington, OH: Charles A. Jones, 1970.

Ploski, H. A., and R. C. Brown. *The Negro Almanac.* New York: Belleweather Publishing Corporation, 1967.

Potter, Robert E. *The Stream of American Education.* New York: American Book Company, 1967.

Psacharopoulos, George, and Maureen Woodhall. *Education for Development.* New York: Oxford University Press, 1985.

Pulliam, John D. *History of Education in America.* 5th ed. New York: Merrill, 1991.

Pulliam, John D., and James van Patten. *History of Education in America.* 6th ed. Englewood Cliffs, NJ: Merrill, 1995.

Ravitch, Diane. *The Troubled Crusade: American Education, 1945–1980.* New York: Basic Books, 1983.

Riche, John Martin. *Innovations in Education: Reformers and Their Critics.* Boston: Allyn and Bacon, 1988.

Rippa, S. Alexander. *Education in a Free Society: An American History.* 6th ed. White Plains, NY: Longman, 1988.

Robinson, Allen W. *A Critical Evaluation of the American Federation of Teachers.* Chicago: American Federation of Teachers, 1934.

Roche, John F. *The Colonial Colleges in the War for American Independence.* Millwood, NY: Associated Faculty Press, 1986.

Rouceck, J. S., and T. Kierman. *The Negro Impact on Western Civilization.* New York: Philosophical Library, 1970.

Seeley, Levi. *History of Education.* New York: American Book Company, 1899.

Shane, H. G. *Curriculum Change: Toward the 21st Century*. Washington, DC: National Education Association, 1977.

Shields, James, and Colin Greer. *Foundations of Education: Dissenting Views*. New York: Wiley, 1974.

Silver, Harold. *Robert Owen on Education*. New York: Cambridge University Press, 1960.

Sizer, Theodore R. *The Age of Academies*. New York: Bureau of Publications, Teachers College, 1962.

———. *Horace's Compromise: The Dilemma of the American High School*. Boston: Houghton Mifflin Company, 1984.

Sloan, Douglas. *The Scottish Enlightenment and the American College Ideal*. New York: Teachers College Press, 1971.

Spring, Joel. *American Education: An Introduction to Social and Political Aspects*. New York: Longman, 1978.

———. *The American School, 1642–1985*. White Plains, NY: Longman, 1986.

———. *Conflict of Interest: The Politics of American Education*. New York: Longman, 1993.

———. *Deculturalization and the Struggle for Equality: A Brief History of Education of Dominated Culture in the United States*. New York: McGraw-Hill, 1997.

———. *Wheels in the Head: Educational Philosophies of Authority, Freedom, and Culture from Socrates to Paulo Freire*. New York: McGraw-Hill, 1994.

Stinnett, Timothy M. *Turmoil in Teaching: A History of the Organizational Struggle for America's Teachers*. New York: Macmillan, 1968.

Strouse, Joan H. *Exploring Themes of Social Justice in Education: Readings in Social Foundations*. New York: Merrill, 1997.

Taft, Phillip. *United They Teach: The Story of the United Federation of Teachers*. Los Angeles: Nash Publishing, 1974.

Talbott, Strobe, Edward Crankshaw, and Jerrald Schecter. *Khrushchev Remembers: The Last Testament*. Boston: Little, Brown and Company, 1974.

Tewksbury, Donald G. *The Founding of American Colleges and Universities before the Civil War*. New York: Bureau of Publications, Teachers College, Columbia University, 1932.

Thursfield, Richard E. *Henry Barnard's American Journal of Education*. Baltimore: Johns Hopkins University Press, 1945.

Thwing, Charles F. *A History of Higher Education in America*. New York: Appleton, 1906.

Tiedt, Sidney W. *The Role of the Federal Government in Education*. New York: Oxford University Press, 1966.

Traper, Andrew. *A Teaching Profession: An Address before the Massachusetts State Teachers Association*. Albany, NY: Weed, Parsons, and Company, 1890.

Tussman, J., ed. *The Supreme Court on Racial Discrimination*. New York: Oxford University Press, 1963.

Ulich, Robert, ed. *Education and the Idea of Mankind*. Chicago: University of Chicago Press, 1964.

van Til, William. *Education: A Beginning*. Boston: Houghton Mifflin Company, 1974.

Warren, Donald, ed. *American Teachers: Histories of a Profession at Work*. New York: Macmillan, 1989.

Washington, Booker T. *Up From Slavery*. New York: Doubleday, 1916.
————. *Working with the Hands*. New York: Doubleday, Page and Company, 1902.
Wattenberg, William W. *On the Educational Front: The Reactions of Teachers' Associations in New York and Chicago*. New York: Columbia University Press, 1936.
Webster, S. W. *The Education of Black Americans*. Berkeley: University of California Press, 1974.
White, Anne T. *George Washington Carver: Boy Scientist*. New York: Randolph House, 1954.
Whitfield, Stephen J. *Scott Nearing: Apostle of American Radicalism*. New York: Columbia University Press, 1974.
Woodring, Paul. *Introduction to American Education*. New York: Harcourt, Brace, 1965.
————. *The Persistent Problems of Education*. Bloomington, IN: Phi Delta Kappan, 1983.
Woody, Thomas. *Educational Views of Benjamin Franklin*. New York: McGraw-Hill Book Company, 1931.
Wright, Edmund. *Franklin of Philadelphia*. Cambridge, MA: Harvard University Press, 1988.
Yogodin, Gennadi. *Towards Higher Standards in Education Through Its Humanization and Democratization*. Moscow: Novosti Press, 1989.

GOVERNMENT MATERIALS

Andrews, Benjamin F. *The Land Grant of 1862 and Land Grant Colleges*. Washington, DC: U.S. Government Printing Office, 1918.
Bayh, B. *Challenge for the Third Century: Education in a Safe Environment: Final Report on the Nature and Presentation of School Violence and Vandalism*. Washington, DC: U.S. Government Printing Office, 1977.
Bell, T. H. *Report by the Secretary on the Regional Fortunes on Excellence in Education*. Washington, DC: U.S. Department of Education, 1983.
Brown v. Board of Education of Topeka, 347 U.S. 483, 1954.
Brunner, Henry S. *Land Grant Colleges and Universities, 1862–1962*. Washington, DC: U.S. Government Printing Office, 1962.
Bush, George. *America 2000: An Education Strategy*. Washington, DC: U.S. Department of Education, 1991.
Chicago Division of Illinois Education Association v. the Board of Education of the City of Chicago, 222 NE. 2nd 43 (1967).
City Board of Education, Chicago. *Annual Report*, 1903.
City Board of Education, Chicago. *School Records*, 1902.
Coffman, Lotus D. Address to the NEA, February 1920. NEA Files: Washington, DC.
Department of the Interior. *Biennial Survey of Education*, 1920–24, vol. 2, no. 44. Washington, DC: U.S. Government Printing Office, 1925.
Economic Opportunity Act. U.S. Public Law 88-482. Washington, DC: U.S. Government Printing Office, 1964.
Finot v. Pasadena City Board of Education, 58 Cal. 520 (1967).
La Fleure v. Cleveland Board of Education. Washington (1974).

National Commission on Excellence in Education. *A Nation at Risk*. Washington, DC: U.S. Department of Education, 1983.

National Commission on Excellence in Education. *A Nation at Risk: The Imperative for Educational Reform*. Washington, DC: Government Printing Office, 1983.

National Defense Education Act. U.S. Public Law 85-864, 85th Congress. Washington, DC: U.S. Government Printing Office, 1958.

NEA. "NEA and AFT Continue Merger Talks" (minutes). Washington, DC, November 4, 1993.

———. "Teachers Salaries and Cost of Living, 1918." NEA Files, Washington, DC.

Perry v. Sindermann, 408, U.S. 593 (1972).

Roosevelt, Franklin D. *State of the Union Message*. Washington, DC: U.S. Government Printing Office, 1941.

Roosevelt, Franklin D., and Winston Churchill. *The Atlantic Charter*. Washington, DC: U.S. Government Printing Office, 1941.

Roth v. Board of Regents of California, 408 U.S. 564 (1972).

State of New York. *Report and Recommendations of the Joint Legislative Committee Investigating Seditious Activities*, Legislative Document no. 52 (Clayton R. Lusk, chairman). Albany: Government Printer, 1920.

Tinker v. Des Moines Independent School District, U.S. Supreme Court 393 U.S. 503 (1969).

U.S. Department of Education. "Secretary Riley Defines Education Challenges." In *Community Update*. Washington, DC, March 1996.

U.S. Senate. Committee on Labor and Public Welfare. *Enactment by the 89th Congress Concerning Education and Training*. Washington, DC: U.S. Government Printing Office, 1966.

U.S. Senate. *The Challenge in the Third Century: Education in a Safe Environment* (Birch Bayh, chairman). Washington, DC: U.S. Government Printing Office, 1977.

Virginia Board of Education. Rules of Conduct for Female Teachers. Williamsburg, VA, 1902.

MATERIALS ON TEACHER ORGANIZATIONS

Adler, Mortimer, to Albert Shanker, AFT Files, Walter Reuther Archives of Labor and Urban Affairs, Wayne State University, Detroit, MI, May 22, 1986.

Aexlrod, Donald. "How 'Red' Is the Teacher's Union? Fellow Travelers Lose Control But Liberalism Remains Unshaken." *Common Sense* (February 1940).

"Albert Shanker, President of the American Federation of Teachers." October 1990. AFT Files, Washington DC.

"Annual Convention Proceedings." 1937. AFT Files, Washington, DC.

The AFT. "Annual Convention Proceedings, Chicago." 1939. AFT Files, Washington, DC.

———. "The Big Question for 1976: More Vetoes or a Pro-education President." An editorial. *The American Teacher* (April 1976): 52.

———. "Carter on Education." *The American Teacher* (October 1976).

———. "Human Rights and Community Relations." *The American Teacher* (September 1975): 54.

————. Ida Fursman's CTF Collection. AFT Files, Walter Reuther Archives of Labor and Urban Affairs, Wayne State University, Detroit, MI.

————. Linville Collection. AFT Files, Walter Reuther Archives of Labor and Urban Affairs, Wayne State University, Detroit, MI.

————. "The Need for the AFT to Be Inclusive." *The American Teacher* 23 (March 1939): 5–7.

————. "Profile of Carl Megel." *The American Teacher* (February 1977): 52.

————. "Quality Educational Standards in Teaching" (abstract of a conference held in Washington, DC), July 9, 1993.

————. "Report of the Resolutions Committee of the Twenty-third Annual Convention of the AFT." August 1939. AFT Files, Washington, DC.

————. "Shanker on Student Seminar." *The American Teacher* (March 1977): 53.

————. "Study of Teachers, Pay. The United States Compared With Other Countries." July 1993. AFT Files, Washington, DC.

————. "Teacher Wins $40,000 Award for Fighting Firing Since 1968." *The American Teacher* (June 1975): 6.

————. "Tribute to Margaret A. Haley and Catherine Goggin." *The American Teacher* (November 1975): 58.

————. Twelfth Annual Convention held in Chicago, June 1928. AFT Files. Washington, DC.

Alexander, Lamar. "A Message from the U.S. Secretary of Education." Introduction to George Bush, *America 2000: An Education Strategy*. Washington, DC: U.S. Government Printing Office, 1992.

Arts and Entertainment. *Five Rings under the Swastika: Olympic Games in Berlin, 1936* (a documentary film), 1988.

Atkin, Myron J. Letter to Albert Shanker, March 9, 1987, AFT Files, Washington, DC.

Baltimore Teachers Union. "Resolution on Denial of Academic and Political Rights to Teachers." August 10, 1935. AFT Files, Walter Reuther Archives of Labor and Urban Affairs, Wayne State University, Detroit, MI.

————. "Resolution on Tenure Rights for Teachers." August 1935. AFT Files, Walter Reuther Archives of Labor and Urban Affairs, Wayne State University, Detroit, MI.

————. "Resolution on the Position of Teachers." August 10, 1935. AFT Files, Walter Reuther Archives of Labor and Urban Affairs, Wayne State University, Detroit, MI.

Barker, Mary C. "Address of President Mary C. Barker." *The American Teacher* (October 1930).

————. "Address of the President." *The American Teacher* (September 1927).

————. "The Atlanta Public School Teachers Association." *The American Teacher* (March 1928).

————. "Federation of Teachers Issues Program of Action." *American Federation of Teachers Monthly Bulletin* 5 (September 1925): 1.

————. Letter to Florence Hanson, June 23, 1929. The AFT Files, Walter Reuther Archives of Labor, Wayne State University, Detroit, MI.

————. "Presidential Address." June 26, 1928. The AFT Files, Walter Reuther Archives of Labor, Wayne State University, Detroit, MI.

————. "Presidential Address," July 2, 1929. AFT Files, Walter Reuther Archives of Labor and Urban Affairs, Wayne State University, Detroit, MI.

————. "Presidential Address," June 30, 1930. AFT Files, Walter Reuther Archives of Labor and Urban Affairs, Wayne State University, Detroit, MI.

————. "President's Address." *The American Teacher* (September 1926).

————. "President's Address to the Thirteenth Convention of the American Federation of Teachers." *The American Teacher* (October 1929).

Botel, Morten. Letter to Albert Shanker, March 19, 1986. AFT Files, Walter Reuther Archives of Labor and Urban Affairs, Wayne State University, Detroit, MI.

Bowen, John J. "Better Working Conditions, Better Education." *The American Teacher* (February 1961).

Callahan, Ray. Letter to Albert Shanker, July 14, 1985. AFT Files, Washington, DC.

"Chicago Teachers Federation and the Board of Education." *School and Society* 5 (May 5, 1917): 5.

Chicago Teachers Federation. "Committee on Commercial Education of the New York Chamber of Commerce." *The American Teacher*, no. 6. (June 1916).

————. "The Dismissal of Chicago Teachers." *School and Society* 4, no. 94 (July 15, 1916).

Clinton, Bill. *Goals 2000: Educate America*. Washington, DC: U.S. Government Printing Office, 1994.

Cogen, Charles. "Education in the United States Today." 1967. AFT Files, Washington, DC.

Collette, Earnest B. Letter to Freeland B. Stecker, June 19, 1921. AFT Files, Washington, DC.

Douglas, Paul. "Why I Joined the AFT: Brief Statements by Individuals." 1957. AFT Files, Washington, DC.

"Early Childhood Education: A National Program." December 17, 1974. AFT Files, Washington, DC.

"Early Childhood Education: A National Program." October 20, 1976. AFT Files, Washington, DC.

Feldman, Sandra. "The Marvelous Revolutionist." An editorial. *The American Teacher* 6, no. 6 (June 1917).

————. Response to the author, August 12, 1997.

————. "Through the Fluoroscope." An editorial. *The American Teacher* 6, no. 6 (June 1917).

Fiske, Edward B. "Where He Stands: Profile of Albert Shanker, 1980." AFT Files, Washington, DC.

Goggin, Catherine. Letter to Cynthia Leet, October 15, 1905. AFT Files, Washington, DC.

Goldberg, Kalman. Letter to Albert Shanker, April 1, 1986. AFT Files, Walter Reuther Archives of Labor and Urban Affairs, Wayne State University, Detroit, MI.

Haley, Margaret A. Letter to Florence C. Hanson, May 23, 1934. AFT Files, Walter Reuther Archives of Labor and Urban Affairs, Wayne State University, Detroit, MI.

————. "Tribute to Catherine Goggin." January 1916. AFT Files, Washington, DC.

Hanson, Florence C. Letter to Mary Barker. June 19, 1929. AFT Files, Washington, DC.

Linville, Henry R. Letter to Members of the AFT Executive Council, April 23, 1934. AFT Files, Walter Reuther Archives of Labor and Urban Affairs, Wayne State University, Detroit, MI.

Loeb, Jacob. "Stenographic Report: the Chicago Teachers Federation." Presented to the Chicago Board of Education, February 2, 1917. AFT Files, Washington, DC.

McElroy, Edward J. Letter to Albert Shanker, January 8, 1987. AFT Files, Washington, DC.

Meyers, Ellen. Letter to Albert Shanker, March 11, 1986. AFT Files, Walter Reuther Archives of Labor and Urban Affairs, Wayne State University, Detroit, MI.

The New York Teachers Union. "Shanker Meets the Press." *The American Teacher* (September 1974): 51.

———. "Shanker Urges Affirmative Action through Better Training and More Jobs." in *The American Teacher* (October 1974): 51.

———. "Statement on Collective Bargaining." April 12, 1962. AFT Files, Washington, DC.

Newman, Edwin. "Meet the Press." April 15, 1974. AFT Files, Washington, DC.

Selden, David. Memo to Albert Shanker, January 19, 1967. AFT Files, Washington, DC.

———. "Reconstructing the AFT Executive Council." Memo to the Constitutional Amendment Committee of the AFT, January 17, 1967. AFT Files, Washington, DC.

Smith, William D. "Teaching: Not Just a Job, But a Profession." Draft article sent to Albert Shanker with letter dated March 11, 1986. AFT Files, Washington, DC.

Stecker, Freeland G. Letter to Earnest B. Collette, June 17, 1921. AFT Files, Washington, DC.

———. Letter to Florine E. Francis, president of the Gary, Indiana, Teachers Federation, December 11, 1924. AFT Files, Washington, DC.

Wayne, Edward A. Letter to Albert Shanker, January 16, 1986. AFT Files, Washington, DC.

NEWSPAPERS AND PERIODICALS

"Bill Clinton, Man of the Year: The Torch Is Passed." *Time*, January 4, 1993.

Bernstein, Harry. "No Backing for Reagan: Shanker Says." *The American Teacher* (July 6, 1983).

———. "Teacher Union Leader Assails Reagan Stand." *The American Teacher* (July 5, 1983).

Bloom, Arnold M. "A More Militant Profession." *American School and University* (October 1964).

Boyer, Ernest. "On Shanker." *USA Today* (January 9, 1990).

Bremfoerder, Alice. "Toledo Wins Full Restoration." *The American Teacher* (January 1943).

Brewer, John M. "The Question of Unions in the Teachers' Profession." *School and Society* (January 14, 1922).

Bruce, William C. "An Illegal Strike." *American School Board Journal* (June 1962).

Byrnes, Mary. "Teacher Tenure: Report of the Permanent Committee to the A.F.T. 1929 Convention." *The American Teacher* (December 1929).

Callis, H. A. "The Negro Teacher and the AFT." *Journal of Negro Education* (April 1937).

Capen, Samuel P. "The Teaching Profession and Labor Unions." *Journal of General Education* (July 1947).

Carr, William G. "Response to the AFT Memo." 1962. NEA Files, Washington, DC.

———. "The Education of William G. Carr." 1962. NEA Files, Washington, DC.

Chambers, M. M. "Teachers' Union and the Law." *National Schools* (November 1938).

Chenery, William L. "Adulterated Education." *The New Republic* (October 23, 1975).

Christian Science Monitor. "Statistics for Teacher Professionalism," December 9, 1985.

Clark, C. B. "Why Educational Technology Is Failing." *Educational Technology* (1979).

Clohesy, Agnes B. "Some Objectives of the Elementary Teachers Union." *The American Teacher* (May 1928).

Coaldigger, Adam. "What the American Federation of Teachers Is Doing and Attempting to Do." *The American Teacher* (September 1929).

———. "Teachers' Associations." *M.S.T.A. Quarterly Review* (March 1920).

Cook, Carla. "Annual Conference of Teachers in Workers' Education." *The American Teacher* (May 1931).

Cook, William A. "Rise and Significance of the American Federation of Teachers." *Elementary School Journal* (February 1921).

Corey, Arthur M. "Strikes or Sanctions?" *NEA Journal* (October 1962).

Counts, George. "Communists in the AFT." *New York Times* (December 15, 1939).

———. "Farewell Address." *The American Teacher* (October 1942).

———. "Is Our Union Controlled by Communists?" *The American Teacher* (December 1939).

———. "The Teacher's Responsibilities." *The American Teacher* (October 1939).

———. "Dare Progressive Education Be Progressive." *Progressive Education* (April 1932).

Dawson, George G. "Doctoral Studies on the Relationship between the Labor Movement and Public Education." *Journal of Educational Sociology* (February 1961).

Davis, Jerome. "America's Educational Retreat." *Christian Century* (July 1937).

DeLacy, Hugh. "Retreat to the Mountain." *Social Frontier* (March 1937).

Dewey, John. "The Bearings of Pragmatism upon Education." *Progressive Journal of Education* (December 1, 1908).

Diamant, Gertrude. "The Teachers' Union." *The American Mercury* (September 1934).

Dorr, Rheta Childe. "What's the Matter with the Public Schools?" *Delineator* (January 1909).

Elam, Stanley M. "NEA-AFT Merger—And Related Matters." *Phi Delta Kappan* (February 1966).

Elsila, David. "AFT Helps Fill a Gap for South's Educationally Starved." *The American Teacher* (September 1966).

Engdahl, J. L. "Chicago Teachers' Federation." *The American Teacher* (October 4, 1915).

Fisher, Lyman B. "Buffalo Industrial Teachers' Association; Local, 39." *The American Teacher* (February 1931).

Fordyce, Wellington G. "The American Federation of Teachers—Its History and Organization." *American School Board Journal* (June 1946).

Frank, Glenn. "Should Teachers Unionize?" *Century Magazine* (February 1921).

Frayne, Hugh. "Public School Teachers in Affiliation with the American Federation of Labor." *The American Teacher* (February 1916).

Frohlich, May T. "New Orleans Teachers Organize." *The American Teacher* (April 1919).

Fuller, Edward H. "Educational Associations and Organizations in the United States." *Educational Review* (April 1918).

Furdycee, Wellington G. "The Historical Background of American Teacher Union." *American School Board Journal* (May 1946).

Fursman, Ida L. M. "Freedom, Ignorance, and Poverty." *The American Teacher* (October 1916).

Gaines, W. W. "The Atlanta Public School Teachers Association and the Board of Education." *The American Teacher* (March 12, 1928).

Gilman, Charlotte Perkins. "Education and Social Progress." *The American Teacher* (December 1912).

Glassberg, Benjamin. "The Organization of Teachers in the United States." *Dial* (September 20, 1919).

Gogen, Charles. "Blueprint for Democracy in Teacher Bargaining." *The American Teacher* (September 15, 1965).

———. "Inaugural Address." *Chicago Teacher and School Board Journal* (June 1899).

Gompers, Samuel. "The American School and the Working Man." *Addresses and Proceedings of the National Education Association* (July 1916).

Gregg, Russell T., and Roland A. Koyen. "Teacher Association, Organization, and Unions." *Review of Educational Research* (June 1949).

Haley, Margaret A. "Why Teachers Should Organize." *Addresses and Proceedings of the National Education Association*. August 1904. NEA, Washington, DC.

Hall, G. Stanley. "The American Federation of Teachers and Strikes." *School and Society* (January 8, 1927).

———. "Certain Degenerative Tendencies Among Teachers." *Pedagogical Seminary* (December 1905).

Hard, William. "Chicago's Five Maiden Aunts." *American Magazine* (September 1906).

Healy, Robert. "Tribute to Carl Megel." *The American Teacher* (February 1977).

Hibbard, Walter H. "Courage and Co-Operation: Providence, R.I., Local 197." *The American Teacher* (January 13, 1929).

Jackman, Wilbur S. "Teachers' Federation and Labor Unionism." *Elementary School Teacher* (March 1905).

Jones, Jerome. "The Relation of the Atlanta Public School Teachers Association to Organized Labor." *The American Teacher* (March 12, 1928).

Kelly, Florence, et al. "A Symposium on Teachers' Unions." *The American Teacher* (February 1919).

Kennedy, John C. "Labor Unions and the Schools." *The American Teacher* (October 1915).

Kerchen, J. L. "Mutual Aid of American Federation of Teachers and Workers' Education." *The American Teacher* (June 1927).

Kimball, Hattie. "Federation of Teachers." *Journal of Education* (September 1919).

Lefkowitz, Abraham. "Affiliation with Labor." *The American Teacher* (January 1928).

———. "Letting the Professor." *Survey* (May 1919).

————. "The Teachers' Union: Past, Present, Future." *The American Teacher* (June 1917).

Lieberman, Myron. "Are Teachers Underpaid?" *The Public Interests* (Summer 1986).

Linville, Henry R. "Plans for the Development of the Teachers Union." *The American Teacher* (April 1919).

————. "Program of Action of the Teachers' Union of New York City for the Year 1921–1922." *School and Society* (October 22, 1921).

————. "Through the Fluoroscope." *The American Teacher* (June 1917).

Little, Mary V., and Elizabeth E. Dix. "Present and Future Objectives of Local No. 52." *The American Teacher* (March 1, 1928).

Lloyd, Ralph. "New York Teachers Don't Want War with the NEA." *The American Teacher* (April 1975).

Loeb, Max. "The Radical Movement in Education." *Survey* (December 1916).

————. "The Teacher and the Union." *The American Teacher* (February 1917).

Lovett, John L. "Fighting for Chicago Public Schools." *Chamberlain's* (June 1917).

Lowry, Raymond F. "United for Democracy in Education and the Nation." *The American Teacher* (September-October 1935).

MacKenzie, Stewart. "Teachers' Strikes, a Professional Disgrace." *Nation's Schools* (July 1947).

"The Maid of Chicago." *Journal of Education* (August 15, 1901).

Mayer, Milton S. "When Teachers Strike: Chicago Learns Another Lesson." *Forum and Century* (August 1974).

Mayman, J. Edward. "Business and Education." *The American Teacher* (June 1917).

McAndrew, William. "The Control of the Teacher's Job." *The American Teacher* (September 1916).

McCoy, W. T. "What We Have Accomplished." *The American Teacher* (June 1919).

Meany, George. "For a People's Congress: Now More than Ever." *The American Teacher* (September 1974).

Megel, Carl J., et al. "Economic Conditions for Teachers." *The American Teacher* (October 1952).

————. "Goals of the American Federation of Teachers: A Symposium by Executive Council Members Sums Up Our Objectives for Teachers of America." *The American Teacher* (April 4, 1956).

————. "The 93rd Congress: An AFT Report Card." *The American Teacher* (September 1974).

"Milk Drivers and Professors." *Literary Digest* (July 19, 1919).

Miller, Frederick. "Teachers' Unions at Work." *The American Teacher* (February 1916).

————. "What a Teacher's Union is Not." *The American Teacher* (April 1916).

Milwaukee Evening Wisconsian, December 30, 1915.

Minton, Bruce. "The Plot against the Teachers." *New Masses* (November 12, 1940).

"Miss Margaret A. Haley." *Current Literature* (June 1904).

Morrison, Benjamin. "The Cleveland School Board and the Teachers Union." *The American Teacher* (September 1914).

Mortimer, Florence C. "The Value of Labor Unions." *The American Teacher* (December 1919).

Myers, C. E. "Should Teachers' Organizations Affiliate with the American Federation of Labor?" *School and Society* (November 22, 1919).

Nearing, Scott, "The New Education." *The American Teacher* (January 1916).

The New Republic. "Albert Shanker on Social Integration Through Educational Reform," June 24, 1985.

New York Times. "The AFL-CIO and Shanker," February 16, 1976.

———. "Bilingual Education," November 5–6, 1974.

———. "Inauguration of Jimmy Carter and Shanker," December 6, 1976.

———. "New York City Board of Education and Shanker," March 24, 1976.

———. "Shanker on Equal Educational Opportunity," January 19, 1978.

———. "Shanker on Grading Students," November 20, 1977.

———. "Shanker on Reagan's Policy," September 27, 1982.

———. "Shanker on Special Education," February 3, 1980.

———. "Shanker and the Position of Teachers," January 5, 1979.

———. "The Rise of Albert Shanker," January 15, September 14, 1975.

Noah, Timothy. "The Fiery Unionist as Educational Leader: Albert Shanker." *The New Republic* (June 24, 1993).

O'Hanlon, John M. "Why Organized Labor Welcomes the Teachers." *The American Teacher* (December 1928).

O'Hare, Kate Richards. "Who Said Jurisdiction?" *The American Teacher* (October 13, 1928).

O'Reilly, Mary. "What Organization of the Teachers Means to Labor." *Life and Labor* (November 1915).

Overstreet, Harry A., and Davis Snedden. "Should Teachers Affiliate with Organized Labor?" *Survey* (March 13, 1920).

Peirce, Neal. "Obstacles to Change in Schools." *The Arizona Republic* (October 16, 1989).

Persons, Warren M. "The Chicago Teachers Federation." *Commons* (August 1905).

Peterson, Ester, et al. "A Symposium on Organization." *The American Teacher* (March-April 1937).

Pifer, Alan. "When Fashionable Rhetoric Fails." *The Education Week* (February 23, 1983).

Price, Richard R. "Should Teachers Unionize under the American Federation of Labor?" *School and Society* (April 3, 1920).

Ramsay, Charles Cornell. "Impressions of the NEA Convention for 13." *Education* (September 1903).

Rankin, Jeanette. "Unionism among Teachers." *The American Teacher* (May-June 1918).

Reese, Arthur. "Freedom Schools: 1965 and 1966." *The American Teacher* (April 1966).

Reeves, Floyd. "Current Educational Problems and the Work of the AFT Commission on Educational Reconstruction." *The American Teacher* (October 1946).

Roach, Stephen F. "School Boards and Teacher Strikes." *American School Board Journal* (November 1957).

Rood, Florence. "A New Type of City School Administration." *The American Teacher* (June 1914).

———. "It's the First Step that Counts." *The American Teacher* (October 1928).

Rosenfeld, Stephen. "Bilingualism." *Washington Post* (September 27, 1974).

Roth, Herrick S. "Colorado Fights Faceless Informers." *The American Teacher* (December 1954).

Ruediger, W. C. "Unionism among Teachers." *School and Society* (November 1918).

Russell, James E. "Organization of Teachers." *Educational Review* (September 1920).

Satterthwaite, W. B. "What Seattle Has Been Doing." *The American Teacher* (April 13, 1929).

Savage, David. "Teacher Union Leader: Shanker Out Front again in Push for School Reform." *The American Teacher* (July 2, 1983).

Schnaufer, Pete. "Collective Bargaining Contracts." *The American Teacher* (March 1967).

Schwanke, Marie L., and Sylvia J. Solomon. "How Local 250 Became a Majority Union." *The American Teacher* (December 1954).

Scully, John. "America's Choice." *USA Today* (December 15, 1992).

Selden, David. "Evaluate Teachers?" QuEST Papers Series, #4. Washington, DC, 1969. Available from ERIC, Document #ED 032 271.

———. "Parent's Role as AFT Sees It." *Senior Scholastic* (teacher supplement) (November 1, 1968).

———. "The Professional Improvement of Teachers and Teaching through Organization." *School and Society* (November 8, 1919).

Shukotoff, Arnold. "A Program of Defense." *The American Teacher* (November-December, 1937).

Sibelman. "A Philosophy of Splendid Isolation: The NEA v. the AFL-CIO." *The American Teacher* (October 1974).

Smith, H. P. "How Far Can Teachers' Organizations Go and Be Professional?" *Midland Schools* (April 1920).

Snodgrass, Margaret. "The American Federation of Teachers." *American Federalist* (September 1916).

Stair, Bird. "The Unionizing of Teachers." *School and Society* 10 (December 13, 1919): 699–703.

Stecker, Freeland G. "Report of the Financial Secretary of the American Federation of Teachers." *The American Teacher* (September 1918).

Stillman, Charles B., and C. C. Willard. "Educational Recommendations of the Atlantic City Convention of the American Federation of Labor." *The American Teacher* (September 1919).

———. "Four Months of Progress." *The American Teacher* (January 1919).

———. "Response to a Strike by Teachers in Seattle, March 20, 1919." *The American Teacher* (February 1919).

———. "The Teachers' Outlook." *Public* (March 1918).

Sutton, Willis A. "Relation of Superintendent to Teachers Association, Atlanta, Georgia, Public Schools." *The American Teacher* (March 1928).

Toch, Thomas. "Teacher Reform: Does Albert Shanker Still Believe?" *America's Agenda* (1993).

"Toward Better Race Relations in Detroit." *The American Teacher* (February 1948).

Turley, Ira S. "Full Salary Restored to Chicago after Ten Years." *The American Teacher* (February 1943).

U.S. News & World Report, February 8, 1988.

Varnum, Walter C. "ETV Messiah or Minister?" *The American Teacher* (October 1958).

Wall Street Journal. "Albert Shanker's Vision of America," November 24, 1987.

Wood, Charles W. "Professor John Dewey on the Hysteria Which Holds Teaching in a Check." *American Federation of Teachers Semi-Monthly Bulletin* (November 5, 1922).

Yabroff, Barnard, and Lily Mary David. "Collective Bargaining and Work Stoppages Involving Teachers." *Monthly Labor Review* (May 1953).

DISSERTATIONS AND THESES

Browder, Lesley Hughes, Jr. "Teacher Unionism in America: A Descriptive Analysis of the Structure, Force, and Membership of the American Federation of Teachers." Ed.D. diss., Cornell University, 1965.

Christensen, John Edward. "A History of Teacher Unions." M.A. thesis, Arizona State Teachers College, 1940.

Clarke, James Earl. "The American Federation of Teachers: Origins and History from 1870 to 1952." Ph.D. diss., Cornell University, 1966.

Close, William Edward. "An Historical Study of the American Federation of Labor-Congress of Industrial Organizations Involvement in Higher Education with an Emphasis on the Period 1960–1969." Ph.D. diss., Catholic University of America, 1972.

Dewing, Rolland Lloyd. "Teacher Organizations and Desegregation, 1959–1964." Ph.D. diss., Ball State University, 1967.

Eaton, William Edward. "The Social and Educational Position of the American Federation of Teachers, 1929–1941." Ph.D. diss., Washington University, 1971.

Gilmer, Mary Fant. "History, Activities, and Present Status of the Atlanta Public School Teachers' Association." M.A. thesis, Emory University, 1939.

Goulding, Joel Arthur. "The History of Unionism in American Higher Education." Ed.D. diss., Wayne State University, 1970.

Graybiel, John M. "The American Federation of Teachers, 1916–1928." M.A. thesis, University of California, 1928.

Hobbs, Edward Henry. "The American Federation of Teachers: A Study in Politics and Administration." M.A. thesis, University of Alabama, 1947.

Lester, Jeanette. "The American Federation of Teachers in Higher Education: A History of Union Organization of Faculty Members in Colleges and Universities, 1946–1966." Ed.D. diss., University of Toledo, 1968.

Levitan, Sar A. "A Study of the American Federation of Teachers." M.A. thesis, Columbia University, 1939

Lowman, Fern Elizabeth. "The Rise, Objectives, and Mode of Operation of the American Federation of Teachers." M.A. thesis, State University of Iowa, 1945.

McLaughlin, Samuel J. "The Educational Policies and Activities of the American Federation of Labor during the Present Century." Ph.D. diss., New York University, 1936.

Miller, Charles William. "Democracy in Education: A Study of How the American Federation of Teachers Met the Threat of Communist Subversion through the Democratic Process." Ed.D. diss., Northwestern University, 1967.

Miller, Oscar Edward. "A Comparative Study, as to Organization and Functions, of the San Antonio Teachers Council with Local Teacher Associations of Cities of the United States, of 100,000 Population or More." M.A. thesis, University of Texas, 1936.

Newman, Joseph Whitworth. "A History of the Atlanta Public Teachers' Association: Local 89 of the American Federation of Teachers, 1919–1956." Ph.D. diss., Georgia State University, 1978.
Nottenburg, Robert A. "The Relationship of Organized Labor to Public School Legislation in Illinois, 1880–1948." Ph.D. diss., University of Chicago, 1950.
Pearse, Robert Francis. "Studies in White Collar Unionism: The Development of a Teachers Union." Ph.D. diss., University of Chicago, 1950.
Pootishman, Nancy. "Jane Addams and Education." M.A. thesis, Columbia University, 1960.
Reid, Robert Louis. "The Professionalization of Public School Teachers: The Chicago Experience 1895–1920." Ph.D. diss., Northwestern University, 1968.
Salerno, Michael Philip. "A Study of Various Aspects of Teacher Unionism in the United States." Ph.D. diss., University of Wyoming, 1967.
Schiff, Albert. "A Study and Evaluation of Teachers' Strikes in the United States." Ed.D. diss., Wayne State University, 1952.
Tomlinson, James L. "Teacher Organization and Labor Affiliation with the Educational Activities of the American Federation of Labor." M.A. thesis, Cornell University, 1944.
Tostberg, Robert Dugene. "Educational Ferment in Chicago, 1883–1904." Ph.D. diss., University of Wisconsin, 1960.
Waskiewicz, Leon S. "Organized Labor and Public Education in Michigan from 1880 to 1938." Ph.D. diss., University of Michigan, 1939.
Welsh, James W. "A Brief History of the Union Movement among Teachers in the Public Schools of the United States." M.A. thesis, University of Michigan, 1930.

OTHER MATERIALS

Berg, J. Otto. "America Faces a Choice." Lecture to a graduate class in education at Northern Arizona University, December 3, 1992.
Hardison, Carolyn. "Correspondence between Janie Kerr and Charles Wallis, April 1885." Arlington, Arizona, February 27, 1997.
Mungazi, Dickson A. "Crisis in Literacy in the World after the Second World War." Paper presented at the Literacy Volunteers of Coconino County, Flagstaff, Arizona, October 23–24, 1992.
———. Interview with Albert Shanker, President, American Federation of Teachers (1974–1997). Washington, DC, May 17, 1993.
———. "The March to the Promised Land: The Development of Black Education in the United States, 1875–1975." Paper written for Graduate Class, University of Nebraska, Lincoln, 1975.
———. "Some Reflections on the Presidential Election Campaign of 1996." Memo to Republican Headquarters, Washington, DC, February 20, 1997.
Sacks, Eve. "Shanker's Impact on American Education and Society." Interview conducted by Dickson A. Mungazi. Washington, DC, May 17, 1993.

Index

About the Author

DICKSON A. MUNGAZI is Regent's Professor of History at the Center for Excellence in Education at Northern Arizona University. He is the author of numerous books on African political history and education, including *The Mind of Black Africa* (Praeger, 1996), *Educational Reform and the Transformation of Southern Africa* (Praeger, 1997), and *The Last Defenders of the Laager: Ian D. Smith and F. W. de Klerk* (Praeger, 1997).